EXPERT SYSTEMS

EXPERT SYSTEMS

Principles and case studies

SECOND EDITION

Edited by

Richard Forsyth

LONDON   NEW YORK
Chapman and Hall Computing

501.535 E

First published in 1984 by
Chapman and Hall Ltd
11 New Fetter Lane, London EC4P 4EE
Published in the USA by
Chapman and Hall
29 West 35th Street, New York NY 10001
Second edition 1989

Printed in Great Britain by
J. W. Arrowsmith Ltd, Bristol

Typeset in Photina 10/12
by Thomson Press (India) Ltd, New Delhi
ISBN 0 412 30460 0 (hardback)
0 412 30470 8 (paperback)

British Library Cataloguing in Publication Data

Expert systems: principles and case studies.
  2nd ed.—(Chapman and Hall computing).
  1. Expert systems
  I. Forsyth, Richard, 1948–
  006.3'3

  ISBN 0–412–30460–0

Library of Congress Cataloging in Publication Data

Expert systems: principles and case studies/edited by Richard
  Forsyth.—2nd ed.
    p. cm.
  Bibliography: p.
  Includes index.
  ISBN 0–412–30460–0. ISBN 0–412–30470–8 (pbk.)
    1. Expert systems (Computer science) I. Forsyth, Richard.
  QA76.76.E95E9825 1989
  006.3'3—dc 19

Contents

REASONING

REPRESENTATION

Preface to the first edition

An expert system is a computer system that encapsulates specialist knowledge about a particular domain of expertise and is capable of making intelligent decisions within that domain. Areas successfully tackled so far within the expert systems framework include medical diagnosis, geological exploration, organic chemistry and fault-finding in electronic equipment.

Although expert systems typically focus on a very narrow domain, they have achieved dramatic success with real-life problems. This has excited widespread interest outside the research laboratories from which they emerged.

Expert systems have given rise to a new set of **knowledge engineering** methods constituting a new approach to the design of high-performance software systems. This new approach represents an evolutionary change with revolutionary consequences.

Many people, whether they think of themselves as computer professionals or not, are aware that something momentous is taking place in the field of computing, and want to educate themselves to the point where they can evaluate and, if necessary, apply the new techniques.

This book serves that need by explaining the concepts behind expert systems to computer users unfamiliar with the latest research. It has been written as an introductory handbook for people who want to find out how expert systems work. It is not an academic text: it is a practical guide written by active practitioners in the field, designed to open your eyes to developments in a new and dynamic area of computer science. After reading it you should be able to begin work on practical knowledge engineering projects of your own.

Richard Forsyth,
March 1984.

Preface to the second edition

When the first edition of this book was published, only four years ago, the **expert system** was a new and exciting concept, fresh out of the research laboratory. Today expert systems are part of the accepted scenery of information technology.

Because the change from avant-garde idea to standard practice has been so fast and so complete, a new kind of book is needed. In the first edition we were promoting the concept and trying to convey the excitement that the break-through into knowledge-based computing had given us, the authors. Now there is no need to sell the basic concept, indeed it has been over-sold already; instead, we have tried to distil some of the practical experiences gained over the last four years in the application of knowledge-based computer systems to real-world problems – for the benefit of those who do not wish to repeat our mistakes.

Like the first edition, however, this book is intended as a practical introductory guide for people who actually want to make use of expert systems in their own work.

Richard Forsyth,
March 1988.

Notes on contributors

MAX BRAMER

Dr Max Bramer is manager of the Knowledge Engineering Programme at Hewlett-Packard's Research Laboratories in Bristol. Until March 1988 he was Head of the School of Computing and Information Technology at Thames Polytechnic in London. He has been actively involved in artificial intelligence since 1972 and was awarded the degree of Doctor of Philosophy for research in the field in 1977. His current principal interests are in the automatic derivation of rules from examples, and more generally in the establishment of a sound theoretical and methodological basis for expert systems development.

He has been a committee member of the BCS Specialist Group on Expert Systems since its inception in 1980 (and is currently its Chairman) and was a committee member of SSAISB (the Society for the Study of Artificial Intelligence and the Simulation of Behaviour) from 1982 to 1987. He is also Vice-Chairman of professional group committee C4 (Artificial Intelligence) of the Institution of Electrical Engineers, a member of the Council of the British Computer Society and a member of the Computing Science sub-committee of the Science and Engineering Research Council. Dr Bramer is the author of over 60 publications and has lectured extensively on expert systems and artificial intelligence in Britain and abroad. He has acted as an expert systems consultant for a number of companies and is a frequent referee for technical conferences, journals and funding bodies.

RICHARD FORSYTH

Richard Forsyth is a failed poet who now makes a living as a computer expert. He holds a BA hons. in Psychology from Sheffield University (1970) and an MSc in Computer Science from the City University (1980) but so far no reputable institution has seen fit to grant him an honorary doctorate. From 1979 to 1984 he was a lecturer, latterly senior lecturer, in computing at the Polytechnic of North London. Since 1984 he has run his own business, Warm Boot Limited, which is a software house specializing in machine intelligence, and especially machine learning.

GILLY FURSE

Gilly Furse is a founder director of Cognitive Applications Limited, which specializes in expert systems and knowledge engineering. She has written and presented courses on knowledge engineering techniques and on the methodology used by Cognitive Applications. She has been involved in a number of expert systems projects, including software diagnosis, machine monitoring and financial assessment. These projects and others provided the basis for the development of techniques of knowledge acquisition, protocol analysis, concept definition and knowledge representation. Her previous computing work experience includes the design of on-line medical systems, and she believes that many of the principles of systems analysis and software engineering are applicable to expert systems projects. Her special interests include the theory of cognition as studied by cognitive scientists. Her original degree was in theology, and her research work on images in near-eastern religion. She has also worked in publishing and lived in a community. She has had close brushes with philosophy, psychology, photography and being a writer, all of which (and more) have contributed to her outlook as a knowledge engineer.

ALEX GOODALL

Alex was born in 1951 and is married with a young daughter. He graduated from Exeter University with a degree in Mathematics and Theoretical Physics. During his subsequent employment as a systems programmer with Plessey, he attended a part-time course at Brunel University and obtained a Master's degree in Computer Science. His interest in expert systems goes back as far as 1978. This interest led him to form and run Expert Systems Limited (now Expert Systems International Limited) in 1980. Alex is now operating as an independent consultant in expert systems, advising on how to integrate the technology into business environments, and providing project audit, evaluation and management services. He is author of *The Guide to Expert Systems*, published in 1985 by Learned Information. He is on the editorial board of the *Expert Systems Journal* and holds posts on a number of professional and technical committees – including chairmanship of the BCS/SGES-sponsored ES88 Conference.

IAN GRAHAM

Ian Graham obtained BSc and MSc degrees in mathematics from the Universities of Hull and London in 1969 and 1971 respectively. He then studied Category Theory at Sussex, worked as a teacher and began actuarial training. Between 1974 and 1979 he worked in the field of transportation modelling and operations research, before finally making his career in computing, where he has consulted in modelling and management information systems ever since. He has advised several prominent organizations on management information strategy and knowledge-based systems. He is currently working on the development of several expert systems. His research interests are in artificial intelligence, management science, fuzzy mathematics and philosophy. He has published papers on transportation modelling, fuzzy mathematics and knowledge engineering. With Peter Llewelyn Jones he is co-author of the book *Expert Systems: Knowledge, Uncertainty and Decision* which is published by Chapman and Hall Ltd. Ian Graham is a member of the British Computer Society, the London Mathematical Society and the International Fuzzy Systems Association. He is currently on the editorial board of the international journal *Fuzzy Sets and Systems.*

PETER LLEWELYN JONES

Peter Jones is Chairman of Creative Logic Limited, and the chief architect of the Leonardo range of experts systems environments. He has been active in knowledge engineering since 1979, and before founding Creative Logic was the author of the REVEAL intelligent decision support system. He has lectured widely on fuzzy set theory and expert systems on both sides of the Atlantic, and with Ian Graham is the co-author of *Expert Systems: Knowledge, Uncertainty and Decision.* He is married with two children and lives in Weybridge.

CHRIS NAYLOR

Chris Naylor holds degrees in Psychology and Philosophy from the University of Keele and in Mathematics and Statistics from the University of London. He is a member of the British Psychological Society, the Institute of Mathematics and its Applications, the Institute of Statisticians, the British Computer Society and several other learned bodies. Presently he is a full-time author, researcher and freelance journalist. His recent books include *Build Your Own Expert System* and *The PC Compendium*, both from Sigma Press. He is also a regular contributor on artificial intelligence and allied topics to a number of publications, including *PC Week* and *The Times.*

NIGEL SHADBOLT

Nigel Shadbolt graduated from Newcastle University with a first-class Honours degree in Psychology and Philosophy. His doctorate was obtained from the department of Artificial Intelligence at Edinburgh University for work in the area of natural language processing. On completing his PhD, Dr Shadbolt spent a year as Research Fellow in Edinburgh's department of Linguistics, working on the explanation of features in naturally occurring discourse. In October 1983 he was appointed lecturer in Cognitive Science at the University of Nottingham. He teaches courses in AI programming, AI methods, expert systems, computational linguistics and cognitive psychology. Dr Shadbolt currently holds research grants from the Alvey organization, the Science and Engineering Research Council and the Economic and Social Research Council. Since 1984 he has been a consultant to the Artificial Intelligence Group of Cambridge Consultants Limited. His book, written with Mike Burton, *POP-11 Programming for Artificial Intelligence* was published by Addison-Wesley in 1987.

TOM STONIER

Professor Stonier is the Head of the Postgraduate School of Science and Society at the University of Bradford, Yorkshire. He obtained his AB from Drew University in 1950 and his MS (1951) and PhD (1955) from Yale University. A New Yorker, he is based in Britain and well-known in the UK as an expert on the impact of technology on society. He is a prolific speaker and author, and one of his recent books, *The Wealth of Information* (Methuen), is a detailed study of the economics of information. He is currently involved with totally computerizing Bradford University.

MASOUD YAZDANI

Masoud Yazdani was born in Iran, but has lived in England since 1975. He obtained a BSc in Computer Science at Essex University in 1978 before moving on to do research in artificial intelligence at the University of Sussex. From 1981 to 1987 he was a lecturer in the Computer Science Department at Exeter University. Recently he has moved to Oxford to work as the training manager of Expert Systems International Ltd. His special interests include educational computing and computer creativity. He has authored numerous technical papers and edited a number of publications, most notably *Artificial Intelligence Review*, a quarterly survey and tutorial journal published by Blackwell Scientific Publications of Oxford.

Background

1

The expert systems phenomenon

RICHARD FORSYTH

The aim of this introductory chapter is to say what expert systems are by setting them in their historical context. In order to understand the phenomenon of the expert system, we must step back and examine the soil from which it sprang – the fertile field of artificial intelligence, or AI for short.

1.1 AI: FROM Dr FRANKENSTEIN TO Dr FEIGENBAUM

AI has a long and chequered prehistory, stretching back at least as far as the legend of Pygmalion and Galatea. Mankind's enduring fascination with intelligent artefacts is a long and sometimes blood-curdling tale of golems, talking heads and, most notably, Frankenstein's monster. (See Aldiss, 1975; McCorduck, 1979.) We can skip over the first 2000 years of AI and pick up the story in the 1950s, when the fantasy at last showed signs of becoming fact, thanks to the digital computer.

Table 1.1 is a brief synopsis of AI history in the computer age. It has been boiled down to four digestible decade-size chunks and therefore, of course, simplified drastically. Nevertheless, it highlights the important milestones.

The column labelled Paradigm is the answer you would have got if you had asked an AI worker of the time what AI research was all about. The column labelled Workers identifies one or two key figures who seem to characterize the

Table 1.1 A bottled history of AI.

	Paradigm	*Workers*	*System*
1950s	Neural networks	Rosenblatt (Wiener, McCulloch)	Perceptron
1960s	Heuristic search	Newell & Simon (Shannon, Turing)	GPS
1970s	Knowledge engineering	Shortliffe (Minsky, Feigenbaum)	MYCIN
1980s	Machine learning	Lenat (Samuel, McCarthy)	EURISKO

spirit of their times in AI. (Underneath the main worker or workers I have put, in brackets, the thinkers or theorists whose ideas laid the foundations for their work.) Finally, the column headed System picks out one typical system (not necessarily the best) which exemplifies the underlying trend or fashion.

1.1.1 Neural nets

In the 1950s AI researchers – who mostly called themselves cyberneticians – tried to build intelligent machinery essentially by imitating the brain. With hindsight, it is hardly surprising that they failed: the hardware was just not up to the job, to say nothing of the software.

The key system I have picked out was the Perceptron (Rosenblatt, 1957; 1962). This was a trainable automaton which can be thought of as a crude model of the retina in the Vertebrate eye. It could be taught to recognize patterns, but only a limited class of patterns, as Minsky and Papert (1969) proved later.

At the time there was a good deal of enthusiasm for systems such as Rosenblatt's, based on the pioneering cybernetic ideas of Norbert Wiener (1948) and Warren McCulloch (1965) about abstract neural networks. It was felt that a richly interconnected system of simulated neurons could start off knowing nothing, be subjected to a training regime of reward and punishment, and end up doing whatever its inventor wanted. The fact that the human brain contains ten billion neurons, each as complex as, say, an Intel 8088 microprocessor, was conveniently overlooked.

This false optimism had evaporated even before Minsky and Papert did their comprehensive theoretical demolition job on the Perceptron concept. The empirical results were simply not good enough. And so a new idea took hold of the imagination of AI workers, who swept the cybernetic approach into the dustbin of recent history – which was a pity in so far as the cyberneticians had recognized two important facts which would later have to be rediscovered:

1. There can be no machine intelligence without machine learning;
2. Human intelligence is approximately 99% pattern recognition and only 1% reasoning.

1.1.2 Heuristic search

The trailblazers on this new frontier of AI were Allen Newell and Herbert Simon at Carnegie-Mellon University; and their work culminated in GPS, the 'General Problem Solver' (Ernst and Newell, 1969).

Central to their approach was the notion of heuristic search. They believed that human thinking is accomplished by the coordination of simple symbol-manipulating tasks such as comparing, searching, modifying a symbol and the like – the kind of things a computer can do. They viewed problem solving as a search through a space of potential solutions, guided by heuristic rules which helped direct the search to its destination without exploring every possible avenue.

Thus they threw out the neural-net model. They pointed out that even to design a frog's nervous system was beyond the limits of current technology; and in any case they were chiefly interested in processes which could be realized on a variety of hardware, including brains as well as computers (Newell and Simon, 1972).

Newell and Simon began their work with a theorem-proving program and moved on to computer chess. Then they turned their attention to the formulation of general techniques that could be applied to a wide variety of problems and came up with GPS.

GPS was general in that it made 'no specific reference to the subject-matter of the problem'. The user had to define a task environment in terms of objects and the operators applicable to those objects. This was a kind of finesse by which they side-stepped the difficulties of knowledge representation and of the user interface.

But the generality of GPS was confined to a restricted domain of puzzles with a relatively small set of states and well-defined formal rules. Like most of its contemporary systems, GPS functioned in a formalized micro-world where the problems (e.g. the Towers of Hanoi) are, in human terms, no problem.

From a technical standpoint, moreover, it can be said that the GPS procedure, known as depth-first search, of breaking down a problem repeatedly into pieces until a sub-problem is reached small enough to be solved directly, is inefficient, since many blind alleys are explored rather thoroughly. Later workers have devised more efficient 'best-first' search strategies, as discussed in Chapter 3 (though blind depth-first search is alive and well and living inside innumerable Prolog interpreters!).

Nevertheless the GPS project stands out from the ruck. Its authors, like the cyberneticists before them, fell victim to misplaced optimism, as when Herbert Simon predicted in 1957 that within ten years a computer would be world chess champion; but there is a place for overconfidence in science. (Simon now has a Nobel Prize to his name, which shows that scientific reputation does not depend on perfect foresight.) And by attempting to prove that both minds and computers were examples of general-purpose serial symbol-manipulating devices, they carried out the experimental *reductio ad absurdum* which cleared the way for the next advance in AI.

1.1.3 Knowledge engineering

What GPS could not do was solve real-world problems. In the 1970s a team led by Edward Feigenbaum at Stanford University began to remedy that deficiency. Instead of trying to discover a few very powerful and very general problem-solving methods, they narrowed their focus. What a human specialist seems to have is plenty of know-how – a large number of useful tricks or rules of thumb.

And so the expert system was born, almost as a caricature of the real human expert who is said to know more and more about less and less. The mass spectrogram interpreter DENDRAL (Feigenbaum *et al.*, 1971) was the prototype of them all. But its immediate successor, MYCIN (Shortliffe, 1976) has been even more influential.

MYCIN is a computer system which diagnoses bacterial infections of the blood, and prescribes suitable drug therapy. Though it has never been accepted by doctors as an everyday tool, it has spawned a whole series of medical-diagnostic 'clones', several of which are in routine clinical use. For instance, PUFF, a lung function diagnostic program built on the MYCIN plan, is routinely used at the Pacific Medical Center near San Francisco.

MYCIN introduced several new features which have become the hallmarks of the expert system.

Firstly, its 'knowledge' consists principally of hundreds of rules such as the following.

IF   1. the infection is primary-bacteriaemia, and
      2. the site of the culture is a sterile site, and
      3. the suspected portal of entry of the organism is the gastro-intestinal tract,

THEN
      there is suggestive evidence (0.7) that the identity of the organism is bacteroides.

Secondly, these rules are probabilistic. Shortliffe devised a scheme based on 'certainty factors' (not, strictly speaking, probabilities) to allow the system to reach plausible conclusions from uncertain evidence. This is highly significant. MYCIN, and systems like it, are robust enough to arrive at correct conclusions even when some of the evidence is missing or incorrect. This is because they have methods for combining fragmentary and possibly inaccurate information to derive a good estimate of the truth – whether based on probability theory, fuzzy logic, certainty factors or some other calculus of likelihood.

Thirdly, MYCIN can explain its own reasoning processes. The user (a physician, not the patient) can interrogate it in various ways – by enquiring why it asked a particular question or how it reached an intermediate conclusion, for example. It was one of the first genuinely 'user-friendly' computer systems. This degree of user-friendliness was a by-product of the rule-based style of programming. Each rule can be treated as an independent packet of knowledge; if the user wants to know why a certain question was asked, the system simply constructs a descriptive trace of the rules which led to that question.

Fourthly, and crucially, MYCIN actually works. A trial in 1979 (reported by Jackson, 1986) showed that MYCIN's performance compared favourably with that of clinicians on patients with bacteriaemia and meningitis. Its conclusions were rated by eight adjudicators on ten cases, giving a perfect score of 80. MYCIN's score was 52 which compared with 50 for the best physician on the Stanford faculty, 46 for the therapy actually given and 24 for a medical student. In summary, it performed as well as the experts and significantly better than the non-experts. Thus, it does a job that takes a human being years of training. Actually MYCIN is very limited in scope, even compared to your hard-pressed neighbourhood practitioner, but it gets closer to intelligence than the crude pattern-recognizers of phase 1 or the abstract problem-solvers of phase 2 in the progress of AI.

Expert systems have finally disposed of the old dictum: if it works, it's not AI! People and corporations are starting to use knowledge-based systems to make and/or save money. Two famous money-spinners have entered the folklore of the subject: Prospector and XCON.

Prospector is a geological expert system (Gashnig, 1982) which was used to discover a previously unknown deposit of the mineral molybdenum near Mount Tolman in Washington state, and later found another in Alberta, Canada. The value of the latter has been estimated as $100 million. XCON is a development of R1, a system originated at Carnegie-Mellon University by John McDermott (Bachant and McDermott, 1984). It has been used by Digital Equipment Corporation (DEC) to configure VAX computer systems from customer orders for the past seven years, resulting, according to DEC personnel, in a net saving in the order of $18–20 million per annum. These two cases are often held up as beacons lighting the way for others to tread, and while their semi-legendary status suggests that savings on this order are very rare, it is no longer possible to doubt that knowledge-based systems can be sources of considerable profit.

For example, Wheat Counsellor, developed by ICI in the UK which advises farmers about the usage of herbicides and fertilizers on wheat crops, and Tom, developed by Cognitech for the French Ministry of Agriculture which advises agricultural inspectors on tomato diseases, are both success stories by normal commercial standards (see Hewett, 1987).

1.1.4 Machine learning

However, while the world of commercial data processing is living off the intellectual capital of the 1970s, AI in the 1980s has moved on to focus on the problems of machine learning. This is a natural progression, since the 'magic ingredient' of expert systems is knowledge. It is the extent and quality of its knowledge base which determine the success of an expert system.

But knowledge is hard to acquire. Most present-day expert systems contain a knowledge base that has been laboriously hand-crafted. The extraction and codification of expertise from a domain specialist by a **knowledge engineer** is an expensive and time-consuming process. It is natural to ask whether the computer cannot, in some sense, synthesize that knowledge for itself – for instance, by analysing a database of training examples.

This brings us to the fourth and final section of Table 1.1. One of the most impressive AI systems of the present decade is a machine learning system called EURISKO (Lenat, 1982) which automatically improves and extends its own body of heuristic rules. Apart from winning the Trillion Credit Squadron naval wargame three years in succession (despite rule-changes designed to thwart it), EURISKO made a breakthrough in VLSI (Very Large Scale Integration) by inventing a three-dimensional AND/OR logic gate.

Even more significant, perhaps, is the work of Michalski and colleagues at the University of Illinois. Michalski and Chilausky (1980) reported what can only be described as the *experimentum crucis* for machine learning. They collaborated with an expert plant pathologist, Barry Jacobsen, to produce a hand-crafted set of decision rules for identifying soybean diseases. This was refined using standard knowledge-engineering techniques until it was 72% correct in its first-choice diagnosis. In parallel with this work, they fed several hundred example descriptions of diseased soybean plants to an inductive rule generator named AQ11. The program produced a set of diagnostic rules that were over 97% correct in their first-choice diagnosis.

Spurred on by this challenge, Jacobsen revised his original formulation – using a more powerful rule-language than that available to AQ11 – until it was 83% correct on unseen samples. Then he abandoned that approach, and taught himself the machine-generated rules, which he now uses in his own professional work. (See Michie and Johnston, 1985.) This is the first recorded case of a machine-derived knowledge base which exceeded the performance of a human expert. The story also neatly illustrates the fact that rules generated by machine induction can contribute to the sum of human knowledge (provided they are expressed in a comprehensible notation).

More recently, some AI scientists have turned their back altogether on the rule-based representation of knowledge and attempted to build connectionist models (Hinton and Anderson, 1981; Hinton, 1986). The essential features of a connectionist machine are 1. that its expertise is distributed throughout a network, not encoded in localized symbolic form; and 2. that it can learn new concepts for itself on the basis of input–output pairings.

So machine learning in general, and connectionist modelling in particular, are the 'flavours of the month' in AI as we teeter towards the 1990s. Which brings us full circle, or rather round one spiral in the staircase of AI history, because machine learning was precisely the key problem that cyberneticians like Wiener, McCulloch, Ashby and Rosenblatt were attacking with different methods and more primitive technology in the 1940s and 1950s. Whether we will 'crack' the problem of learning this time around – with the aid of modern parallel hardware – remains an open question. Even if we do not, however, it is highly likely that machine-learning research will have a significant impact on the commercial world over the next five to ten years, just as the early expert systems, for all their faults, are having a profound impact on advanced software technology at this moment.

AI is, and always has been, a moving target. But however far or fast it moves, learning will remain one of the central issues of intelligence.

(For those who like a quick look into the future, it is just about possible to hazard a guess at the central theme of AI in the 1990s. It is variously labelled 'reflexivity', 'self-reference', 'meta-level reasoning' and under other aliases. Like the preceding four phases, it arises out of a deficiency in the previously accepted framework. If a machine is to learn effectively, it must re-structure its own representations, its **vocabulary of concepts**, from time to time. That will require a degree of self-reference that has been absent from computer systems in the past – the first glimmerings of self-consciousness. Remember: you read that prediction here first (though reflexivity has been entertainingly discussed already by, among others, Hofstadter, 1985).)

1.2 THE ANATOMY OF EXPERT SYSTEMS

Returning to the present day, expert systems are still the most important contribution of AI to the wider world of computing. The expert systems bandwagon was given a push start by the Japanese Fifth Generation initiative (JIPDEC, 1981) and received further momentum from the various Western responses to that plan (e.g. Alvey, 1982). These projects are discussed further in Chapter 3, but whether they succeed or fail in their long-term aims the notion of the expert system is now too firmly embedded in commercial computing to be dismissed as a passing fad.

Most people now know that a knowledge-based system consists of a **knowledge base** (to store expertise) and an **inference engine** (to put it to work). But, as a matter of fact, there are four essential components of a fully fledged expert system (Forsyth, 1984):

1. the knowledge base
2. the inference engine
3. a knowledge-acquisition module
4. an explanatory interface.

To put it another way, if you stand back far enough from a modern expert system so that the details fade away, you will see that it has the kind of top-level architecture illustrated in Fig. 1.1.

The knowledge-acquisition module can be seen as a kind of back-end to the knowledge base; and the explanatory interface as a front-end to the inference engine. But perhaps the most fruitful way of looking at this diagram is as a pointer to the four central unsolved problems in expert systems methodology. These are:

1. the problem of knowledge representation
2. the problem of approximate reasoning
3. the problem of knowledge acquisition
4. the problem of human–machine interfacing.

It may seem paradoxical to say that the state of the art in expert systems is a collection of unsolved problems, when hundreds of practical expert systems are in use worldwide, but it is true.

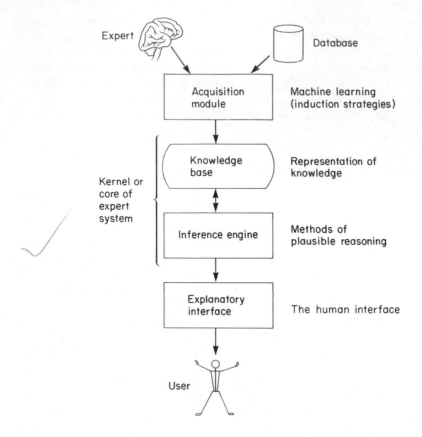

Fig. 1.1 Expert systems: a ground plan

We will consider each of the four modules in Fig. 1.1 in turn, along with the problems that they raise.

1.2.1 Knowledge representation

The two fundamental components of an expert system are the knowledge base and the inference engine. The knowledge base stores information about the subject domain; however, information in a knowledge base is not a passive collection of records and fields such as you would expect to find in a conventional database. Instead it contains symbolic representation of experts' rules of judgement in a format that allows the inference engine to perform deductions upon it.

The knowledge representation problem concerns the mismatch between human and computer 'memory' – i.e. how to encode knowledge so that 1. it is a faithful reflection of what the expert knows and 2. it can be manipulated by a computer. The task of the knowledge engineer is to bridge this conceptual gap – i.e. to find a way of storing expertise symbolically. Four main methods have evolved:

1. Rules in IF-THEN format: the condition specifies some pattern and the conclusion may be an action or assertion;
2. Semantic nets: these represent relationships among objects in the domain (e.g. granite is an igneous rock) by links between nodes;
3. Frames: these are generalized record structures which are more flexible than is usual in traditional data-processing in that they may have default values or procedural entries as the values of certain fields or slots;
4. Horn clauses: these are expressions in a form of predicate logic on which Prolog is based and with which the Prolog system can perform inferences.

Early expert systems tended to use the rule-based formalism almost exclusively, e.g. the MYCIN system for diagnosing blood infections (Shortliffe, 1976). Below is a sample MYCIN rule.

IF   1. the infection is meningitis, and
         2. the sub-type of meningitis is bacterial, and
         3. only circumstantial evidence is available, and
         4. the patient is at least 17 years old, and
         5. the patient is an alcoholic

THEN

         there is suggestive evidence that Diplococcus pneumoniae is an organism causing the meningitis.

Rules are still the predominant form of encoding knowledge in expert systems. However, both MYCIN and Prospector (Gashnig, 1982), which are quoted, quite rightly, as rule-based systems, make use of other structures for background knowledge. In the case of MYCIN a 'context tree' is used to guide the course of the consultation. The precise structure of the tree varies with each consultation; and it is used to determine whether certain rules of inference (in the primary knowledge base) may fire. In the case of Prospector a semantic net is utilized to provide background geological knowledge. Networks or tree-like structures are useful in setting up what are often called inheritance hierarchies like that shown in Fig. 1.2. The arcs represent links relating sets to subsets and supersets. Coding such information in terms of a sequence of production rules would simply be clumsy.

Other significant expert systems have made use of frames to represent knowledge. The frame below (called a unit) is one of the concepts used by EURISKO in tackling the naval wargame (Trillion Credit Squadron fleet design challenge) which it won.

Name: Energygun.
Generalizations: (anything, weapon).

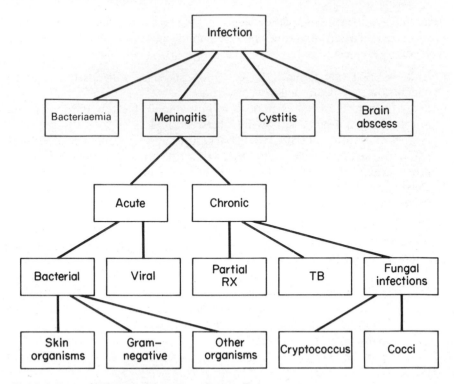

Fig. 1.2 Part of MYCIN's inheritance hierarchy

Allisa:	(gameconcept, gameobj, abstractobj, physicalobj, physgameobj, ... anything).
Isa:	(defensiveweapontype, offensiveweapon, physgameobj).
Myworth:	400.
Myinitialworth:	500.
Worth:	100.
Initialworth:	500.
Damageinfo:	(smallweapondamage).
Attackinfo:	(energygun-attackinfo).
Numpresent:	Nenergyguns.
USPpresent:	energygunUSP.
Defendas:	(beamdefense).
Rarity:	(0.11/19).
Focustask:	(Focusonenergygun).
Mycreator:	DLenat.
Mytimeofcreation:	4-June-81 16:19:46.
Mymodeofcreation:	(EDIT nucmissile).

Frame-like representations have many advantages. They can contain default values. Not all slots need to be filled in all examples of a particular type of frame. The contents of a slot may be of any data type – numbers, strings, procedures, lists, pointers and so on. Above all, frames may be linked to other frames, providing the same sort of inheritance lattice as that provided by a semantic net. Indeed the **object-oriented** style of programming, pioneered by the Smalltalk programming language, is finding its way into more and more expert systems environments. As this happens, the frame is beginning to displace the condition–action rule as the basic building block of computerized knowledge.

Finally, the Horn-clause form of logic has been brought to prominence by the popularity of Prolog among certain AI researchers. Prolog provides a flexible representation scheme that allows both rules and facts to be coded in essentially the same way. For example the clauses

mother (eve, cain).
father (adam, cain).

express simple assertions or facts in the database, while the clause

maternal_grandfather (X, Z):-
father (X, Y), mother (Y, Z).

expresses a relationship or rule. It states that X is the maternal grandfather of Z if X is the father of Y and Y is the mother of Z. This relation can be treated as an inference rule that can be evaluated directly by Prolog's built-in theorem prover. (Variables are in upper case and constants in lower case: this is the so-called 'Edinburgh syntax' as standardized by Clocksin and Mellish, 1981.)

To pretend that there is one accepted method of representing knowledge in expert systems would be quite wrong. Indeed there are those who argue that the whole concept of representing knowledge as atomic chunks of information in a well-formed symbolism is misleading (Dreyfus and Dreyfus, 1985; Winograd and Flores, 1986). They present compelling evidence that human experts simply do not 'have knowledge' in any well-defined sense even when they 'know' what to do in a given situation. How far the engineering-type AI workers can push the notion of knowledge as something you can store in a machine while the philosophically inclined AI workers strive to work out what is actually going on is an unanswered question. For practical purposes the best advice is: tread warily, you may be on shakier ground than you think when you build your first knowledge base, even if it appears to work. (See also Chapters 7 and 8 of this volume.)

1.2.2 The inference engine

Inference is the deployment of evidence in order to arrive at new conclusions. An inference engine consists of search and reasoning procedures that enable an expert system to find solutions and, if required, provide justifications for its conclusions. Inference engines typically follow one of two top-level reasoning strategies – **forward chaining** or **backward chaining.**

Forward chaining involves working forward from the evidence or symptoms to the conclusions or diagnoses. In a rule-based system it simply involves matching the IF conditions to the facts, possibly in a predetermined order. Forward chaining is easy to computerize and is suitable in cases where all the data has to be gathered anyway – for example, when the data is produced automatically by a recording instrument or when a form has to be filled in as a matter of standard practice.

Backward chaining works from hypothesis to evidence. The system selects a hypothesis and looks for data to support or refute it. It is normally programmed in a recursive manner. Its main advantage is that it typically leads to a more natural dialogue in consultation-style systems, since the system can at any stage describe its current goal. (And very many expert systems still follow the MYCIN plan and interact with the user in a consultation session.)

However, the problem of which hypothesis to investigate next in backward chaining is not yet solved; and so, in practice, most systems combine forward with backward chaining. For example, Naylor (1983) has developed the 'rule-value' method which decides what evidence to ask for next on the basis of how much it would reduce the overall uncertainty in the system. And the Leonardo expert system shell (Creative Logic, 1987) employs backward chaining 'with opportunistic forward chaining' as its default strategy.

Apart from the overall inference strategy (forward or backward chaining) an inference engine must address the issue of uncertainty. Many expert systems allow for uncertainty in the facts obtained from the user and in the rules themselves. Shortliffe (1976) devised an approximate reasoning scheme for MYCIN based on what he termed 'certainty factors'. This has been criticized for being *ad hoc*, though it proved quite effective in practice. Other systems have been based on fuzzy-set theory, which extends the operations of Boolean algebra to cover fractional truth-values intermediate between 0 (false) and 1 (true). (See Chapters 4–6 of this volume.)

The most immediately appealing calculus of uncertainty, however, is probability theory. Most expert systems that use probabilities follow the lead of Prospector, rather than MYCIN, and use Bayes's theorem as the thread which ties together chains of uncertain inference. Bayes's rule can be encapsulated in the following expression.

$$P(H:E) = P(E:H) \times P(H)/P(E)$$

This states that the probability of a hypothesis (H) given some evidence (E) is the probability of the evidence given the hypothesis times the probability of the hypothesis divided by the probability of the evidence. This may not seem a very magnificent piece of mathematics, but it has important ramifications. It is useful primarily because it is easier to find out the proportion of measles patients who have spots than the proportion of spotty people who have chicken pox (for instance).

For computational convenience, most Bayesian systems work with odds rather than probabilities (at least internally) which allows them to use an updating scheme based on the likelihood ratio (LR).

$$O(H:E) = O(H) \times LR(H:E)$$

This formula equates the odds in favour of the hypothesis (H) given a piece of evidence (E) to the odds in favour of the hypothesis prior to the observation of that evidence multiplied by the likelihood ratio for the hypothesis given the evidence. It is simply a condensation of Bayes's original formula. The value O (H:E) is known as the posterior odds, while O(H) is the prior odds.

Likelihood ratios can be calculated from two-way contingency tables. Table 1.2 is a frequency tabulation of some data compiled from the 1986 English flat-racing season. It is taken from a random selection of 266 races (with less than 18 runners) in which only the two horses with the lowest odds in the *Guardian* newspaper betting forecast were considered. This gave 529 runners (after removing the late withdrawals). The item of evidence under consideration is whether the horse was top-ranked according to the Formcast ratings published in the *Daily Mail*. In brief the idea is to see the extent to which being top-rated on the Formcast improves the probability of a horse which is first or second in the *Guardian* betting forecast winning.

Bayes's rule provides a way to compute how much more likely the presence of the evidence (top ranking) makes the hypothesized outcome (winning the race). The likelihood ratio is usually defined as

$$LR(H:E) = P(E:H)/P(E:H')$$

where H' means not-H. But a simpler way to compute it from a contingency table like Table 1.2 is to label the four cells

A   B
C   D

and then calculate

$$LR(H:E) = (A \times (B + D))/(B \times (A + C))$$

which gives in the present case

Table 1.2 Contingency table for racehorses.

		Frequencies and Percent (%)			
		Winners		Losers	Total
Daily Mail	Top Formcast	72	(39%)	112	184
Daily Mail	not Top	70	(20%)	275	345
		142	(27%)	387	529

LR (Win:Topform) = $(72 \times 387)/(112 \times 142) = 1.7520$.

The likelihood ratio when the horse is known not to be top ranked LR (Win:not-Topform) can also be computed in a similar fashion. It is 0.6937. This says that the odds in favour of a horse winning its race can be multiplied by 1.752 if it is top ranked in the *Daily Mail* ratings (or by 0.6937 if it is not).

Other potential indicators can be treated sequentially by using the posterior odds after taking into account one piece of evidence as the prior odds for a second piece of evidence – although this procedure is only valid, strictly speaking, if the two items of evidence are uncorrelated.

The great attraction of Bayesianism is that it permits – indeed en-courages – detailed statistical investigation. It does not have to rely on sub-jective numerical estimates. Thus it offers a remedy for the unfortunate breach between statisticians and knowledge engineers (Spiegelhalter and Knill-Jones, 1984). Simple-minded Bayesianism has two serious disadvantages, however. In the first place the estimation of prior probabilities or odds (before any evidence is gathered) is problematical. It all depends on the reference population (e.g. patients who report to a particular hospital, the adult population of the UK, the population of Europe, everybody in the world. . . etc.) In the second place the various items of evidence must be statistically independent; otherwise some rather complex re-calibrations are required.

The first criticism loses some of its force if a large number of evidential indicators is considered. As the evidence piles up one way or the other, the effect of prior odds is swamped. The second drawback is more fundamental, but in most practical systems the knowledge engineer is warned during the rule-construction phase if two sources of evidence are strongly associated, and given the opportunity to combine several correlated variables into a single index. Generally speaking, correlated items of evidence should not be in separate rules but should be integrated into a single rule with a single likelihood ratio attached. To give an example: it would be inadvisable in a weather-forecasting system to have one rule relating cloudiness to the probability of rain tomorrow and another rule relating humidity to the probability of rain tomorrow, since cloudiness and humidity are causally connected. It would be preferable to combine the two raw variables into some kind of 'dull-dampness' index and use that composite measure in a rule predicting rainfall.

From all this it should be clear that there is no one way of handling uncertainty in knowledge-based systems. Indeed the whole question of approximate reason-ing is an active and controversial research area.

1.2.3 Knowledge acquisition

Experts are notoriously bad at introspection: when it comes to describing their own reasoning processes they tend to tell tall tales. Coaxing and cajoling their knowledge out of them is a process more akin to psychoanalysis than data transfer. So **knowledge acquisition** has come to be widely regarded as the main bottleneck in the development of expert systems. (See Feigenbaum and McCorduck, 1984; Michie, 1986.)

Getting knowledge out of the expert may be difficult for any of three main reasons:

1. deliberate resistance
2. inarticulacy
3. cognitive mismatch between brains and programs.

problems

The first reason has received a good deal of attention (although it is less serious than the other two). Consider an expert trader in coffee futures on the London commodities exchange. His future earning potential depends on his unique 'feel' for the way the market is going – a skill built up over many hundreds of hours spent poring over price-movement charts and many years spent huddled over a flickering screen. Now his firm wants to put his expertise in a box, with the implied message that he (and his salary) will become dispensible. It is hardly surprising if he asks himself: whose knowledge is it anyway? (A question to which it is very difficult to give a definitive answer.) What is surprising is that so many experts do in fact try their best to be cooperative in situations precisely analogous to the fictitious example just quoted. Clearly the flattery of being treated as a guru, even if only temporarily, and having a team of knowledge engineers respectfully immortalize your hard-won expertise for posterity, is almost irresistible. But as the consequences of knowledge engineering – including the de-skilling of intellectual workers – become widely apparent, resistance by domain specialists will become more and more common.

The second major problem, inarticulacy, affects even cooperative experts. They tend to be busy people who seek results and do not spend a lot of time analysing their own behaviour and thought processes. The stories they initially tell the knowledge engineers tend to be half-remembered fragments of theories they learnt at college woven into an appearance of coherence with the aid of the folklore that surrounds every specialist subject. In particular, the expert almost always places too much relevance on superficial scientific respectability and too little on the real tricks of the trade. Experienced knowledge engineers, however, gain their own expertise with time – the ability to see behind the façade which professionals habitually present to the public and discern the 'back-room' activities which actually get the job done.

The third problem, cognitive mismatch, is the most serious of all. If the progress of AI has revealed anything, it has made it abundantly clear that people do not think in the way that computers process information – if they did there would be no need for four decades of (partially successful) research effort in order to get computers to recognize images or understand speech. Yet expert systems are founded on the premise that human expertise can be codified and replicated by rule-following machines. This is a daring hypothesis which has led to some spectacular successes (and failures), not by any means a proven fact. How much further the knowledge-based approach can be pushed before it breaks down is an unsolved research issue. The conscientious knowledge engineer should be aware that rendering human skill into computable form is an art which has limitations.

Because of the well-known difficulties in knowledge acquisition, people have tried to devise ways of automating the procedure. (See Hart, 1985.) Experts may not be much good at articulating their knowledge, but they are, by definition, good at making the right decision. They are also good at criticizing the decisions of others, including decisions made by machines. So software tools have been developed recently (e.g. EXTRAN) which allow computers to generate rules from pre-classified examples, by induction. (See, for example, Asgari and Modesitt, 1986.)

These systems generally work in the following mode: the expert enters a set of example situations, described in terms of the attributes that are considered important, and assigns each situation a class (which indicates the correct decision). Then the induction program generates a rule or rule-set for classifying those examples in the same way as the expert. Then the expert tests the rule or rules on a novel case, realizes that something is wrong, and introduces a new training example (or sometimes a new attribute) to 'teach' the computer how to cover the wrongly classified case.

This process can continue over many cycles. It has two advantages over the conventional knowledge-engineering route: 1. the expert takes a more active role; 2. it resembles something that comes more naturally to human experts – i.e. repeatedly 'boxing the ear' of an apprentice or pupil until he or she finally picks up the unspoken skills needed to make the correct decision most of the time. In other words, induction packages help to humanize the knowledge acquisition task; though they do not remove the need for other means of knowledge elicitation.

(Induction, of course, is at the heart of machine learning, and is considered more fully in Chapter 11 of this volume.)

1.2.4 The explanatory interface

One of the good ideas introduced by the classic expert systems such as MYCIN and Prospector is the idea that a decision support system should be able to justify its conclusions on request. Obviously when life-and-death or even profit-and-loss decisions are being handed over to a computer it is essential for the system to explain its own reasoning.

Below is an extract from a session showing how MYCIN replies to a WHY? question posed by its user, who is a physician, not the patient, and should not accept diagnoses on trust without any explanation.

Is meningitis a hospital-acquired infection?
** WHY
[2.0] This will aid in determining the organisms (other than those seen on cultures or smears) which might be causing the infection. It has already been determined that:

[2.1] the infection which requires therapy is meningitis, and

[2.2] organisms were not seen on the pending csf culture, and

[2.3] the type of infection is bacterial, and

[2.4] neurosurgery is not one of the relevant items from the history of this patient, and

[2.5] the age of this patient is greater than 10 days.

Therefore, if:

[2.6] the infection was acquired while the patient was hospitalized, then there is evidence that the organisms (other than those seen on cultures and smears) which might be causing the infection are E. coli (0.75), Staphylococcus coag pos (0.3), Pseudomonas aeruginosa (0.3), Klebsiella pneumoniae (0.5).

–from [RULE545]

**

This explanation is, in effect, a partial trace through the program's reasoning steps, couched in medical-jargon English. Explanations of this type can be produced fairly easily and cheaply in rule-based systems by regurgitating the rules used, and their predecessors, until the user gets tired of asking for more. In the 1970s such facilities constituted a genuine advance (and many modern computer systems do not yet have anything comparable) but they would not satisfy the more sophisticated users of today.

Second-generation expert systems are now starting to incorporate the ideas about human–machine interaction developed at the Xerox Palo Alto Research Center and given commercial backing by the Apple Macintosh. But there is still a long way to go before we see the truly 'handy' systems prefigured in the Japanese Fifth Generation plan (JIPDEC, 1981). One thing becoming clearer is that we will probably not get there without jettisoning the cherished consultation model pioneered by MYCIN and carried over almost as an article of faith into most of today's expert systems (Pollitt, 1986).

1.3 SUMMARY

Expert systems have moved out from AI research into the mainstream of commercial computing. They represent a new approach to the design of software for intelligent decision support. Knowledge engineering is the methodology for building expert systems.

A typical expert system has four major components:

1. the knowledge base
2. the inference engine
3. the acquisition module
4. the explanatory interface.

2oo words

① The knowledge base consists of information structures for encoding expertise. Usually this is elicited from a human specialist and reformulated as a collection of rules, a network of facts or a frame-based structure. A knowledge base differs from a database in several ways: in particular, it is more active. That is, it contains rules for deducing facts that are not stored explicitly.

② The inference engine uses the facts and rules in the knowledge base to derive new conclusions leading to a recommendation or diagnosis. Very often it can cope with missing or unreliable data by means of some method of approximate reasoning.

③ The acquisition module eases the knowledge acquisition process by testing proposed rules for inconsistency, redundancy and syntactic validity. More advanced systems use inductive methods to create rules from examples, thereby discovering new knowledge. (This topic is dealt with in depth in Chapter 11.)

④ The importance of an explanatory interface is that it allows the user to interrogate the system, normally by posing 'how' or 'why' questions. 'How' questions ask the system to justify its line of reasoning ('How did you reach that conclusion?'). 'Why' questions ask it to explain why it requires some piece of information ('Why are you asking me that?'). Both facilities help make the system more usable; but human–machine interaction is still the weakest link in expert systems technology.

While many organizations have found that knowledge engineering projects can have useful payoffs in a realistic time-scale, the theory of knowledge-based computing remains in a surprisingly primitive state. Two decades after the first expert system (DENDRAL, working in 1967) the field of expert systems is best characterized as a collection of interesting unsolved problems.

1.4 REFERENCES

Aldiss, B. (1975) *Billion Year Spree*, Corgi, London.
Alvey Directorate (1982) *The Alvey Report*, HMSO, London.
Asgari, D. and Modesitt, K. (1986) Space shuttle main engine test analysis: a case study for inductive knowledge-based systems involving very large databases, *Proc. IEEE* 65–71.
Bachant, J. and McDermott, J. (1984) R1 revisited after four years in the trenches, *AI Magazine*, **5**, 21–32.
Clocksin, W. and Mellish, C. (1981) *Programming in PROLOG*, Springer-Verlag, Berlin.
Creative Logic (1987) *Leonardo, The Manual*, Creative Logic Ltd., Middx.
Dreyfus, H. and Dreyfus, S. (1985) *Mind over Machine*, Macmillan/The Free Press, New York.
Ernst, G. and Newell, A. (1969) *GPS: A Case Study in Generality and Problem Solving*, Academic Press, New York.
Feigenbaum, E., Buchanan, B. and Lederberg, J. (1971) On generality and problem solving, *Machine Intelligence*, **6**.
Feigenbaum, E. and McCorduck, P. (1984) *The Fifth Generation*, Michael Joseph, London.
Forsyth, R. (ed.) (1984) *Expert Systems: Principles and Case Studies*, 1st edition, Chapman and Hall, London.

Gashnig, J. (1982) PROSPECTOR: An expert system for mineral exploration. In *Introductory Readings in Expert Systems* (ed. D. Michie) Gordon & Breach, New York.

Hart, A. (1985) The role of induction in knowledge elicitation. *Expert Systems*, 2, 24–8.

Hewett, J. (1987) Commercial progress in Europe. *Proc. 3rd Int. Expert Systems Conf.*, Learned Information Ltd, Oxford.

Hinton, G. (1986) Learning distributed representations of concepts. *Proc. 8th Annual Conf. Cog. Sci. Soc.*, Amherst, Mass.

Hinton, G. and Anderson, J. (eds) (1981) *Parallel Models of Associative Memory*, Erlbaum, New Jersey.

Hofstadter, D. (1985) *Metamagical Themas*, Viking, New York.

Jackson, P. (1986) *Introduction to Expert Systems*, Addison-Wesley, Reading, Mass.

JIPDEC (1981) *Preliminary Report on Study and Research on Fifth Generation Computers*, Japan Information Processing Development Centre, Tokyo.

Lenat, D. (1982) The nature of heuristics, *Artificial Intelligence*, 19, 189–249.

McCorduck, P. (1979) *Machines Who Think*, Freeman, San Francisco.

McCulloch, W. (1965) *Embodiments of Mind*, MIT Press, Mass.

Michalski, R. and Chilausky, R. (1980) Learning by being told and learning from examples..., *Internat. J. of Man-Machine Studies*, 12, 63–87.

Michie, D. (1986) The superarticulacy phenomenon in the context of software manufacture, *Proc. Royal Soc.*, A, 405, 185–212.

Michie, D. and Johnston, R. (1985) *The Creative Computer*, Pelican, London.

Minsky, M. and Papert, S. (1969) *Perceptrons: An Introduction to Computational Geometry*, MIT Press, Mass.

Naylor, C. (1983) *Build Your Own Expert System*, Sigma Press, Cheshire.

Newell, A. and Simon, H. (1972) *Human Problem Solving*, Prentice-Hall, New Jersey.

Pollitt, S. (1986) Reducing complexity by rejecting the consultation model as a basis for the design of expert systems, *Expert Systems*, 3, 234–8.

Rosenblatt, F. (1957) *The PERCEPTRON: A Perceiving and Recognizing Automaton*, Cornell Aeronautical Lab, New York.

Rosenblatt, F. (1962) *Principles of Neurodynamics*, Spartan Books, London.

Shortliffe, E. (1976) *Computer Based Medical Consultations: MYCIN*, American Elsevier, New York.

Spiegelhalter, D. and Knill-Jones, R. (1984) Statistical and knowledge-based approaches to clinical decision-support systems, *J. Royal Statis. Soc.*, 147, 35–77.

Wiener, N. (1948) *Cybernetics*, MIT Press, Mass.

Winograd, T. and Flores, F. (1986) *Understanding Computers and Cognition*, Ablex, New Jersey.

2

An introduction to expert systems

ALEX GOODALL

2.1 ORIGINS OF EXPERT SYSTEMS

In the Beginning was **reason.** And Reason was with Intelligence. And Reason WAS Intelligence.

Or so the early researchers into AI (artificial intelligence) thought. Their argument went something like this:

> 'Let us find some formal and powerful notation in which we can describe any aspect of the world. Because it is formal, a computer will easily be able to manipulate such a notation. Let us then define various reasoning methods which will allow a computer to draw inferences, make deductions and prove or disprove statements about the world as described by this notation. Given enough facts about the world, and given a powerful enough reasoning mechanism, this approach should enable us to build a machine that is "intelligent".'

Various forms of notation were defined, some extremely clever reasoning mechanisms were devised, and much effort was expended in trying to implement these efficiently on limited hardware. The results of this effort have given us as a side-effect many of the techniques now commonly used in computer science: virtual memory, garbage collection, compiling techniques, and complex data manipulation. But the major goal of AI remained unachieved.

The problem was two-fold. Firstly, in order to describe even a small subset of the world, an enormous number of facts and relationships are needed. And even worse, when the reasoning mechanism starts adding to and changing these facts and relationships, the effects of these changes on all the other facts and relationships have to be taken into consideration, resulting in an exponential growth due to a sort of 'knock-on' effect. Even with today's very much more powerful hardware, this approach is almost certain to fail.

The birth of expert systems came when it was realized that at least one aspect of intelligence was not based on reasoning. An expert performing a specialist task often uses very simple reasoning. His or her expertise comes from years of experience and training, not from a built-in ability to reason better than the non-specialist. And what is it that the expert gains over the years? It is knowledge.

To take an example, what is the distinctive aspect of the intelligence that goes into the advice an accountant gives for minimizing tax liabilities? Is it that the

An accountant's tax liability are not only acquire from deduction and reasoning, but also gain from experience over years of how the Revenue may interpret them.

accountant has superior powers of deduction and reasoning? Certainly he or she needs to have good reasoning ability, but then, so does a logician. In fact, the distinction is the accountant's knowledge of the tax laws and his knowledge gained from experience over the years of how the Inland Revenue may interpret them.

This insight into the key role played by knowledge encouraged the AI community to build systems that attempted to be intelligent not in a general way, but about some very specific area of expertise. And they did this by applying relatively simple reasoning mechanisms to knowledge about just that area of expertise. This specialization circumvented the problem of having to re-check the state of the world every time someone blew their nose. The knowledge is the expertise.

And thus was born the area of expert systems – the first commercially viable application of artificial intelligence.

2.2 STRUCTURE, COMPONENTS AND SOME TERMINOLOGY

It is instructive to make an analogy between expert systems and more traditional programs. A traditional program can be thought of as follows:

Program   =   Algorithm   +   Data

If you were to analyse the algorithm part from an expert system perspective, it is possible you would divide it into a control component and descriptive component. Thus:

Program   =   Control   +   Data

            +

        Problem description

If this distinction is now made explicit in the structure of the program, we can equate control with inference engine and problem description with knowledge base. We finally therefore get:

Expert system   =   Inference engine   +   Data

            +

        Knowledge base

This is not meant to show how expert systems can be formally derived from traditional programs. It is just a helpful way of showing the distinction between the two types of program. In fact, expert systems are more often than not used in cases where an algorithmic approach is inappropriate, so the analogy usually breaks down when applied to actual cases.

We have now identified the two major components of an expert system – the inference engine and the knowledge base. The 'control' aspects of the system are inherent in the inference engine. It is this component that supplies the reasoning ability of expert systems, and it is the knowledge about which it reasons.

In order to support these two components, other components are also needed. For example, a 'knowledge editor' or 'knowledge compiler' (or both) to convert from a human-readable form of the knowledge into an 'inference engine understandable' form. This editor/compiler also performs any validation/consistency checking functions. Of equal importance to all these components is the user interface.

For example, a human-readable form of a 'rule' within the knowledge base may look like this:

Rule 3:

> IF   surplus_income > 25,000   AND
>   capital_gain_reduction = critical
> THEN
>   advise 'Consider BES investment',
>   BES_scheme = considered

After conversion by a compiler/editor, the internal form may be completely unreadable, or may look something like this (for a system written in the AI language Prolog):

rule (3, cond (1) & cond (2) →
                advise (text (1)), assert ('BES_scheme' (considered))).
cond (1, surplus_income > 25,000).
cond (2, capital_gain_reduction = critical).
text (1, 'Consider BES investment').

The user interface is not just a collection of screen layouts. It also includes a set of commands which the user can invoke during a consultation with the system. The usual sequence of an interaction with an expert system is for the system to ask questions and the user to answer them. However, instead of answering a question, the user can often interrupt the consultation and take actions himself or interrogate the system. There are usually three types of command available:

1. Modifying the flow of the interaction. This can be by volunteering information which has not been asked for, but which the user thinks should be taken into account; by changing the answer to a question which has already been asked; by explicitly telling the system to consider a particular line of reasoning, thus overriding any control mechanisms inherent in the knowledge base.
2. Interrogating the status of the consultation. These types of command allow the user to ask for the current values of variables or parameters; to request a display of the line of reasoning (this is the almost mandatory 'why' facility – i.e. 'why are you asking me this question?'); to request a justification for a conclusion (this is the almost equally mandatory 'how' facility – i.e. 'How did you reach this conclusion?' or 'How did this parameter obtain this value?').
3. Examining the knowledge base. These commands do not give any information

about the current consultation, but it is often very useful – particularly during the development of a knowledge base – to be able to look at the rules or other components of the knowledge base part way through a consultation. Thus, you may be able to ask for a particular rule to be displayed, or, on more sophisticated systems, for all rules that refer to a particular parameter in their condition (for example).

Certain features of the user interface – most particularly those which allow interrogation of the status of the consultation – require very careful consideration during the design of the inference engine. Implementing features such as the ability to change an already established parameter can be quite difficult, especially for some of the more complex forms of knowledge representation.

2.3 WHY IS THE INTEREST LEVEL SO HIGH?

The idea of expert systems seems to have captured the imagination of very many people in the computer industry – including both suppliers and users. In some sense, expert systems are what newcomers to computers always think computers should be. They should be clever, they should be knowledgeable, they should understand what the user is trying to do, they should be tolerant of the user's incomplete information, typing errors and woolly thinking, they should be able to learn about the user and about the problem domain. In short, they should be intelligent.

All of us who have worked with computers for even a very short period know that, alas, computers are just not like that. But we never quite stop believing that, given the right design methodology, the right relational database, the right specification language, the best designers and programmers, the right hardware, the right computer language and enough time... perhaps...

Then along come the artificial intelligence researchers and say 'Well, we've been working hard since computers were invented trying to make them like you always thought they should be, and although we are not there yet, what we have achieved is... "Expert Systems"...'

Their descriptions sound both enticing and eminently plausible, and they seem to offer solutions to many of the problems facing the computer industry:

1. systems too complex for the users to use directly/effectively
2. systems too complex to maintain
3. systems too complex to update

and to suggest that it may be possible to implement applications which were previously not even considered. They seem to offer the missing ingredient which is the difference between an intelligent application and a non-intelligent one. Once again, the focus leads us to knowledge. This is the missing ingredient.

In summary, therefore, expert systems have become a very popular concept so quickly because they suggest a plausible way to program computers to make them fulfil our largely subconscious expectations of how they should behave. But what is the reality?

The techniques suggested by expert systems technology offer the best chance of building applications that are even very slightly intelligent. However, getting to that stage requires a great deal of effort in extracting the knowledge, representing it in a suitable formalism, and selecting and/or writing a suitable inference engine. Again, knowledge is the key. Most of the time will be spent extracting and representing knowledge. Intelligence never comes cheaply.

On the other hand, many people recommend that a modest microcomputer is a perfectly adequate tool on which to develop an expert system, and that it can be done in a matter of a few days. The crucial point to bear in mind is this:

> The technology of expert systems is of value in its own right, and can be used to good effect to build both small and large systems. Because the small systems, by definition, do not contain much knowledge, they will not be regarded as 'intelligent', but they will, nevertheless, be useful applications that would have been difficult to implement using non-expert systems technology.

Here are some examples of small systems that are very easy to write using a simple shell, but would be hard to cost-justify if developed using conventional programming techniques:

1. A system for use by a bank to quickly confirm whether or not an applicant may open a bank account, and if so, whether a cheque guarantee card may be issued.
2. A system to record the rules for administering a corporate pension scheme.
3. A simple 'help desk' adviser for dealing with regular queries from, say, users of a computer application.

2.4 HOW TO RECOGNIZE AN EXPERT SYSTEMS PROJECT

It is often very difficult for someone not closely associated with an area of expertise to even realize it exists. It is such areas that, by their nature, are best suited to implementing as an expert system. Areas of expertise which everyone knows exist – weather forecasting, predicting market trends, deciding on marketing strategies and so on – are almost always far too general and complex for today's technology. To be suitable for an expert systems application a much more focused description is required. For example, deciding on the advertising strategy for a particular product type for a company in a particular area in a particular country over some specified period to be used by a particular type of user; that might just be a suitable application – all other considerations being acceptable.

The 'other considerations' concern the identification of the expert and the practicality of the system. Long checklists can be produced to aid in identifying a suitable application, but reproduced below is a summary of some of the preliminary considerations often used for selecting an expert systems application:

1. Identifying an expert and his expertise

   (a) He or she should be regarded as an expert by virtue of experience, and not just because of his or her intelligence, title or status.
   (b) The task to be performed by the system must be clearly definable. It will almost certainly be a subset of one of the many tasks performed by the expert.
   (c) The selected task should take the expert no more that a few hours to perform, but more than a few minutes.
   (d) The expert must have sufficient time to devote to the project, and be committed to it. Without the expert's enthusiasm, the project will fail.

2. Appropriateness of the technology

   (a) Is it immediately obvious that the system could be implemented almost entirely by a simple look-up table (at one extreme) or a mathematical equation (at the other)? If so, forget expert systems technology.
   (b) If there is a high proportion of 'common sense' reasoning involved, choose another domain. This should have been eliminated by 1. (a), anyway.

3. Practicality of the system

   (a) Determine whether you want the system to replace the expert (often very difficult, technically and politically) or to assist the expert (safer approach), and then decide if this is practicable.
   (b) Try to choose an application where the maintenance of the knowledge base will not present difficulties.
   (c) Are there sufficient test cases available? If not, you will never be able properly to evaluate or test the system.
   (d) Is the end-user well-identified, and would he/she be happy to use the system?
   (e) Is there sufficient management support and commitment?

2.5 EXPERT SYSTEMS POTENTIAL ON MICROCOMPUTERS: YESTERDAY, TODAY AND TOMORROW

A few years ago there were two or three versions of Prolog available on IBM PC computers, two or three versions of LISP, and perhaps half a dozen shells.

Today there are at least 15 versions of Prolog, 9 versions of LISP and 30 shells.

The power of these tools has increased enormously during this period, and there is no sign of the development process easing off. It is possible today to build expert systems with several thousand (simple) rules on a desk-top micro. Prolog-2, for example, now offers module architectures, virtual memory management, automatic overlay management, window handling, compilation, interfaces to other languages (C, FORTRAN, Pascal, Assembler) and utilities (such as dBase III,

Lotus, GSX etc.) and development environments which more than match those offered by other languages.

For the future, it seems likely that the rate of development will increase rather than decrease. The suppliers of these tools have been ingenious in making the best possible use of the limited speed and memory of the PC, and using the windowing capabilities to best effect. AI programs had a reputation for being extremely memory and processor hungry, so the results obtained have surprised many of the traditional AI researchers who were used to using $100 000 machines as single-user workstations.

The 'second generation' of languages and tools are beginning to come on the scene, such as Prometheus. These offer more sophisticated forms of knowledge representation and start moving towards the power of the integrated AI development toolkits previously only available on the dedicated AI workstations.

The new generation of PCs based on the Intel 80386 chip have been eagerly awaited by the expert system suppliers. With the traditional limitations removed, these now allow the full potential of these second generation tools to be released.

2.6 REASONS FOR ADOPTING EXPERT SYSTEMS TECHNOLOGY

There are two possible reasons:

1. Everyone else seems to be doing so, so it must be important.
2. You have a perceived need for an application which appears to fit the criteria for an expert system.

The most common sequence of events is that an individual in an organization decides he wants to become involved in expert systems based on reason 1. and the inherent interest in the subject, then tries to apply reason 2. to persuade his company to apply sufficient resources.

The question 'Why adopt expert systems technology?' is analogous to the question 'Why adopt computer technology?'. There is no single answer, but it is possible to make general statements which carry over the analogy. Whilst computers have assisted companies in making the best possible use of one of their more valuable resources (data or information), expert systems can now help organizations make the best possible use of what is probably its most valuable resource – knowledge or expertise. Just as in the early days of computing the application of computers to data processing was rather crude and not applicable to all forms of data within an organization, so too – at present – is the application of expert systems. The tools and technology are 'adequate to very good' for the right applications, but these have to be chosen very carefully (see above).

The short-sighted might decide that they can quite safely completely ignore expert systems technology for the next two years or so. However, in two years' time many organizations will have already invested hundreds of person-years in the technology and have the technical and managerial infrastructure set up to maximize their expertise using the, by then, mature expert systems technology. Some of those organizations may be your competition. That is when the far-sighted will be clearly distinguished from the short.

2.7 A STRATEGY FOR ADOPTING EXPERT SYSTEMS TECHNOLOGY

The most common path being followed by organizations developing an interest in the subject starts with a seminar on expert systems, followed by the purchase of a shell. A great deal can be learned by buying an inexpensive shell (£400–£3000) that runs on an IBM PC and building small demonstration systems. This can go on indefinitely, and can be great fun, but after a while there is no more to learn from this approach, and a larger, serious application should be built. This should entail real knowledge engineering on a real expert, and the system should be planned to be installed in a real site for use by real users. It should not, preferably, be a critical application for your organization at such an early stage in your organization's adoption of the technology.

An alternative approach to building your own application is to purchase a ready-made application. This has the disadvantage of not teaching you so much about the technology, but the compensating advantage of being much less risky; you would be able to demonstrate the effectiveness of expert systems immediately with an operational system to refer to as an example. These are now available in increasing numbers. Three examples are:

1. a system which advises on how to tune your VAX computer
2. a system to advise on dismissal legislation
3. a system for market analysis and forecasting.

At the point where you decide to build your own application, you should have a team of at least three people, not necessarily all on the same project, but all involved in expert systems with at least one being well experienced. Fewer than three people is unlikely to achieve critical mass. It can also be cost-effective to use a specialist expert systems consultancy for at least part of the work, and serious consideration should be given to the selection of the correct tools. It is far too easy to choose an inappropriate tool (too simple or too complex), and more often than not the choice is made too early.

And choose your consultancy carefully. A software house (not in the UK) was asked to recommend a tool for an expert system application for its client. The application was presented as being very complex, requiring an AI tool costing tens of thousands of pounds. Whilst the recommendation was being considered, the software house negotiated the marketing rights to said product for that country, and eventually made a sale to their client. They are probably still learning about the product themselves at the client's expense.

For the more advanced applications, an AI language, an advanced shell or a toolkit is likely to be required, and it is at this point that serious training becomes a necessity. Two or three days' training by the right people can save weeks of frustration.

An extreme example occurred in Holland. Dutch companies have a tendency to use university students as cheap labour to investigate expert systems for them in the mistaken belief that most expert systems expertise still resides in academia. Our Dutch associate company reported to us that a customer in just such a situation had spent weeks writing elaborate Prolog code to input characters in a particular way – without success. We sent back an electronic mail message immediately with a two-line solution.

It is worth bearing in mind that some aspects of AI require a different approach to problem solving that cannot be adequately learned from books or manuals.

Because the costs begin to grow at this stage, it is important to get the commitment and enthusiasm of higher management who must be persuaded that expert systems have a strategic value to the organization. So, choose your demonstration/prototype application with great care and make sure it not only is intelligent, but it looks intelligent!

The steps beyond this point are, naturally, different for each organization. Those organizations that do take those steps and fully embrace expert systems technology will, I predict, gain benefits comparable to and possibly greater than those gained by using computers for data processing.

Knowledge is a fundamental component of all activities in an organization. Harnessing, distributing and amplifying that key resource is the goal of expert systems.

3

Expert systems: where are we and where are we going?

MAX BRAMER

3.1 INTRODUCTION

Although expert systems have become a fashionable area of computing activity only in the last few years, the earliest expert system – DENDRAL – had its origins as long ago as 1965, and much of the influential work on the MYCIN family of systems (described in e.g. Buchanan and Shortliffe, 1984) took place over a decade ago, also by the Stanford University Heuristic Programming Project.

Expert systems are themselves an outgrowth from work in artificial intelligence (AI), a field of study which can be traced back well beyond the development of the electronic computer itself (see for example McCorduck, 1979).

Many of the early pioneers of computing were interested in the idea of the 'intelligent machine', two notable examples being Charles Babbage (1792–1871), who talked of the possibility of using his 'Analytical Engine' to play chess and even considered building a special chess-playing version of the Engine as a means of fund-raising, and Alan Turing (1912–1954), who proposed the 'imitation game' – now known as the Turing test for intelligence – in 1950 and wrote and hand-simulated a chess-playing program in the 1950s.

However, AI as a field has probably attracted more opponents (and even outright enemies) than any other area of computing and its development until recent years was frequently problematic at best (the development of AI in Britain has been described elsewhere, e.g. Bramer, 1987).

The transformation of artificial intelligence from an esoteric research field to one of major industrial significance (principally through the medium of expert systems but also through work in computer vision, speech recognition, intelligent robotics etc.) is a remarkable one but easy to trace back to its origin in the Japanese announcement towards the end of 1981 of its Fifth Generation Computer Systems initiative.

The Fifth Generation programme envisaged a collaboration of industry, academic institutions and government departments in a nationally coordinated programme which was clearly of great potential importance to the Japanese computer industry and (if successful) could propel Japan into a worldwide lead in the field of advanced information technology.

What was most significant – and unexpected – about the Japanese programme was its concentration on the development of work (on speech, vision, logic programming, etc.) which had originated in the artificial intelligence research community in the West and particularly the identification of expert systems as a key area of application of the advanced computer systems of the 1990s. In a memorable phrase, it was asserted that in fifth-generation systems 'Intelligence will be greatly improved to approach that of a human being' (JIPDEC, 1981).

The explosive growth of interest and activity in expert systems worldwide that was catalysed by the Japanese announcement and its aftermath is already well-known. The list of commercial companies (from the very large down to the very small) actively involved in the field is both long and impressive, with an ever-growing 'support industry' of commercial conferences, workshops, management tutorials etc. of all kinds, plus a plethora of new magazines and journals.

The availability of both hardware and software tools has changed out of all recognition, with dozens of products now competing for attention, including powerful programming languages, expert system shells and artificial intelligence development environments, running on a variety of mainframes, personal computers and workstations. Pre-packaged expert systems are also becoming available, although not yet in large numbers.

The remaining sections of this chapter look at a number of aspects of this growth of work in expert systems. Section 3.2 looks at the kinds of application to which expert systems can usefully be put and reviews progress to date. Some of the technical and organizational issues raised by this work are discussed in Section 3.3. Social considerations (both potential benefits and problems) are discussed in Section 3.4 and Section 3.5 looks briefly at future trends in the field. Section 3.6 offers some overall conclusions.

3.2 EXPERT SYSTEMS IN PRACTICE

3.2.1 Applications of expert systems

The range of tasks to which expert systems have been applied is now very large and rapidly growing. One reference source, *The CRI Directory of Expert Systems* (CRI, 1986) lists over 600 systems developed worldwide and described in the technical literature (in English) up to the end of 1985.

Overall, the European market for expert systems has been predicted to be growing to a value of several billions of pounds per annum by the early 1990s. In the United States, where industrial applications projects started somewhat earlier than in Britain, a recent report indicates that there are at least a thousand major (i.e. million-dollar) projects currently in progress, covering a wide range of applications in a variety of industries (Hewett, 1986).

The systems listed in CRI (1986) cover a range of applications as diverse as accountancy, angiography, archaeology, wafer fabrication and X-ray crystallography. However, it is inevitable in compiling any such list that some problems of both inclusion and exclusion will arise. There is no universal agreement on the precise definition of an expert system and there is a natural tendency for software developers to adopt fashionable new terms such as expert system to describe their systems on the slightest pretext, whatever tasks they actually perform. (In some circles, there seems to be an assumption that any rule-based system written in Prolog must be an expert system, almost by definition!)

The current position is reminiscent of the early days of databases, when anyone with a program using a sequential file – or better still a random-access file – felt free to reclassify himself as a database administrator (with a corresponding rise in status and perhaps salary). Expert systems demonstrated at conferences etc. are often nothing of the sort, but straightforward rule-based programs performing tasks which could perfectly well have been achieved in other ways.

On the other hand, certain kinds of expert system are inevitably substantially under-represented in the published literature:

1. the large number of small systems which have undoubtedly been built using standard shells, e.g. by management for 'familiarization' purposes, but not converted into fully operational systems, documented or named
2. systems still under development (which includes many of those for the more complex kinds of application)
3. systems treated as commercially confidential by the companies concerned (this category will inevitably include some of the largest and most interesting systems!).

Although expert systems were initially seen by many as an entirely new form of software for standalone applications, different from those of conventional computing, attention is increasingly becoming focused on forming links between expert systems and the conventional problems of data processing and commercial computing, including the interface between expert systems and database management systems, the development of intelligent front ends to complex software packages and information retrieval systems, applications in real-time process control and embedding expert modules in otherwise standard data processing software. Although most systems have been implemented on 'standard' hardware, some systems have recently appeared implemented on portable hand-held micros for use 'out in the field'.

3.2.2 Expert systems in practical use

Despite the undoubtedly high level of effort put into expert systems development worldwide in the last few years, it is salutary to observe that there are still very few substantial systems in regular use in industry, a particularly notable exception being the series of systems produced by Digital Equipment Corporation (DEC) in the USA.

Doubtless a proportion of the many small-scale systems which have been developed using simple rule-based shells on business PCs are also in practical use.

These systems are somewhat analogous to the large number of applications developed using spreadsheet software (often by users who are certainly not computer professionals). Whilst some of them are no doubt of commercial value, observation suggests that in many cases the applications could equally well have been implemented using conventional programming techniques.

The return so far obtained by industry for all the effort expended on expert systems would seem to have been very low and hard to reconcile with the previously quoted projections of the worldwide expert system market growing to a value of many billions of pounds per annum by the early 1990s. It has been unkindly remarked that more money has been made by suppliers of software for developers of expert systems than by anyone else.

Naturally, the lack of serious operational systems is partly a function of the timescales involved. A substantial practical problem currently facing companies wishing to move into the expert systems field is the shortage of skilled manpower. This is a direct legacy of the widespread neglect of artificial intelligence and expert systems in the past, which led to very few individuals emerging from the higher education system with any experience of the relevant techniques, tools and languages until the last few years.

The position is slowly improving, with a growing number of courses on expert systems and AI, which now also form a part of many computer science degree syllabi. However the demand is still increasing each year, with the need for skilled staff seemingly exceeding the supply several times over.

One reason why more expert systems have not been put into practical use would seem to be that systems have been developed (frequently to gain experience of the necessary techniques) which are not particularly wanted or needed or do not match the working practices of the organization. It is often pointed out that even MYCIN has never been put to regular use, but this is hardly surprising – consultants in hospitals are unlikely to spend 30 minutes or so answering simple questions at a terminal for each patient (and are even less likely to have a terminal on their desks for other purposes) and the normal delays in hospitals notifying the results of laboratory tests to a general practitioner make it pointless for the latter to use a computer system designed to produce a rapid diagnosis.

Other frequently-made mistakes are to underestimate the amount of work involved (especially in going from a prototype to a completed system), forcing projects into an inappropriate development cycle (specify, then code, then test, etc.), more suitable for commercial data processing applications and – perhaps most important of all – undervaluing the role of the domain expert in the development process.

Perhaps more than any other consideration in choosing an application it is imperative to find an expert who is articulate, willing to cooperate and has time to spare. Such individuals are relatively rare. They should be consulted at the start of a project (i.e. before contracts are signed, staff employed, etc.) to gain their support (and if possible enthusiasm). This advice may seem obvious, but many projects seem to have been chosen without any consultation with domain experts.

With the present state-of-the-art of developing expert systems (and unlike the position for most conventional applications) it is only seldom likely to be possible to develop a system without the expert's active (as opposed to nominal) support. It would seem sensible therefore to avoid applications that downgrade the expert or make the expert feel that he or she is in imminent danger of replacement by a machine!

3.2.3 The need for theory

As well as the practical pitfalls already outlined, there are a number of obstacles to success of a more theoretical nature. Although the number of people involved in the expert systems field has increased enormously in the last five years, as has the field's commercial recognition, the theoretical and methodological basis of the subject has advanced very little. In all the euphoria, long-standing technical problems have been forgotten or ignored but not solved.

Unfortunately, the need to solve such problems and more generally to develop a satisfactory methodology for all aspects of the development and maintenance of expert systems seems little appreciated by many of those developing systems 'in the field' – as indeed the need for well-formulated development methodologies for conventional data processing systems was not widely recognized in the 1960s and early 1970s.

It is not surprising that business and industry frequently do not see the solving of such problems as their direct concern, but there are obvious dangers in overestimating the soundness of the foundations on which expert systems are being built. Problems which do not show up in developing small-scale demonstration systems may well be of crucial importance with more complex systems. Given the nature of the tasks performed by expert systems, even very substantial errors in a knowledge base may easily pass undetected for a long period, but may lead to seriously mistaken decisions being taken.

Some of the problems that will need to be addressed if companies are to achieve the full potential of expert systems in the future are discussed in the following section.

3.3 TECHNICAL AND ORGANIZATIONAL ISSUES

3.3.1 Development methodologies

Up to now the development of expert systems has frequently been conducted on an *ad hoc*, largely experimental basis (generally using the common AI approach of rapid prototyping, followed by cycles of iterative refinement in which the subject expert is directly involved in examining the consequences of applying in a range of cases the knowledge which he or she has imparted).

Although developing expert systems for relatively simple rule-based applications does not seem to present much difficulty in practice, developing even one high-performance system for a complex application is a skilled task, far more a craft than an exact science.

The position has similarities to the early days of data processing. Most of the early applications in business and industry were implemented using techniques which seem extremely crude by today's standards, but many straightforward applications were still implemented and generally worked successfully.

This work was clearly of great practical value to business and industry. Only later, when more complex tasks (and 'maintenance' of software already written) were attempted, did the limitations of the tools available manifest themselves and the need for more powerful languages and properly thought-out development methodologies become apparent.

There is no reason to believe that today's methods of developing expert systems will prove more successful in the long run than the early pioneering methods used for data processing applications in the 1960s and early 1970s. Companies that remember the spectacular failures produced by undue (although at that time unavoidable) reliance on *ad hoc* methods will not lightly repeat the process with expert systems for very long.

Whereas with conventional software, there was no realistic alternative to learning from experience (and failure), in the case of expert systems it should be possible to short-cut the learning process, particularly since there is already considerable experience (in the research community) of developing large and complex artificial intelligence software. This experience has not yet been analysed and codified as it needs to be and this should surely be a high priority in the next few years.

Although regarding expert system development as fully-understood with a clear-cut methodology would be a serious error, it would be equally questionable to regard an expert system as merely a simple variant of a conventional computing system and thus susceptible to existing methodologies such as entity analysis, JSP etc. It is worth pointing out that all is not yet ideal even with routine computer applications – which still seem to take many times longer to implement than the time which can be spared before they are needed. It is notable that fourth-generation languages and the technique of prototyping are increasingly being used in the world of commercial computing.

As expert systems become more widespread and particularly as the value of embedded expertise in conventional software is more widely recognized, a reconciliation will be needed between the traditional prototyping style of expert systems and the development methodologies of conventional commercial software. It would be most strange if there were not a large area of common ground between these two kinds of software, even if in the most extreme cases different methodologies were needed.

3.3.2 Software for expert system development

There are essentially four kinds of software tool available for expert system development:

1. conventional languages (such as Pascal and C)
2. AI languages (such as LISP and Prolog)
3. AI development environments (such as ART and KEE)
4. AI shells (such as Savoir).

Apart from those brave individuals who insist on applying their favourite conventional languages to tasks for which they were not designed, almost all expert system development has taken place using 2, 3 and 4.

Using a 'raw' AI language gives the implementer most flexibility but requires him or her to expend a great deal of effort on implementing facilities such as the user interface which are not generally the principal focus of the work and for which the AI language may not be particularly well suited. In addition, Prolog is still very much in need of the good program debugging and development aids which have long been a feature of the major LISP systems.

It is probable that most large-scale applications in the USA have been implemented using AI development environments. Unfortunately these are generally large items of software, correspondingly expensive and usually require a computer of the speed and size of a personal workstation (as opposed to a PC) to run satisfactorily. Such machines are themselves relatively expensive and still by no means common in business and industry, although with the rapid advances in hardware technology (and corresponding reductions in price) this position could easily change in the next few years.

In Britain, the position is markedly different. For reasons which would seem to be mainly those of cost and availability, up to now the principal development vehicles for expert systems in business and industry have been relatively unsophisticated rule-based shells (derived from MYCIN, Prospector or their near relatives), running on IBM PC and compatible systems. A large number of small-scale systems (and some larger-scale ones) have been constructed, frequently in a matter of a few days or a few weeks only.

At present the use of shells is a matter of considerable controversy in the British expert systems community. Although the research community has consistently expressed the view that shells are of limited value, some software suppliers have been extremely vigorous in their advocacy, citing in support of their position the numerous systems developed using shells and the relative scarcity of those developed using more sophisticated software.

Some software suppliers have gone so far as to decry the use of AI development environments on personal workstations and to suggest that the PC shell is a major British contribution to the expert systems field. However, it is not surprising that rule-based systems developed using shells are far more numerous than those developed using more expensive development systems and more complex representations such as frames and causal models. The latter tend to be used for more complex applications, where progress is much less rapid, success less certain and development times are likely to be far longer. It is probable that the number of such more complex systems will increase significantly in the next few years.

It is also a matter of observation that some of the expert systems implemented with shells are barely deserving of the name and could easily have been implemented in a conventional language (such as BASIC).

Although expert system shells have been embellished substantially in the last year or so, with interfaces to spreadsheets, interactive video, external data sources etc. in recent products, they remain inherently limited to a specific choice of representation, specific means of dealing with missing knowledge etc., regardless of the task domain in question, and in general are most unlikely to be suitable for developing more complex systems (for which the choice of the most appropriate representation, means of reasoning with uncertain information, etc. is likely to be of crucial importance).

Prototyping is often very rapid using a shell, but developing a fully operational system from a prototype may require the prototype to be completely recoded using an entirely different choice of software.

For those who prefer to use shells, the choice of product often seems to be based on commercial decisions rather than on technical criteria as is necessary. In this respect, therefore, it may be that much of the British expert systems community is at present deliberately handicapping itself.

3.3.3 Knowledge acquisition

The expert systems of today contain a few hundred (or in some cases a few thousand) rules and perform relatively straightforward tasks.

In order to perform the more complex tasks which are likely to be required in the future, the expert systems of tomorrow may need to contain many thousands (or even tens of thousands) of rules. This begs the question of how these rules will be found.

An often-cited review of the literature on knowledge acquisition is Welbank (1983). The customary techniques (such as introspection, interviewing, protocol analysis, analysis of critical events, etc.) all seem significantly limited and past experience, even with the most acclaimed expert systems, is not encouraging.

To take only two examples from many, Buchanan *et al.* (1969) describing their experience with DENDRAL state: '... one of the greatest bottlenecks... has been eliciting and programming new pieces of information... the theory does not exist in any sort of comprehensive codified form', and Shortliffe (1976) says of MYCIN: 'The formulation of new decision rules is no straightforward matter. Physicians have not in general structured their decision processes and the expert... may have difficulty describing the steps in reasoning that he uses to make decisions.'

Knowledge acquisition is frequently described as a major bottleneck in the building of expert systems. However, it is not really surprising that it should be difficult to extract rules from an expert, whose skill will generally lie in performing a given task, not in explaining to others how it should be done. To this may be added the natural reluctance which many experts may well feel to pass on their knowledge to an outsider, especially one who may appear to be threatening the expert's own position in his or her organization (remembering the slogan 'in the knowledge lies the power').

Although knowledge acquisition is widely held to be the most difficult phase of expert system development, there have been remarkably few experiments aimed at deciding which criteria (such as task domain, nature of expertise or psychological characteristics of either the expert or the intended user) determine the choice of approach to follow. One exception is the work of Burton *et al.* (1988). In general, system developers seem uninterested in selection criteria and are content to rely on a fixed choice of one 'standard' method or on their intuition about the best approach to adopt.

An alternative approach to the traditional methods of knowledge acquisition which has become increasingly popular in recent years is the so-called **rule induction** approach, where the expert's role is confined to supplying a database of example cases and an induction algorithm is then used to discover the underlying rules automatically.

It could be argued that for experts to supply significant case examples to an induction program is a natural means of knowledge transfer, far more so than explaining how a skilled task is performed, and the hope is that induction will provide a practical way round the problem of the knowledge acquisition bottleneck.

Although a very promising approach, rule induction itself presents a number of technical difficulties. At present it should therefore be regarded as another tool in the knowledge engineer's armoury, most likely to be of use when a large number of example cases are available, but not a panacea suitable for routine use by the inexperienced. A good review of some of the best-known work on rule induction is in Quinlan (1986).

The widely-held view of knowledge acquisition as a bottleneck has been challenged by Gammack and Young (1985), who have drawn attention to the crucial role of representation in developing expert systems and suggested that knowledge acquisition may seem unduly difficult on those occasions when production rules are an inappropriate representation for expert knowledge (see Section 3.3.4). Thus the solution to the problem of developing a system with tens of thousands of rules may lie in finding a different representation in which such a large number of rules is not necessary.

3.3.4 Using 'deep knowledge'

When expert systems first entered the spotlight, the idea of using rules as a representation for knowledge seems to have struck many with the force of revelation. So much so, that some have not fully realized the need for more complex representations for some (probably most) domains.

By contrast, the choice of representation has long been recognized as a major consideration in the AI research community. Such more complex representations were, in fact, used in most of the original (and now 'classic') expert systems, even in MYCIN, but this was not fully appreciated at first.

This misconception is now dissolving as more and more practical systems are being developed, with an increasing use of sophisticated artificial intelligence development environments combining several representations (for example, LOOPS combines the features of four different programming paradigms).

The use of the term **deep knowledge based systems** (DKBS) to describe those systems which use representations of knowledge more sophisticated than heuristic rules (a 'shallow' representation) reflects the new awareness that rules alone are often insufficient as a representation for expert knowledge.

Steels (1986) uses the term 'second generation' expert systems to denote those that combine heuristic reasoning based on rules with deep reasoning based on a causal model of the problem domain ('first generation' systems being those which rely purely on heuristic knowledge in the form of rules). Using causal models avoids the need to construct large rule sets and makes good explanation facilities much easier to provide (see Section 3.3.10).

With the coming of the second generation, it would seem that the expert systems field is in the process of rejoining its parent field of artificial intelligence, a development which is probably essential if the full potential of such systems is to be achieved.

3.3.5 Missing knowledge

A problem which frequently arises in practice is that a piece of knowledge is not available to an expert system (or is of dubious reliability), but is nevertheless essential to the system's inferencing process, for example when making use of a rule such as

IF A and B and C then conclude X

where A and C are known to be true, but the truth or falsity of B cannot be determined.

It is important to distinguish between the cases of what are known as 'open' and 'closed' worlds. An everyday example of a closed world is a railway timetable. If one wishes to know whether there is a train from London to Aberdeen leaving at 4 p.m. on a Sunday and no such train appears in the timetable, it can safely be assumed that no such train exists – if it did, it would be included in the timetable.

Unfortunately most expert systems operate in domains which are open. In general, there is no reason to imagine that an expert system contains all imaginable rules about its task domain and the inability to prove that a certain proposition is true may simply indicate that additional knowledge is needed.

There seems to be no clear-cut and completely satisfactory way of dealing with this problem of missing knowledge, but a straightforward approach would be to use *a priori* probabilities every time it is not possible to form a conclusion about the value of some variable.

It is interesting to note that the 'closed world assumption' was made in no less a system than MYCIN (Shortliffe, 1976), where any proposition not capable of being evaluated (with a reasonably high certainty factor) was treated as false. This would only be justified if there were no possibility of relevant rules being left out of the system.

3.3.6 Reasoning with uncertain information

Many expert systems unavoidably operate in task domains where the available information is inherently imprecise (rules derived from experts are inexact, data values are unreliable, etc.).

An early approach to the problem of reasoning with such uncertain information was the model of inexact reasoning used in MYCIN, described in Shortliffe and Buchanan (1975). This was subsequently carried over to the very influential EMYCIN family of systems and its derivatives.

Although the MYCIN model of uncertain reasoning was presented as an alternative to standard probability theory, an analysis by Adams (1976) showed that a substantial part of the model can be derived from and is equivalent to probability theory, with assumptions of statistical independence. Amongst other difficulties, such assumptions of independence are not generally valid and it is evident that the MYCIN model has serious limitations. Naturally, it may turn out that such limitations make little practical difference in many cases, but it would be unwise to place excessive reliance on any model which did not have a strong theoretical underpinning.

Other models of inexact reasoning have been tried in practical systems, notably in Prospector, but many of these are little more than *ad hoc*. A number of competing theoretical approaches have also been developed, such as fuzzy logic, possibility theory, belief theory, and the use of non-standard logics (e.g. for 'default reasoning'). However, none of these has yet gained wide acceptance.

Others have attempted to develop methods more akin to human reasoning such as the use of formal definitions of linguistic concepts of certainty, such as 'X is likely' or 'X is suspected' (see, for example, Ellam and Maisey, 1986 for an example of inexact reasoning in a medical domain).

At the present time, however, the question of how best to reason with uncertain information must be considered as an open research problem.

3.3.7 Consistency maintenance

A serious problem which arises when knowledge is represented in rules, used in conjunction with an automatic system of reasoning, is how to avoid inconsistent rules occurring in a system's knowledge base.

This can occur in two ways:

1. direct contradictions such as

    (a) all dogs like cats
    (b) some dogs do not like cats

which are easy to detect by a simple check whenever a new rule or new fact is to be added to a knowledge base, and

2. indirect contradictions such as

    (a) all children like all dogs
    (b) John is a child
    (c) Rover is a dog
    (d) John does not like Rover

which are much more difficult to detect. Note that such inconsistencies can be hidden, e.g. if (c) were replaced by

    (c)(i) Rover is a dog or Fido is a cat

the inconsistency would only occur in situations where it could be shown that 'Fido is a cat' was false.

The indirect form of inconsistency can be extremely difficult to detect, indeed it can be proved that no general algorithm for detecting inconsistency can be constructed in the case of rules that are essentially identical to sentences of first order predicate logic.

The significance of allowing even one inconsistency to get into a rule base is the well-known result in formal logic that given any inconsistency, there will be some sequence of reasoning which will enable the system to establish any conclusion whatsoever, i.e. its output will be entirely unreliable.

It is interesting to note that people seem perfectly able to reason reliably despite the – surely universal – existence of inconsistencies in their knowledge (perhaps of only some obscure topic of little importance). It would be worthwhile to consider how an expert system might somehow 'compartmentalize' its knowledge to avoid minor inconsistencies producing incorrect conclusions on topics completely unrelated to the area of inconsistency.

3.3.8 System maintenance

The problem of maintaining a knowledge base once constructed seems to have been largely disregarded up to now. However, it is more than likely that additional knowledge will need to be added to a knowledge base or existing knowledge deleted or changed at a later stage, e.g. as errors in the system's performance are found or as understanding of the task domain increases.

Although a subject expert may be able to detect a necessary change in a knowledge base (using the explanation facilities provided) it would be most unwise to allow such an individual to make a change directly, or in general to allow a number of different experts to modify a knowledge base. Interactions between different pieces of knowledge (such as different rules) can be very complex, making modification a hazardous process.

It is clearly desirable for some facility to be available to ensure that no piece of knowledge is inserted which directly contradicts knowledge already in the knowledge base and to check that crucial test cases still produce the expected results after a proposed modification is made. More generally, it would seem that a knowledge base management system (analogous to a database management system for conventional software) to control access to the knowledge base may be needed. Research into such systems has been reported by Black and Manley (1987).

It may well be that once expert systems gain regular use in industry staff with the role of knowledge base administrator (analogous to database administrator) will be needed. As an example of the effort involved in maintaining a knowledge base, it has been reported that as many as ten people are employed by DEC solely for the purpose of maintaining the XCON system.

3.3.9 Validation

Validating the correctness of any significant computer system is well-known to present difficulties, but these are considerably accentuated in the case of expert systems.

It is necessary to validate an expert system in at least three situations: whilst under development (since it is only by testing the performance of a system for errors that improvements can be made and a satisfactory knowledge base developed), for acceptance by a customer and whilst in use 'in the field'.

Whilst purchasers of expert systems might insist that the systems delivered to them must first be infallibly correct it would clearly be pointless to do so. In many (probably most) expert system domains the 'correct' solutions are not known (e.g. in the case of much medical diagnosis) or are not 'knowable' (e.g. in deciding on a company's long-term financial strategy). Apart from obvious major errors it will thus frequently be difficult to determine whether a system's conclusions are right or wrong.

The most that can be determined is that the system's conclusions differ from those of an expert. However, experts themselves unavoidably make mistakes and it is frequently the case that experts disagree amongst themselves. A demand for evidence of absolute correctness is thus likely to prove fruitless. Refusal by companies to accept systems under such conditions will simply guarantee that those companies do not use expert systems solutions at all – this would be irrational as companies have never refused to employ human experts on the grounds of their fallibility or the difficulty involved in testing their performance!

As a further complicating factor, it seems inevitable that as confidence in expert systems increases, they will be applied to the solution of problems which occur only rarely and where human expertise is at best fragmentary and widely dispersed (such as how to deal with different forms of environmental pollution or natural disaster). Such systems are inherently almost impossible to validate.

Even in cases where absolute solutions can be determined, it is important to realize that all errors are not equally significant. A system may well be forgiven occasional minor errors if sometimes it out-performs the best human experts. However, even one major error (such as prescribing a fatal overdose of drugs for a patient) is likely to be sufficient to justify rejecting the system altogether.

It would seem that considerations of correctness need to be replaced by those of acceptability of performance and some new techniques of validation may be needed.

Such new techniques might well be based on those by which humans (but not computer programs) are traditionally judged now. No one expects a new graduate engineer (say) never to make a mistake. He or she is unlikely to be entrusted with a project such as designing the Channel Tunnel in the first week of employment. However, a period of working successfully (but not necessarily without error) under supervision will inspire trust and confidence, enabling the graduate to rise to a higher level with a greater degree of responsibility and autonomy.

Thus questions such as 'Does this system work?' may need to be replaced by ones more like 'What class of degree would you give this system?', 'Would you offer it a job – if so, at what level?' or 'Does this system deserve promotion?'. Whether companies will be willing to adapt to this radically different way of viewing their computing systems remains to be seen.

3.3.10 'User-centred' issues

Two important areas of recent research concern the interaction of an expert system with its users.

Kidd (1985) has considered the question of how the advice provided by a system can be related to the expertise of a given user, demonstrating that advice which is perfectly reasonable for one user may be entirely unhelpful to another. The alternative paradigm of 'cooperative problem-solving systems' is proposed, believed to be much closer to the style of human interactions with subject experts, whereby the system and the user 'negotiate' the solution to a problem.

Hughes (1986) has challenged the appropriateness of the explanation facilities frequently provided by expert systems, which are typically little more than the ability to ask how and why questions. Although interrogating an expert system in that way is a facility which is notably lacking with most other computer software, its weakness is that the explanations obtained may be very shallow ones (rather like being quoted the contents of a textbook).

The ability to provide deeper explanations of the underlying reasons for conclusions would doubtless be valuable in many cases, but may well imply the need for a more sophisticated representation of expert knowledge than rules alone, in particular the need for at least a partial causal model of the domain.

3.4 SOCIAL BENEFITS AND ISSUES

Even when expert systems eventually develop a firm theoretical and methodological basis, the field will not cease to be a focus for discussion and probably controversy.

Expert systems development, along with most other areas of technological change, cannot be viewed in isolation from the social and political context in which it takes place.

It is often pointed out that all technology has the potential for both positive and negative uses, as if this is a justification for neglecting any further analysis. This argument is particularly inadequate in the case of expert systems.

What is fundamentally different about expert systems, in contrast to technological developments such as, say, telephones, cars, computerized stock control systems or bank cash dispensers, all of which have their negative side but are fundamentally helpful, [is that expert systems are frequently (although not always) concerned with the judgements made by highly-skilled experts who collectively comprise the leaders of society.[

The inherent suspicion that expert systems may take major decisions out of the hands of people and place computers in charge of tasks such as diagnosing their illnesses, handling their legal problems, running the financial affairs of the companies in which they work and controlling weapons systems may be expressed far more often by the 'outsider' to the field than by those on the inside, but (however far removed from current practice or possibility) would seem to reflect a genuine concern that technological developments may easily lead to people having less control over their lives in the future, rather than more.

3.4.1 Effects on employment

A further natural cause for concern about the growing use of expert systems is that this new technology may follow in the tradition of industrial automation by leading to a large increase in unemployment.

Although such concerns may, of course, prove justified, this consequence seems much less inevitable than with other forms of automation. It is hard to imagine top human experts in fields such as medicine – where the demand for access to experts would rapidly increase to match any increase in availability and there seems to be no limit to the new problems waiting to be tackled by the leading experts – being displaced by computer systems. It is far more likely that in practice expert systems would have the beneficial effect of releasing some of the time of medical experts for more valuable work.

In the case of 'lower-level' (and in some cases lowly-paid) experts such as those controlling industrial processes, the introduction of expert systems is likely to lead to reductions in staffing levels, although it is to be hoped that as with other technological developments appropriate retraining and redeployment will be found for those replaced. Companies rash enough to dispense entirely with their expert staff might well find themselves extremely vulnerable on those occasions when their expert systems failed to perform satisfactorily.

In any case, unlike other forms of automation the development of expert systems depends critically on the support of those human experts who initially are the prime source of the expertise concerned. Widespread use of expert systems as a means of dispensing with skilled staff would quickly lead to retaliation in the form of withdrawal of support, without which (in contrast to the case of most conventional computer applications) the knowledge engineer's task would become very difficult indeed, if not completely impossible.

3.4.2 Military applications

The most sensitive uses to which expert systems are likely to be put are in military applications. The possibilities for signal interpretation systems and for command and control systems (to name only two areas of application) are already clear. The expert systems community would seem to include all shades of opinion on the desirability of such uses, from those who are directly involved in them and regard them as self-evidently right to those who see them as self-evidently wrong and immoral.

The danger with applying any new technology in the military area and perhaps most of all with incorporating human judgement or expertise into computer programs for military applications is that it may act as a destabilizing factor by introducing ever more complexity into a world-wide system of defence/offence that is already precariously balanced and barely controllable.

If successful, the incorporation of human judgement might also act as a stabilizing factor, of course, but the notorious problems and failures of the computer industry even with entirely deterministic and routine tasks such as payroll (hardware errors, software bugs, difficulties of maintenance etc.) do not inspire confidence. To these must be added the rudimentary state of the knowledge engineer's art and the embryonic nature of the development methodology currently employed for building expert systems.

An associated problem is the growing involvement of the military in the funding of academic research. This is happening but is not yet a cause for serious alarm in Britain, but is certainly becoming so in the USA not least as the pressure grows for academic institutions to become involved in the US Government's Strategic Defence Initiative (SDI), popularly known as 'Star Wars'. The risk is, of course, that those who disapprove of such programmes or regard them as unsound or excessively dangerous will be forced to smother their concerns or abandon research altogether.

3.4.3 Deskilling society?

Another part of the impact that some fear expert systems may come to make on society, even where the applications domains are not themselves open to suspicion or criticism, is in the 'deskilling' of expert tasks, where the availability of expert systems may enable expert-level decisions to be made by those with considerably less expertise (or none at all) themselves.

To take a medical example, it may be possible for the general practitioner to operate at the level of skill of a top consultant in some specialized area.

It could well be argued that this is highly beneficial as a way of transferring expertise from the skilled to the less skilled. It could mean that the skills of leading experts could be made available in even the remotest (or poorest) parts of the world where there are no human experts and rapid decisions are often required.

On the other hand, it is possible that such a transfer of skills could operate in a detrimental way, by fostering an increasing reliance on relatively junior members of staff. To pursue the example of medicine, it would be possible to use the availability of expert systems as an excuse for dispensing with access to consultants altogether for the large majority of patients (for example, those making use of the British National Health Service), rather than making more of the consultants' time available to deal with the most difficult cases.

3.4.4 Accountability

A problem which has not attracted much attention up to now, but which cannot be neglected indefinitely is that of accountability for the actions, decisions or recommendations of expert systems.

At present, few expert systems are in everyday use and far fewer are available for the general public to purchase 'off the shelf'. However, as the number of systems of both kinds increases in the future, the potential for their misuse (not to mention errors resulting from bugs in the systems) will increase correspondingly.

There is of course a problem of accountability with the use of all software, but these problems are significantly increased when systems are expected to fail occasionally. Purchasers who will not freely accept expert systems on that basis will not use them at all and it is difficult to see how software writers who openly admit that the systems they develop will occasionally give wrong results, poor diagnoses etc. can be held liable when they do. The software writer can hardly be blamed if the user is not skilled enough to realize when such a case has occurred.

The potential hazards for the unwary in using expert systems are undoubtedly serious. Most individuals would not even consider taking on for themselves the role of a highly-skilled professional such as a solicitor, a doctor or an accountant (even assuming it were always legal to do so), without possessing the necessary technical knowledge and experience. However, it is perfectly possible for anyone to make use of books incorporating the expertise of such experts, as the readily available medical textbooks and the growth of books with titles such as *Do your own House Conveyancing* illustrates. Incorporating knowledge of this kind in expert systems makes its accessibility still greater, potentially giving almost anyone access to, for example, medical or legal advice of the highest quality and thus enabling them to perform as their own professional experts and advisers, should they choose to do so.

While the supply of such software is restricted to software houses with considerable skill and high integrity and their users are appropriately chosen, this might be regarded as highly desirable, indeed a way of breaking down the 'power of the priesthood' in a number of professions.

Unfortunately, the reality is likely to be very different. It is easy to predict a flood of low-cost software produced for the hobbyist/home-computer market. No one who has followed the progress of this market could feel confident that low cost will not not lead to low quality and low reliability. The dangers of giving even good information to those without the ability to interpret it correctly are also well-known. ('A little knowledge is a dangerous thing'.)

The risks are real enough even with high-performance expert systems, which are still likely to make errors on occasions (just like human experts), but are far greater with low-cost versions which may be badly programmed, make use of low-grade 'experts' to build the systems and so on, with a corresponding increase in the risk of major errors occurring.

Authors of software of this kind may include disclaimers about the quality of their performance. Such disclaimers might or might not have any legal force. Equally, it is notoriously difficult to successfully (and usefully) take legal action against very small companies or private individuals.

It is difficult to see how the proliferation of low-grade expert system software could possibly be stopped if it took hold amongst computer hobbyists. Although not a problem now, this could easily become one.

Of course, this is little different from the position in the computer industry as a whole. The essential difference is the much greater risk involved in giving a large number of individuals access to professional-level expertise which is in fact erroneous, or possibly correct but misleading. Compared with this, the risk of a games program containing a bug or a word processing program occasionally losing a line of text is quite insignificant.

3.4.5 Codifying knowledge

A major potential benefit of expert systems is the development over a period of time of improved codifications of expert knowledge.

This would be by no means a new phenomenon. Historically, it is the ability to record its knowledge (in the form of books, or in earlier times in stories, songs, etc.) that has enabled each generation to develop by building on the skills of those that have gone before. There are two aspects to this. Not only does the expertise of the most skilled person in a field in one generation progressively 'filter down' to the ordinary participants in that field in future generations, but the capability of starting at a much higher level enables the most skilled in succeeding generations to progress ever further.

The development of expert systems may enable a major acceleration of this process to occur. Computer programs have important advantages over books etc. as media for the recording of knowledge in that not only can they be updated rapidly but they are necessarily precise and unambiguous. Any dispute over the meaning of a program can ultimately be solved by running it.

The availability of the expertise of a leading practitioner in a field in a fully precise and directly testable form may well enable others to find improved ways of codifying that knowledge, to look for simplifications, to identify errors or omissions, or to find improved ways of teaching the underlying skills. A refined form of the knowledge might again be stored in the form of an expert system, but might instead be communicated in the more conventional form of textbooks, etc.

3.4.6 Expert systems as an aid for education and training

A valuable additional benefit of developing an expert system, which has been little exploited so far, is the possibility that it may be used directly as an aid for education and training.

One approach to this is the development of so-called **intelligent tutoring systems** (ITS), which interface with an existing expert system to produce a system for teaching students about the task domain in question. The best-known of these is probably the Guidon system (Clancey, 1979) for teaching about the bacterial infections domain of MYCIN.

Guidon aims to transfer MYCIN's expertise to a student via a dialogue about a particular case diagnosis.

The student plays the role of a consultant who, after being given general information about a case, asks the system a series of questions (such as 'Is the patient feverish') to enable him or her to arrive at a diagnosis.

Guidon compares the student's questions with those which would have been asked by MYCIN in the same circumstances and comments on that basis.

The fundamental components of such a system are three models:

1. of the knowledge to be learned
2. of the teaching process
3. of the student.

Only the first of these is available in the expert system itself and producing the other two is far from a simple task.

Research into ITS shows the considerable additional complexity involved in teaching others to perform a task rather than performing it oneself and the development of intelligent tutoring systems remains at present a very complex research area.

A much more straightforward but still valuable approach is that of using an expert system unaltered, as a way of training those already fairly skilled in the field in question.

An analogy can be made with the training of pilots using flight simulators. It is not possible to give trainee pilots direct practical experience of every combination of circumstances (many of them extremely dangerous) that can occur in the air. However, it is perfectly possible to present trainees with a series of simulated situations to see how well they respond, without risk of injury to themselves or others.

Expert systems fit in well with this style of training as the student can not only be given personal experience of decision making in a complex case but can see what an expert would do in that situation and interrogate the system as to the reasons for its conclusions.

Such an approach may be very valuable as a way of helping the 'near-expert' to add to his or her skill, but is likely to be much less effective for teaching the novice, who will generally lack the expertise necessary to interpret the explanations given.

3.5 THE FUTURE

Although up to now most applications of expert systems have been in relatively well-understood task areas, it may safely be predicted that in the future expert systems techniques will increasingly be applied in more complex areas, where (in many cases) no 'objective' solutions exist. In order for this to be successfully accomplished, it will be necessary to call more fully on the techniques of knowledge representation, reasoning, etc. of the wider field of AI.

As the field becomes larger, it is likely that it will divide into a variety of specialist sub-fields. (Indeed, there is already a growing number of specialized conferences on topics such as 'Expert systems in computer-aided design', 'Expert systems for structural design' and 'Expert database systems'.)

Alongside this, we may see the current 'generalist' knowledge engineer superseded by specialists who are themselves trained in a field such as insurance, medicine or civil engineering and thus are hopefully better able than the generalist to elicit knowledge from subject experts in that field. If this occurs, it is possible that the apparently major problem of knowledge acquisition will shrink to manageable proportions.

In the next few years, interest is likely to be increasingly focused on high-value applications (particularly financial applications, such as insurance underwriting), where substantial sums of money are involved and thus considerable increases in a company's profits can be made by marginal improvements in performance, without any need for an expert system to achieve anything remotely approaching perfection.

As well as the conventional mode of use, it is likely that we shall see more 'mobile' expert systems in use for outdoor applications. These might for example be mounted in a maintenance engineer's van and connected via a radio link with a mainframe back at his or her base (e.g. for database access) or incorporated in a small hand-held portable computer.

It is also likely that we shall see many more uses of 'expert' modules forming part of systems for 'conventional' applications as well as standalone expert systems – in much the same way that information technology has found far more practical use for the layman in the form of embedded components in standard items such as cars, washing machines and portable telephones, than in standalone videotext or teletext (information retrieval) systems.

3.6 CONCLUSIONS

Although the pace of development in the expert systems field in recent years is extremely impressive, it is hard to escape the feeling that we are still only scratching the surface of a major new technology with potential which as yet is barely appreciated.

The state of the art is now such that relatively simple systems can be built in a straightforward way using low-cost software running on hardware that is widely available. Building more complex systems remains a 'craft' activity in which there is a small but increasing number of practitioners. There is an important need for a careful evaluation and synthesis of the lessons learnt from the development of complex systems for commercial applications up to now, in order to place expert systems building on a sound theoretical and methodological basis for the future.

Alongside this there are a number of fundamental technical problems which remain unsolved, but which must be overcome before expert systems could safely be applied to sensitive commercial tasks on a regular basis.

It is clear that if the field can come to terms with the technical problems that currently exist, the potential payoffs from expert systems are enormous. By way of summary, at least six kinds of use can be identified.

1. to increase expert productivity (by automating the easiest cases and thereby freeing the expert to concentrate on more complex problems)
2. to augment expert capability (by making the skill of a greater expert available to a lesser one)
3. to spread expertise more widely (when human experts are scarce)
4. to provide expert training aids (cf. flight simulators)
5. to preserve expertise ('rare skills archiving', where expertise might otherwise be lost)
6. to provide heuristic solutions (where systems could not otherwise be developed or would be computationally infeasible to use).

Unfortunately, despite the large sums being spent on expert systems development there seems to be little interest in carrying out comparative studies of the effectiveness of different techniques, e.g. of knowledge acquisition or knowledge representation. In the case of Britain, millions of pounds of public funds have been spent on financing a wide range of expert systems projects, mostly involving specific one-off applications, but even for those projects there is little interest in comparative evaluation.

Present indications are that national funding bodies in the West are far more interested in developing further applications than in extending the underlying theory. Unless industry is prepared to take on this important task, much of the potential benefit of expert systems to industry may not be realized, and the vision of a new generation of increasingly 'intelligent' computer systems – with all the benefits they could bring to business and industry – may yet turn out to be a mirage.

3.7 REFERENCES

Adams, J. B. (1976) A probability model of reasoning and the MYCIN model. *Mathematical Biosciences*, **32**, 177–86.

Black, D. and Manley, J. (1987) A logic-based architecture for knowledge management. *Proc. Tenth Int. Joint Conf. on Artificial Intelligence*, Milan.

Bramer, M. A. (1987) Expert systems in business: a British perspective. *Proc. First Int. Symposium on Artificial Intelligence and Expert Systems*, Berlin.

Buchanan, B. G. and Shortliffe, E. H. (eds) (1984) *Rule-Based Expert Systems: the MYCIN Experiments of the Stanford Heuristic Programming Project.* Addison-Wesley, Mass.

Buchanan, B. G., Sutherland, G. L. and Feigenbaum, E. A. (1969) Rediscovering some problems of artificial intelligence in the context of chemistry. In B. Meltzer and D. Michie (eds), *Machine Intelligence 5*, Edinburgh University Press, Edinburgh, pp. 253–80.

Burton, A. M., Shadbolt, N. R., Hedgecock, A. P. and Rugg, G. (1988) A formal evaluation of knowledge elicitation techniques for expert systems: Domain 1. In D. S. Moralee, (ed.) *Research and Development in Expert Systems IV*, Cambridge University Press, Cambridge, pp. 136–45.

Clancey, W. J. (1979) Transfer of rule-based expertise through a tutorial dialogue. PhD Thesis, Stanford University.

CRI (1986) *The CRI Directory of Expert Systems.* Learned Information (Europe) Ltd.

Ellam, S. V. and Maisey, M. N. (1986) A knowledge based system to assist in medical image interpretation: design and evaluation methodology. In M. A. Bramer, (ed.) *Research and Development in Expert Systems III*, Cambridge University Press, Cambridge, pp. 89–98.

Gammack, J. G. and Young, R. M. (1985) Psychological techniques for eliciting expert knowledge. In M. A. Bramer (ed.) *Research and Development in Expert Systems*, Cambridge University Press, Cambridge, pp. 105–12.

Hewett, J. (1986) Commercial expert systems in North America. *Proc. Sixth Int. Workshop on Expert Systems and their Applications*, Avignon, France, pp. 35–41.

Hughes, S. (1986) Question classification in rule-based systems. In M. A. Bramer (ed.) *Research and Development in Expert Systems III*, Cambridge University Press, Cambridge, pp. 123–31.

JIPDEC (1981) *Preliminary Report on Study and Research on Fifth-Generation Computers 1979–1980.* Japan Information Processing Development Center.

Kidd, A. (1985) What do users ask – some thoughts on diagnostic advice. In M. Merry, (ed.) *Expert Systems 85*, Cambridge University Press, Cambridge, pp. 9–19.

McCorduck, P. (1979) *Machines Who Think.* W. H. Freeman and Co., San Francisco.

Quinlan, J. R. (1986) Induction of decision trees. *Machine Learning*, **1**, 81–106.

Shortliffe, E. H. (1976) *Computer-Based Medical Consultations: MYCIN.* Elsevier, New York.

Shortliffe, E. H. and Buchanan, B. G. (1975) A model of inexact reasoning in medicine. *Mathematical Biosciences*, **23**, 351–79.

Steels, L. (1986) Second generation expert systems. In M. A. Bramer, (ed.) *Research and Development in Expert Systems III*, Cambridge University Press, Cambridge, pp. 175–83.

Welbank, M. (1983) *A Review of Knowledge Acquisition Techniques for Expert Systems*. British Telecom Research Laboratories Technical Report.

Reasoning

4

Inside the inference engine

IAN GRAHAM

4.1 KNOWLEDGE-BASED SYSTEMS

This chapter deals with the notion of a knowledge application system, and takes a look at the internal operation of inference engines to be found in many expert systems and expert systems shell products. However, the intimate interpenetration of reasoning and its subject matter, knowledge, precludes a discussion which does not include some treatment of knowledge representation. The question of how human beings store and manipulate knowledge is a question only touched upon. (See also Chapter 8.)

The questions of how knowledge comes about and how it may be substantiated – what philosophers call the problem of cognition, or epistemology – is sufficiently neglected in the current literature of knowledge engineering to deserve a little attention.

We also have to ask how the interconnection between knowledge and inference is mediated. In our view this leads to a study of the management of uncertainty in expert systems, a subject to be dealt with further in Chapters 5 and 6.

This chapter is partly based on material from Graham and Jones (1988), to which the reader is referred for further details and background information.

4.1.1 The components of a knowledge-based system

It has become generally accepted that there are essentially three components of a knowledge-based computer system. First is the underlying environment of symbol and value manipulation which all computer systems share and which can be thought of as the programming languages and support environment: editors, floating point processors, data structures, compilers, etc. Secondly, we have the structure of the knowledge itself including methods of representation and access, and lastly, there must be some techniques for applying the knowledge in a rational manner to the problem at hand. This third element has been called the 'control strategy', the 'inference engine' and, as we prefer, the **knowledge application system.**

The architecture which has emerged in recent years as standard in knowledge-based and expert systems is precisely what we have described in Fig. 4.1. The point to be illustrated is that the knowledge base and the inference strategy are

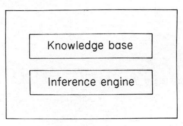

Fig. 4.1 The architecture of an expert system

best separated from one another to facilitate maintenance. After all, in most cases knowledge will change over time and one does not want to rewrite the application system whenever a new rule is added. In real systems this separation is achieved to a greater or lesser extent and may be regarded as an ideal to be strived for. However, from another point of view it is clear that this separation is artificial. The manner of reasoning with knowledge is affected profoundly by the way it is presented to us and represented by us. Conversely, the essential nature of our knowledge about objects is characterized to a large extent by our innate logical processes. We shall see that cognitive and social processes also play a part in human knowledge if not in computer systems.

4.1.2 Knowledge representation and inference

Starting from the point of view of computer science, most of us are familiar with the notion of data, that is unstructured sets of numbers, facts and symbols. These data can convey information only in virtue of some structure or decoding mechanism. In the limiting case this distinction can be illustrated by two people who may communicate via a channel which may only carry one message consisting of a single symbol. The datum, the symbol itself, carries no information except in virtue of the presence of the channel, whose structure determines that the receiver may learn from the absence of a symbol as well from its transmission. Two points emerge from this example. Information always has a context while data may be context free; thus if I say 'she shot up' that is a datum for which I would need to explain whether the person in question was an astronaut or a heroin addict to convey information. Knowledge is usually seen as a concept at a higher level of abstraction, and there is a sense in which this is true. For example, '1000' is a datum, '1000 isobars at noon' could be information about the weather in some situations but 'Most people feel better when the pressure rises above 1000' is knowledge about barometric information and people. The realization that much knowledge is expressed in the form of heuristic descriptions or rules of thumb is what gives rise to the conception of knowledge as more abstract than information.

Apart from asking what it is, epistemologists have been concerned with several other issues concerning knowledge:

1. How may it be classified?
2. How is it obtained?
3. Does it have objective reality?
4. Is it limited in principle?

As a preliminary attempt at classification we might note that there are several evidently different types of knowledge at hand; knowledge about objects, events, task performance, and even about knowledge itself. If we know something about tomatoes we will probably know that tomatoes are red, however, we are still prepared to recognize a green tomato; so that contradictions often coexist within our knowledge. Object knowledge is often expressed in the form of assertions, although this is by no means the only available formalism and frames are particularly well suited to this purpose. Here are a few typical assertions:

TOMATOES ARE RED
THIS BOTTLE IS MADE OF GLASS
ZOE IS VERY LIVELY

Knowledge of causality, however, is expressed typically as a chain of statements relating cause to effect:

IF YOU BOIL TOMATOES WITH THE RIGHT ACCOMPANIMENTS CHUTNEY RESULTS

To perform a task as commonplace as walking in fact requires a very complex interacting system of knowledge about balance, muscle tone, etc. much of which is held subconsciously and is deeply integrated in with our biological hardware. Knowledge about cognition, often called meta-knowledge, also needs to be represented when such questions as 'What do I know?' and 'How useful or complete is a particular knowledge system or inference strategy?' are raised. This, we hope, leads to a clear perception that there is no clear boundary between knowledge and inference as practices. Each interpenetrates the other; we have inference with knowledge and knowledge about inference.

There are various dimensions along which knowledge can be evaluated:

1. Scope – what does it cover?
2. Granularity – how detailed is it?
3. Uncertainty – how certain or plausible is it?
4. Completeness – might we have to retract conclusions if new knowledge comes to light?
5. Consistency – how easily can we live with its contradictions?
6. Modality – can we avoid it?

The above dimensions are all connected with some form of uncertainty. This arises from the contradictory nature of knowledge. Knowledge presents itself in two basic forms as absolute and relative. To understand this consider the whole of the history of science, which is an attempt to arrive at a knowledge of the environment we inhabit. The scientist develops this or that theory or paradigm which explains experimental evidence and is further verified in practice. He or she never suspects that any theory is comprehensively correct, at least not nowadays; Newton's models overthrew the theories of earlier times and were in their turn overthrown by Einstein's. If nature exists beyond, before and apart from us then it represents, in all its complexity, an absolute truth which is (in principle) beyond knowledge because nature is not in itself human and knowledge is. To assume otherwise is to assert that nature is either a totally human construct or that the whole may be totally assimilated by a fragment of itself. This is not to say that the finite may not know the infinite, only that the knowledge may only be relative, otherwise the finite would contain the infinite and thus become infinite itself. Thus all truth seeking aims at the absolute but achieves the relative and here it is that we see why all knowledge must perforce be uncertain. This is why the correct handling of uncertainty is one of the primary concerns for builders of knowledge-based systems of any sort.

The dimensions of knowledge mentioned above all will have some bearing on the techniques used to represent knowledge. If we choose logic as the representation then, if our knowledge is incomplete, non-monotonic logic will be required in preference to first order predicate logic, and in the presence of uncertainty a logic capable of handling it will be requisite. Similar remarks apply to inconsistent knowledge where contradiction must be handled either by the logic or the control structure or meta-logic. Modality will require the use of a logic which can deal with necessity and possibility.

If, on the other hand we choose frames or network representations the scope and granularity will affect the amount of storage we can expect to use. For this it is useful to have some metrics. Granularity is often measured in 'chunks'. Anderson (1976) defines a chunk to be a learned configuration of symbols which comes to act as a single symbol. The passage between levels of representation is an important theme in AI research and has great bearing on the practical question of efficiency of storage and execution. Generally speaking, you should choose a granularity close to that adopted by human experts, if this can be discerned, and use chunking whenever gains are not made at the expense of understandability.

4.1.3 Knowledge and inference – cognition and activity

There are two important questions about the representation of knowledge. First there was the question of how knowledge is represented in the human or animal brain, and now there is that of what structures may be used for computer representation. The first question is the concern of cognitive psychology and psychoanalysis and will not exercise us greatly here. However, the theories of the cognitive psychologists have much to offer in the way of ideas and cognitive simulation has been an important issue in research on expert systems. The interdisciplinary subject of artificial intelligence indeed has been defined as 'the study of mental faculties through the use of computational models' (Charniak and

McDermott, 1985); exactly the reverse of what interests us as builders of knowledge-based systems. Perhaps this is why there is such a considerable overlap and confusion between the fields today. One important point to make categorically is that no one knows how the human brain works and no one can give a prescription for the best computer knowledge representation formalism. Until some pretty fundamental advances are made, our best bet as system builders is to use pragmatically whatever formalism best suits the task at hand.

Quite apart from its ability to be abstract at various levels knowledge is concerned with action. It is concerned with practice in the world. Knowing how people feel under different atmospheric conditions helps us to respond better to their moods, work with them or even improve their air-conditioning (if we have some knowledge about ventilation engineering as well). Incidentally, it also assumes the existence of various socially evolved measuring devices; such as the barometer, thermometer, and so on. Knowledge is a guide to informed practice and relates to information as a processor; that is, we understand knowledge but we process information. It is no use knowing that people respond well to high pressure if you cannot measure that pressure. Effective use of knowledge leads to the formation of plans of action and ultimately to deeper understanding. This leads to a subsidiary definition that knowledge is concerned with using information effectively. The next level of abstraction might be called theory.

From this point of view, inference is to knowledge as processing is to information. It is the method used to transform perceptions (via some symbolic representation) into a form suitable for reconversion into actions. Inference may also be viewed as an abstraction from practical activity. In our experience of the world we observe, both individually and collectively, that certain consequences follow from certain actions. We give this phenomenon the name Causality, and say that action A 'causes' perception B. Later (both in ontogenesis and philogenesis) we generalize this to include causal relations between external events independent of ourselves. From there it is a short step (one originally taken at the end of the Bronze Age) to the idea that ideas are related in a similar way; that symbol A can 'imply' symbol B. This process of abstraction corresponds, according to Piaget, to the process of child development. Historically, it corresponds to the development of the division of labour. In other words just as tool making and social behaviour make knowledge possible, so the interdependencies of the world of nature are developed into the abstract relations of human thinking, part of this system of relationships corresponding to inference.

Of course, computers do not partake of social activity, nor yet do they create tools (although they may manufacture and use them if we include robots in our perception of computing machinery). As far as inference is concerned we cannot expect computers to encompass the richness and depth of human reasoning (at least not in the foreseeable future). For many thousands of years it has been convenient, for certain applications in the special sciences, to reason with a formalized subset of human reasoning. This 'formal logic' has been the basis of most Western technological developments, and while not capturing the scope of human informal reasoning is immensely powerful in resolving many practical problems. Thus we are converging on a definition of inference which will serve the purposes of knowledge engineering. Inference in this sense is the abstract, formal process by which conclusions may be drawn from premises. It is a special kind of meta-knowledge about the abstract relationships between symbols representing knowledge.

Many philosophers have questioned whether true artificial intelligence is possible in principle. In our view the question is merely maladroit. Clearly, if we are able in future to genetically (or otherwise) engineer an artificial human being there is no reason (excluding spurious religious arguments) why the constructed entity should not be 'intelligent' by any normal criteria. If, on the other hand, the question is posed as to whether electronic computers of the type currently existing or foreseeable can pass the Turing test, then matters are a little different. Human cognition is a process mediated by both society and the artefacts of Man's construction. It may well be that no entity (be it a computer or a totally dissimilar organism from outer space) could ever dissemble its true non-social, non-toolmaking character sufficiently to deceive the testers. Our belief is that artificial intelligence in this sense is impossible, but that useful results are to be obtained by trying to achieve an approximation.

Let us now descend from these abstract considerations and return to our programme. How can computers be made to simulate reasoning? It is to this question that we now turn.

4.2 INFERENCE IN KNOWLEDGE-BASED SYSTEMS

Given that knowledge is stored in a computer in some convenient representation or representations, the system will require facilities for navigating through and manipulating the knowledge if anything is to be achieved at all. Inference in the usual logical sense is this process of drawing valid conclusions from premises. In our wider sense it is any computational mechanism whereby stored knowledge can be applied to data and information structures to arrive at conclusions which are to be plausible rather than valid in the strict logical sense. This, of course, poses problems in relation to how to judge whether the conclusions are reasonable, and how to represent knowledge about how to test conclusions and how to evaluate plausibility. Thus we can see that knowledge representation and inference are inextricably bound together. Before exploring the inference strategies of expert systems we introduce some ideas from formal logic. We first deal with the rules for making individual inferences.

4.2.1 Inference methods and logic

Before moving on to the more complex inference strategies to be found in expert systems, we first look at the basics of simple inferences as found in Aristotelian logic. In doing this we follow closely the treatment to be found in McCawley

(1981). We start with some definitions. A **formal system** comes equipped with the connectives

∧ (and), ∨ (or), ¬ (not), ⇒ (implies), ⇔ (if) and (sometimes) =

and with (at least) two quantification symbols

∀ and ∃

The primitive symbols are usually taken to include only 'and', 'or', 'implies' and 'not'. These symbols can be used together with propositions to make up sentences, and these are valid sentences when they follow by specified rules of inference from a few selected sentences called axioms. The rules of inference we will use here fall into two classes called rules of introduction and rules of elimination. The introduction rule for 'and' says that, for example, if the sentences:

Amy is American
Peter is English
Rudolph is French

are all true, then we may infer that the sentence:

Amy is American and Peter is English and Rudolph is French

is also true. The corresponding elimination rule says that if the previous sentence is true then we may infer that any one of the earlier three holds. We may state the rules more succinctly in the following rather general form as **rules of inference.**

∧ introduction	∧ elimination
p	$\dfrac{p \wedge q \wedge r}{p}$
q	
r	
$\dfrac{}{p \wedge q \wedge r}$	

Similarly, we can state rules for the other connectives and the quantifiers.

∨ introduction	∨ elimination
$\dfrac{p}{p \vee q \vee r}$	$\dfrac{p \vee q \vee r}{\text{one of } p, q, r}$

The rules of ¬ introduction and elimination are known as '*reductio ad absurdum*' and 'the law of the excluded middle' respectively. They are not valid in all logical systems. For the purposes of reasoning one of the most interesting rules is ⇒ elimination which is also known as *modus ponens*:

p ⇒ q   (*Modus ponens*, ⇒ elimination)

$$\frac{p}{q}$$

This rule sanctions inferences of the form:

If Socrates is a man, then he is mortal
Socrates is a man
    Therefore
Socrates is mortal.

$\Rightarrow$ introduction sanctions the following type of argument:

Whoever committed the murder left by the window.
Anyone leaving by the window would have mud on his boots.
If the butler committed the murder, then he left by the window.
Therefore he has mud on his boots.
So, if the butler did it he has muddy boots.

This just says that implication is transitive;

$p \Rightarrow q$ ($\Rightarrow$ introduction)
$q \Rightarrow r$
___

$p \Rightarrow r$

Now the rules for the quantifiers.

$\forall$ introduction (generalization)

p
___
$(\overline{\forall} x) p(x)$

$\forall$ elimination

$(\forall x : q(x) \Rightarrow p(x))$

$q(a)$
___
$p(a)$

$\exists$ introduction
$p(a)$
___
$(\exists x) p(x)$

The rule of $\exists$ elimination is left to the reader as an exercise.

Returning to *modus ponens* as a model of reasoning forwards from premises to conclusion, we can put the case as follows. From a fact p and a rule $p \Rightarrow q$ we may deduce a new fact q with certainty. Two other rules of inference which follow from those given above is *modus tollens* and the resolution principle which latter is the basis of automatic theorem proving systems (Robinson, 1965):

Modus tollens	Resolution
$p \Rightarrow q$	$p \lor q$
$\neg q$	$\neg q \lor r$
$\neg p$	$p \lor r$

Modus tollens is clearly very different from *modus ponens*: we are reasoning backwards from the falsity of a conclusion to the falsity of the premise. *Modus tollens* is much harder for humans to understand and compute with although it is similar to a lot of problem-solving behaviour, as we will see later when we encounter backward chaining. For example, suppose p = 'It is raining' and q = 'It is cloudy', then the two kinds of inference are exemplified by:

If it is raining then we know it must be cloudy
If it is not cloudy then we know it can't be raining

In the latter case we are implicitly invoking the rule of *modus tollens* on the implication 'if raining then cloudy'.

4.3 FORWARD AND BACKWARD CHAINING AND MIXED STRATEGIES

Up to now we have only considered the problem of how to infer the truth value of one proposition from another using a rule of inference in just one step. Clearly however, there will be occasions when such inferences (or proofs) will involve long chains of reasoning using the rules of inference and some initial suppositions (or axioms). We now turn to the generalizations of *modus ponens* and *modus tollens* which feature strongly in all expert systems and are supplied as standard code in many expert system shells.

4.3.1 Forward chaining

To fix ideas we will consider an expert system whose knowledge is represented in the form of production rules and whose domain is the truth of abstract propositions: A, B, C, . . .

The knowledge base is as follows.

Rule 1: A and B and C implies D
Rule 2: D and F   implies G
Rule 3: E   implies F
Rule 4: F   implies B
Rule 5: B   implies C
Rule 6: G   implies H
Rule 7: I   implies J
Rule 8: A and F   implies H

To start with, assume that two-valued logic and *modus ponens* are available, and that the expert system has been asked whether proposition H is true given that propositions A and F are true. We will show that the system may approach the problem in two quite distinct ways. Assume for the present that the computer stores these rules on a sequential device such as magnetic tape, so that it must access the rules in order unless it rewinds to rule 1.

What we are about to describe is the forward chaining inference strategy. This itself has several variants. We may pass through the rules until a single rule fires, we may continue until all rules have been processed once, or we may continue firing in either manner until either the conclusion we desire has been achieved or until the database ceases to be changed by the process. A little thought shows that this gives at least four different varieties of forward chaining. This will become clearer as we proceed.

The assumption is that A and F are true. If we apply all the rules to this database the only rules that fire are 5 and 8 and the firing of rule 8 assigns the value true to H, which is what we were after. Suppose now that rule 8 is excised from the knowledge base. Can we still prove H? This time only rule 5 fires, so we have to rewind and apply the rules again to have any chance of proving the target proposition. Below we show what happens to the truth values in the database on successive applications of the rules 1 to 7.

	Iteration number							
	0	1	2	3	4	5	6	7
A	T	T	T	T	T	T	T	T
B		T	T	T	T	T	T	T
C			T	T	T	T	T	T
D				T	T	T	T	T
E								
F	T	T	T	T	T	T	T	T
G					T	T	T	T
H						T	T	T
I								
J								

So, H is proven after five iterations. Note, in passing, that further iterations do not succeed in proving any further propositions in this particular case. Since we are considering a computer strategy, we need to program some means by which the machine is to know when to stop applying rules. From the above example there are two methods; either 'stop when H becomes true' or 'stop when the database ceases to change on rule application'. Which one of these two we select depends on the system's purpose, for one interesting side effect of the latter procedure is that we have proven the proposition B, C, D and G and, were we later to need to know their truth values, we need do no more computation. On the other hand, if this is not an important consideration we might have proved H long before we can prove everything else.

It should be noted that we have assumed that the rules are applied 'in parallel', which is to say that in any one iteration every rule fires on the basis that the data are as they were at the beginning of the cycle. This is not necessary, but we would warn of the confusion which would result from the alternative in any practical applications; a knowledge-based, and thus essentially declarative system, should not be dependent on the order in which the rules are entered, stored or processed unless there is some very good reason for forcing modularity on the rules.

These two strategies are both known as forward chaining or data-directed reasoning, because they begin with the data known and apply *modus ponens* successively to find out what results are implied. In expert systems, this strategy is particularly appropriate in situations where data are expensive to collect but few in quantity. Typical domains are financial planning, process control, the configuration of complex systems and system tuning.

In the example given, the antecedents and consequents of the rules are all of the same type; propositions in some logical system. However, this need not be the case. For example, in industrial control applications the inputs might be measurements but the output control actions. In that case it does not make sense to add these incommensurables together in the database. Variations on forward chaining now include: 'pass through the rules until a single rule fires then act'; 'pass through all the rules once and then act'.

4.3.2 Backward chaining

There is a completely different way we could have set about proving H, and that is to start with the desired goal 'H is true' and attempt to find evidence for this to be the case. This is backward chaining or goal-directed inference. It is usual when the only thing we need to do is prove H and are not interested in the value of other propositions.

Backwards chaining arises typically in situations where the quantity of data is potentially very large and where some specific characteristic of the system under consideration is of interest. Most typical are various problems of diagnosis, such as medical diagnosis or fault finding in electrical or mechanical equipment. Most first generation expert system shells are based on some form of backward chaining, although some early production rule languages such as OPS5 use forward chaining.

Returning to our original eight rules, the system is asked to find a rule which proves H. The only candidate rules are 6 and 8, but 6 is encountered first. At this point we establish a new sub-goal of proving that G is true, for if we can do this then it would follow that H were true by *modus ponens*. Our next sub-goal will be to prove that D and F are true. Recall that we have told the system that A and F are true, so it is only necessary to prove D (by $\wedge$ – introduction). The whole proof proceeds as follows.

Trying to prove H
Try rule 6
Trying to prove G
Try rule 2
F is true, trying to prove D
Try rule 1
A is true, trying to prove B

Try rule 4
It works. B is true
Backtrack to trying rule 1
Trying to prove C
Try rule 5, it works. C is true
Apply rule 1, D is true
Apply rule 2, G is true
Apply rule 6, H is true

The observant reader will have noticed that we could have proved H in one step from rule 8. The point is that rule 8 was not reached and the system could not know in advance that it was going to be quicker to explore that rule than rule 6. On the other hand if the original line of exploration had failed (suppose rule 4 was deleted) then the system would have had to backtrack and try rule 8. Figure 4.2 illustrates the proof strategy.

It is these considerations that lead to viewing backward chaining as a strategy for search through trees built in some solution space. The strategy we have described is usually called depth-first search in that context. In the next section we look at alternative strategies.

Barr and Feigenbaum (1981) point out that most problems may be represented either by search for points in a state space, by reduction to simpler sub-problems or by game trees. The point which emerges quite quickly is that all these representations are formally equivalent in so far as methods of search are concerned, even if they are not always equally convenient in terms of efficiency of search. The problem of mechanically choosing a convenient representation is still a long way from being a solved one. Here we will assume that a representation has been chosen and that the problem is to search for a solution (or solutions) only.

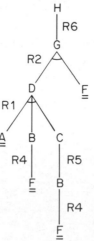

Fig. 4.2 Proving H by backward chaining. Note that underlined symbols are those given as true

4.3.3 Mixed strategies and tree search

We have introduced two fundamental forms of inference, forward and backward chaining. In practice most reasoning is a mixture of at least these two. Given some initial assumption, we infer a conclusion by reasoning forwards and then apply backward chaining to find other data which confirm these conclusions. This process of abduction will be dealt with further in the next section. Alternatively, we start with a goal, backward chain to some plausible reason and then forward chain to exploit the consequences of this new datum. This is often called 'backwards reasoning with opportunistic forward chaining', because the data-directed search exploits the consequences of data as they become available 'opportunistically'. This method is commonly found in the better expert systems shells. Both these methods can be represented as a search through a branching network or tree, and trees may be searched in a number of ways. We turn briefly now to some of the available methods. The subject of tree search is so well covered in the existing literature that we will not attempt exhaustive descriptions of every technique, but try to give the general idea for each one with a view to giving some intuition as to when a particular technique is likely to be appropriate to a problem.

Methods of searching trees may be conveniently divided into blind search and informed search. The latter is often called heuristic or intelligent search. The two basic methods of blind search are called depth-first and breadth-first search. Depth-first search corresponds to what we did in the example given in the preceding section. It is important however not to confuse totally backward chaining with depth-first search; the terms backward and forward chaining refer to the relationship between goals and data, whereas a depth-first search may be applied to either and refers only to the solution strategy. It is convenient sometimes to blur the distinction and think of depth-first search as the 'usual' way of doing backward chaining.

Depth-first search proceeds broadly as follows. Look for the left-most (or first) node beneath the goal node (or initial data in the case of forward chaining) and check if it is terminal (i.e. proven or a goal), if not establish it on a list of sub-goals outstanding. Start again with the node reached as goal. Once there are no lower level nodes then, providing the current node is not terminal, go back to the last sub-goal on the outstanding list and take the next route of descent to the right. If the tree has an AND/OR structure then success indicates going back to the last AND node, while failure indicates a return to the last outstanding OR node. Since we do not know in advance how deep the search may go only to find a failure or dead end before backtracking, it is sometimes convenient to place a restriction on the maximum depth of any one exploration. In fact the search may go on forever with infinite trees, in which case the only course is to set a limit. This is called a depth bound. The danger, of course, is that the required solution may be one step below the bound level. There are two principal methods of implementation for this kind of search, although they are formally equivalent. In languages like Prolog which depend on the idea of pattern matching the implementation technique is called 'backtracking' and is as we have described except that explored paths are explicitly deleted and blocked and variable bindings undone at that stage, whenever failure is encountered. Backtracking accounts for much of the declarative nature of the Prolog language since it is relatively transparent to the user. The other method, prevalent in lower level languages like LISP and Pascal is known as recursive descent. In this case the route recording has to be hand-crafted and the garbage collection done later (in most LISPs, automatically). Recursive algorithms need to beware of one subtlety: if, in the above example, we were to have had rules of the form $A \Rightarrow B$ and $B \Rightarrow A$, then there is every possibility that the search could continue forever in a loop. This must be explicitly checked.

Breadth-first search expands all the nodes immediately below the initial node. Then, working from left to right, expands all these nodes until a solution is reached or the tree is completely expanded. This procedure has one striking advantage over the depth-first method; it guarantees that the shortest solution is found, if it exists. On the other hand, breadth-first search in large solution spaces can lead to huge computational costs; the so-called combinatorial explosion. This is because the cost of expanding the nodes at any level is typically the square of that on the previous level. In some cases it is appropriate to assign costs (other than computational costs) to each link of the tree. A good example is the travelling salesman problem, which is essentially the problem of how to optimize the delivery route of a vehicle which must visit a number of sites once and only once on its tour. The generalized cost in that case is a linear combination of distance, time, fuel and risk costs. In a tree with costs both depth- and breadth-first techniques may be used but will be modified to expand the nodes with lowest cost first. Clearly, if an optimal solution is required breadth-first search will tend to be better.

Combining the ideas of forward and backward chaining with that of breadth-first search leads to the notion of bi-directional search. In this, a goal is expanded backwards and the initial data expanded forwards until the two trees being built can be joined, leading to a complete path. This can sometimes be much more efficient than other blind strategies. The problem we mentioned in the last section of how to avoid blind alleys or unnecessarily long searches can be dealt with in a number of ways. In our current example, we might choose, during a depth-first search, to expand those nodes with the smallest number of clauses in the antecedent. As it happens, this is the wrong strategy in this case, although it does seem a plausible one for this type of problem in general. The reason it is plausible is that it makes the tacit assumption that the computational cost of expanding a node is roughly proportional to the number of its descendants.

In a tree with costs, a slightly more intelligent way to proceed is not to expand nodes with lowest cost but to store the cumulative cost of the exploration so far and expand the node whose expansion keeps the costs at a minimum. This strategy restores to breadth-first search the optimality property. One can go one step further and make an estimate of the cost of completing the search from a particular node and then minimize the sum of the two functions. This is the basic idea behind the A* algorithm. An algorithm designated B* has been suggested by Berliner (1981) which makes much more use of knowledge to terminate the search. These algorithms have been particularly important in game playing machines.

These are our first examples of intelligent search, although the only feature of intelligence being used for the most part is memory (of the costs). Knowledge about the particular problem at hand can often be used to guide a search in several ways. These include deciding which node to expand next in a search, and which sections of a tree to disregard or discard. The latter process is known as pruning. Best-first search seeks to construe an evaluation function for every node reached. This function is often a measure of how much the current state differs from a solution state.

4.4 ABDUCTION, DEDUCTION AND INDUCTION

Using *modus ponens* and breadth-first search to arrive at conclusions is an example of deduction. So are all the other methods we have mentioned. Forward chaining lets us deduce the consequences of an assertion, and backward chaining allows us to deduce a cause for some stated situation or to find a potential cause for a goal. Mixtures of the two strategies also have this character. It is possible for a fact to support the truth of a proposition even though it does not prove it in a strict deductive manner. We are saying that if a consequence of a thing can be proven, then at least there is nothing to contradict its truth, and that this provides evidence of its plausibility. This kind of reasoning is called abduction. It becomes especially important when multivalent logic is in use. Suppose that, in the above tree we can only assign probabilities to propositions A, E and G. Then, it is plausible that F is caused by them but not certain. For example, if a friend says she feels tired and hot and is sneezing we may abduce that she is suffering from the common cold from the implication 'colds cause sneezing, high temperature and lassitude'. The fact that she has pneumonia will be discovered by further questioning, we hope. In other words, abduction is non-monotonic. It is nonetheless an invaluable method in expert systems as in human reasoning about causes.

The other principal mode of inference in everyday thought as in logic is induction. The word 'induction' has two senses; the Aristotelian sense of a syllogism in which the major premise in conjunction with instances entails the generalization, or the sense of empirical generalization from observations. A third sense, the principle of mathematical induction, need not concern us here. It is with the second sense we shall be concerned. Most authorities (Braithwaite, 1953; Haack, 1978; Hempel, 1966) talk about induction in terms of probabilities; if we observe that sheep on two hundred hillsides all have wool and four legs, then we may induce the generalization 'all sheep have wool and four legs'. Every observation we then make increases the probability of this statement being true, but never confirms it completely. Only one observation of a shorn three-legged merino is needed to refute the theory. From our point of view this cannot be correct. There are many kinds of uncertainty, and it can be said equally that our degree of knowledge, belief or the relevance of the rules is what is changed by experience rather than probability. The obsession with probability derives (probably) from the prevailing empiricist climate in the philosophy of science; experience as experiments performed by external observers trying to refute some hypothesis. Another view is possible. The history of quantum physics shows that we can no longer regard observers as independent from what they observe. Marcuse (1955) develops the alternative point of view especially clearly. Experience takes place in a world of which we humans are an internal part but from which we are able to differentiate ourselves. We do this by internalizing a representation of nature and checking the validity of the representation through continuous practice. But the very internalization process is a practice, and practice is guided by the representation so far achieved. From this point of view induction is the process of practice which confirms our existing theories of all kinds. The other important general point to note is that the syllogism of induction moves from the particular to the general, whereas deductive and abductive syllogisms tend to work in the opposite direction; from the general to the particular.

The probabilistic definition of induction does have merit in many cases. Especially in the case of new knowledge, and it is this case that current computer learning systems always face. If we ever get as far as true artificial intelligence, then the situation may call for our broader definition. In nearly every case, computer programs which reason by induction are presented with a number of examples and expected to find a pattern, generalization or program which can reproduce and extend the training set. The complex question of the interaction between theory and practice has not arisen.

Suppose we are given the following training set of examples (an example due originally to Janet Efstathiou).

Eye colour	Hair colour	Sex	Job
blue	blonde	male	programmer
grey	brown	male	programmer
brown	black	female	analyst
brown	brown	male	operator
blue	black	female	analyst

The simplest possible algorithm enables us to infer that:

IF female THEN analyst
IF male AND (blue eyes OR grey eyes) THEN programmer
IF brown hair AND brown eyes THEN operator

However, the addition of a new example (brown eyes, brown hair, female, programmer) makes the position less clear. The first and last rules must be withdrawn, but the second can remain although it no longer has quite the same force.

The first attempts at machine learning came out of the cybernetics movement of the 1950s. Cybernetics, according to its founder Wiener (1948), is the science of control and communication in animal and machine. Several attempts were made, using primitive technology by today's standards, to build machinery simulating aspects of animal behaviour. In particular, analogue machines called homeostats simulated the ability to remain in unstable equilibrium (see Ashby, 1956) Perceptrons are hinted at in Wiener's earliest work on neural networks, and, as the name suggests, were attempts to simulate the functionality of the visual cortex. Learning came in because of the need to classify and recognize physical objects. The technique employed was to weight the input in each of a number of dimensions and, if the resultant vector exceeded a certain threshold, to class the input as a positive example. Recently, neural network – or connection machine – technology has overcome the flaw discovered by Minsky and Papert (1969), and impressive learning systems are beginning to be built.

Apart from Perceptrons, one of the earliest examples of a computer learning algorithm is Langley's BACON program (McCorduck, 1979). BACON was able to 'discover' Ohm's law of electrical resistance from a list a measurements of simple circuit parameters.

An algorithm with more general application is Quinlan's interactive dichotomizer, ID3 (Michalski, Carbonell and Mitchell, 1983) which selects an arbitrary subset of the training set and partitions it according to the variable with the greatest discriminatory power using an information theoretic measure of the latter. This is repeated until a rule is found which is added to the rule set as in the above example on jobs. Next the entire training set is searched for exceptions to the new rule and if any are found they are inserted in the sample and the process repeated. The difficulties with this approach are that the end result is a sometimes huge decision tree which is difficult to understand and modify, and that the algorithm does not do very well in the presence of noisy data. A fuzzy analogue of ID3 might well overcome the latter objection, but it is difficult to see a way round the former one. ID3 forms the basis for the once widely available ExpertEase product.

Another algorithm which depends on searching a space of plausible descriptions is due to Dietterich and Michalski (1981). Their INDUCE program uses a beam search technique to generate rules. This program was used to construct an expert system in the classification of soya bean diseases which achieved notoriety through outperforming an expert system built using conventional knowledge engineering methods. It uses a sophisticated method of generalization and a powerful predicate calculus representation language.

A completely different class of learning algorithm is based on the concept of adaptation or Darwinian selection. The general idea is to generate rules at random and compute some measure of performance for each rule relative to the training set. Inefficient rules are wasted and operations based on the ideas of mutation, crossover and inversion are applied to generate new rules.

One of the problems with totally deterministic algorithms like ID3 is that, although they are guaranteed to find a rule to explain the data in the training set, if one exists, they cannot deal with situations where the rules can only be expressed subject to uncertainty. In complex situations such as weather forecasting or betting, where only some of the contributory variables can be measured and modelled, no exact, dichotomizing rules often exist. With the simple problem of forecasting whether it will rain tomorrow it is well known that a reasonably successful rule is 'if it is raining today then it will rain tomorrow'. This is not always true but it is a reasonable approximation for some purposes. ID3 would reject this as a rule if it found one single counter-example. Statistical tests, however useful, require complex independence assumptions and inter- pretive skills on the part of users. Statistical forecasting has not yet entered on the stage of artificial intelligence although many of its techniques are used internally by some systems. The Beagle system (Forsyth, 1986) is an attempt to fill the gap. Another approach is represented in RuleMaster which extends the basic approach of ID3 to include fuzzy attributes, although other aspects of fuzzy set theory are not included.

The most striking difference between ExpertEase and Beagle (which stands for Bionic [*sic*] Evolutionary Algorithm Generating Logical Expressions) is that the former has a very nice user interface based on a spreadsheet approach and the latter has almost no user interface at all. This is represented in the difference in price, but does not reflect on the functionality of either system. Beagle is presented as a data analysis package designed to extract probabilistic rules from data which is principally numeric. The rules can then be used directly in, say, expert systems or Beagle will generate a subroutine in a conventional language such as C or FORTRAN. Both packages, in our opinion, have a potential role in knowledge acquisition, where a first stab at a rule set can be used to guide later knowledge elicitation as described in the previous chapter. With the current state of technology we think it highly unlikely that pure rule induction systems will enjoy a wide success. ExpertEase has by now been applied to many problems including an advisory system on the postal services operated by Federal Express. Beagle has been applied to the analysis of biochemical data in assessing the likelihood of survival of cardiac patients, predicting alcohol dependency from blood enzyme tests, analysing test bore-hole data in relation to oil exploration and to 'chartist' financial trading. Beagle is a package aimed at helping with forecasting or data analysis. It is not, however, intended for true time-series analysis and its author recommends that trends and suchlike be computed in advance.

Another approach to machine learning is represented by the work of Lenat and his colleagues. As a graduate student Lenat produced a program called AM (which stood for Artificial Mathematician) whose remit was to discover number theory from a base of pre-numerical concepts from set theory (Davis and Lenat, 1982). AM succeeded, admittedly with a fair amount of guidance from its author, in pointing out the interestingness of prime numbers and conjecturing (it had no theorem proving capability) a number of results of number theory, including Goldbach's conjecture: every even number is the sum of two primes. No one has proved or disproved this yet, incidentally, but we forbear setting it as an exercise to the reader. AM, like most mathematicians, thought it was fairly obvious. The next project was EURISKO which, like AM, was based on the idea of frames for which new slots can be created as part of the learning process and meta-rules or heuristics which affect the way rules are generated and generalized. An amusing example of this heuristic approach occurred early on in the development of EURISKO which noticed that rules inserted by humans were generally better than its own attempts at that stage. Thus it generated the meta-rule 'If a rule is machine-generated then delete it'. Fortunately, this was the first rule deleted under the new regime. EURISKO had a number of successes. It participated in the design of a new tesselated VLSI and embarrassed the Pentagon by winning the annual naval war game several times. On one occasion it did so by blasting its own crippled ships out of the water and steaming on to victory. The real success was that the rules were subsequently changed to disallow this rather bloodthirsty option. It should also serve to warn of the very real danger of entrusting dangerous activities like war or nuclear engineering to computer systems. But we digress. Lenat's latest project, CYC, is concerned more with knowledge representation than with learning, since it was the power of the representation language which made EURISKO so successful as well as the meta-rule approach to learning. CYC aims to encode and make available as an expert system all the knowledge contained in the *Encyclopaedia Britannica*.

Machine learning is at the forefront of research in artificial intelligence. Many of the difficulties faced by knowledge engineers, especially those of knowledge elicitation, may be overcome in the future as a result. For the present, though, we view the chief benefit of the commercially available induction systems as only an aid in the acquisition process. Just as human reasoning is a mixture of deductive, abductive and inductive reasoning, so will expert systems be for the foreseeable future.

4.5 INFERENCE IN EXPERT SYSTEM SHELLS

In this section we move from the theoretical consideration of the various available inference strategies to the consideration of commercially available products, and in particular the second generation of expert system shells. The products now emerging are beginning to make the commercial exploitation of the technology of expert systems both relatively easy and cost effective. We will compare the inferencing capabilities of thee products: Crystal, Guru and Leonardo. We are concerned here with the practical implementation of knowledge-based systems, but first let us take a look at the history of knowledge representation languages and expert system shells.

There have been several attempts to construct computer languages specifically for knowledge representation. The best known such languages are probably KRL and OPS5 (Bobrow and Winograd, 1977; Forgy, 1981). OPS5 achieved notoriety because it was used in the highly successful XCON system which is used by Digital Equipment Corporation (DEC) to configure orders for VAX computers. The fact that a large chunk of XCON, concerned with database access, was written in Bliss32 is rarely mentioned, but that does not change the fact that the knowledge incorporated in the system is the key to its success. DEC's success rate in the configuration task has increased by a factor of more than two resulting in huge savings. But even more important is that XCON enables DEC to maintain its distinctive policy of delivering just what the customer asks for, however non-standard. The maintenance of the OPS5 rulebase is in fact a vastly costly operation, because of the continual updates in the product range. The basic form of representation in OPS5 is production rules and in KRL it is frames, so they are chosen here as representative of representation languages.

The so-called 'expert system shell' products which have emerged over the past few years also invariably contain some language for representing knowledge, although it is usually as productions. As far as shells and knowledge engineering environments are concerned we are most interested in their inference systems, but as we have said, discussing these in isolation from some consideration of knowledge representation is nigh impossible.

Two major types of productivity aid are now beginning to emerge as commercial products: expert system shells at the lower end of the market and sophisticated special purpose hardware carrying software to enhance knowledge-based system development at the top end. These latter environments are usually based on hardware optimized for a symbol manipulation language such as LISP or Prolog or sometimes several. On top of these languages are added context-sensitive editors, graphics, object-oriented features such as icons, knowledge representation languages and usually some form of built-in inference method. Typical such systems are KnowledgeCraft, KEE and ART. The idea is to speed system development by providing many of the more commonly used programs and tools and enough raw computer power to build quickly prototypes which might ultimately run on some other machine. The idea is similar to the one behind fourth-generation languages, where program generation is facilitated by exploiting common data processing patterns. If all else fails, these systems give access to the basic languages so that flexibility is not sacrificed; code can be hacked out in LISP, POP11 or C as a last resort. Also programmers can add their own tools to the environment. One problem with the early systems, apart from high cost, is that it is not always easy to run systems written in LISP or such-like on conventional machines at the required speeds. New hardware developments are gradually overcoming this problem. A more serious problem is the lack of more conventional tools: database management, modelling and reporting software. The advantage of such systems is the relative freedom given to the developer to explore ideas – a distinct advantage when building prototypes.

The other kind of product is the shell. The early expert systems such as MYCIN, DENDRAL and Prospector contained very narrow specific knowledge about the subject matter of medicine, mass spectography and geology. It was realized very quickly that it could be useful to excise this knowledge leaving the 'shell' of the inference mechanism and add some means for easily plugging in new knowledge. Thus the shell based on MYCIN (EMYCIN for 'empty MYCIN') could be used to build an expert system in another domain without the overhead of building a knowledge application system. Unfortunately, it was soon found that the inference methods required varied significantly from one domain to another, and that a shell which was good at diagnosing faults in machinery could not be used for a system to tune that machinery or to control it. Ignoring the fact that the systems on which the shells were based were not without problems – MYCIN could not be turned into a training aid for doctors because it contained no knowledge about its reasoning – attempts to build really flexible shells have generally failed. We believe that the solution is to be found in a study of decision support software. What is required is a set of tools, of which shells could form a component, at reasonable cost to aid system development on conventional hardware. Let us look at some of the better established products.

At the low end of the market there are a number of products which will run on microcomputers. AL/X and Savoir for example are broadly based on the Bayesian network approach of Prospector, while M1 and TI Personal consultant are based on the approach in MYCIN or EMYCIN. Other products provide basic forward and backward reasoning mechanisms but have no means of expressing uncertainty other than by the granularity of the terms used, an example being Xi. All these systems come equipped with a fixed inference strategy and allow knowledge to be entered in rule form. They have found a number of applications, principally in domains similar to the Prospector and MYCIN archetypes, such as fault diagnosis and classification of data.

The more elaborate environments such as ART, KEE, and LOOPS typically provide support for LISP and fairly flexible built-in control strategies together with more complex knowledge representation methods as well as production rules; frames for example. Inference is still not under rule control but the degree of flexibility is much greater and a wide range of applications have been tackled. The price to be paid for the additional flexibility is that systems do take longer to build and the systems are, of course, much more expensive. The fact that these systems tend to run on specialized hardware means that there is a problem in delivering applications to end users; either the application must be rewritten for a conventional machine or there is a task in persuading the users to invest in a new type of workstation.

Now we turn to our comparison of inference in the three products announced above (IEL, 1986; Holsapple and Whinston, 1986; CLL, 1987). The rules reproduced in Fig. 4.3 are intended to represent the knowledge of an insurance salesman about the suitability of life assurance products. In the figure they are written in the Leonardo rule language.

Some explanation of the abbreviations may help. The variable 'investment' refers to the type of saving under consideration, permissible answers to the question generated are restricted to the Allowed Values specified in the Leonardo frame structure shown. 'Growth' refers to the desirability of capital growth

1:
2: if investment is 'lump sum'
3: and growth is desirable
4: and pension is desirable
5: and life.cover is unnecessary
6: then advice is annuity
7:
8: if investment is regular
9: and growth is not desirable
10: and income is desirable
11: and pension is not desirable
12: and life.cover is desirable
13: then advice is unit
14:
15: if investment is regular
16: and growth is desirable
17: and risk.aversion is low
18: and life.cover is desirable
19: and funds is ample
20: then advice is equity
21:
22: if investment is regular
23: and growth is desirable
24: and risk.aversion is high
25: and life.cover is desirable
26: then advice is wpend
27:

28: if investment is regular
29: and growth is desirable
30: and life.cover is desirable
31: and funds is limited
32: then advice is whole
33:
34: if no.of.kids > 0
35: then children is yes
36:
37: if no.of.kids < = 0
38: then children is no
39:
40: if married is yes
41: then life.cover is desirable
42:
43: if children is yes
44: then life.cover is desirable
45:
46: if married is no and children is no
47: then life.cover is unnecessary
48:
49: seek advice

Object number: 2g
1:          Name: investment
2:       LongName:
3:          Type:
4:         Value:
5:      Certainty:
6:    DerivedFrom:
7:   DefaultValue:
8:     FixedValue:
9:      ForbidUnk:
10:   AllowedValue: regular, lump sum
11:   ComputeValue:
12:        OnError:
13:    QueryPrompt: What kind of payment are you prepared to make?
14:    QueryPreface:
15: We have to establish first whether you wish to save regularly or
16: merely invest a single lump sum. Later we may explore combined
17: approach.
18:      Expansion:
19:    This is a demonstration of how expert systems can be used in
20:    problems of finding the most suitable product for the needs of
21:    a particular client. In this case we attempt to select a suitable
22:    life assurance linked scheme. The principles however may be
23:    applied to other similar 'product to client matching' problems.
24:     Commentary:
25:   Introduction:
26:     Conclusion:

Fig. 4.3 Rules and an object frame.

as opposed to regular income, and risk.aversion refers to the nervousness of the punter. The remainder of the names are clear from the context, excepting the values taken by the 'advice' variable. These values are to be interpreted as follows.

annuity A conventional deferred annuity
unit   An endowment policy linked to a unit trust
equity   An equity linked endowment
wpend   A conventional with profits endowment
whole   A low cost whole life assurance policy

When we execute these rules in Leonardo, we are asked questions in an order partly determined by the answers we give. A typical consultation might go on as follows. The style of dialogue, of course is nothing like that represented below.

Leonardo	User	Commentary
investment?	regular	Rule 1 is now excluded
growth?	desirable	
income?	unimportant	Now Rule 2 is knocked out
risk.aversion?	low	
married?	no	
no.of.kids?	2	Rule 9 now fires
funds?	ample	Rule 3 can now fire

The advice generated is 'equity' in this case, and at this point a bit of purely procedural code takes over to present this advice to the user in a prettier and more understandable form. One point to note is that the user is never asked to supply a value for 'life.cover'. This is a result of the backward chaining inference being performed, which causes the machine to search for a rule with 'life.cover' in the consequent clause, thus asking the 'married' question in this case. The explanation facilities built into the shell enable the exploration of the chain of reasoning, following it backwards until a point is reached where either the value has been read from some database or put in by the user.

Almost identical rules can be entered into Crystal with identical results in this simple case, but is harder to customize the appearance of the output advice. In Guru this is possible but the coding of the rules is usually a little more tortuous. For example Rules 1 and 6 in the above would appear in Guru as follows:

```
RULE: R1
     IF:  INVESTMENT = "lump sum" AND GROWTH = "desirable"
          AND PENSION = "desirable" AND LIFECOVER = "unnecessary"
     NEEDS: INVESTMENT, LIFECOVER, GROWTH, PENSION
     THEN: ADVICE = "annuity"
     REASON: For someone who wants capital growth and a pension but has no need
             of life cover, the best use of a lump sum is the purchase of a deferred
             annuity
```

RULE: R6
    IF: NOOFKIDS > 0
    THEN: CHILDREN = "yes"
    REASON: I need to know if you have any children

The NEEDS clause changes the order in which the inference engine deals with the variables. This is an example of the great flexibility built into the Guru inference engine which has literally hundreds of fine-tuning devices available. The price paid for this flexibility is the complexity of coding and the need to understand inference and uncertainty at a fairly profound level. Taking the three selected shells along the dimension of flexibility, let us look at an even simpler example. Here are three rules expressed in an arbitrary style:

IF A AND B THEN C
IF A AND B THEN D
IF C THEN E

The point to note is the apparent redundancy of the second rule. In a pure backward-chaining inference strategy this rule is never visited, and so the variable D never has a value assigned. Crystal prides itself on the speed with which it can process large volumes of rules (all three of the shells dealt with here are actually very fast rule processors) and so it operates in the most efficient way on this example and D is not assigned a value – rule 2 is not processed. The difficulty with this approach is that in a more complex application with many more rules, D may be required as part of the antecedent of some rule. In such a case efficiency may dictate that it would have been better if all rules had fired as soon as their antecedents were satisfied; propagating the consequences throughout the database at the earliest opportunity. This mixed strategy is often called 'backward chaining with opportunistic forward chaining' and is in fact the default method in Leonardo. Thus Leonardo would assign a value to D if the above rulebase were consulted; storing the value of the object D for future use. Leonardo supports, in addition to this default strategy, both pure backward and forward chaining, although these are regarded principally as debugging aids. The situation in Guru is a little more complex. Guru's 'environment control variables' allow the designer to control closely the inference strategy. The default strategy is the same as Crystal's, but changing the values of the control variables makes it possible to simulate the mixed strategy of Leonardo along with a large number of others. Understanding which is the correct choice for a particular problem however is a distinctly non-trivial exercise and many users would be happier to be told what to do by the shell. All in all it is a matter of personal preference, the nature of the problem and, of course, cost. Guru is considerably more expensive than the other two products.

4.6 KNOWLEDGE-ENGINEERING ISSUES

A few words need to be said here about how to elicit from human experts the kind of reasoning which they use in problem solving. This is especially true if the system builder envisages using some of the commercial products now available. If an expert system shell is chosen for the development, then it must be established that the logic and reasoning method incorporated in the shell correspond to those used by the human expert in problem solving, otherwise the project is almost certainly doomed to failure. If, on the other hand, a sophisticated knowledge-engineering environment is considered necessary then not only must the extra cost be justified but the developers must have confidence that the tool is sufficiently flexible to model all the strategies which arise in the behaviour of the human subject. This can only be achieved if the knowledge engineers are really able to elicit the inference methods as well as the knowledge representations used.

Very little has been written, and we suspect little more than that is known, on how to elicit inference methods. Our own experience dictates that the two main prerequisites for knowledge engineers in this respect are a sound theoretical understanding of the various methods available and a good helping of common sense. The methods of interview, whether formal or informal, should be constructed to enable comparison of user's and expert's behaviour with a sort of library of standard methods. When no direct match between the standard methods and the real ones identified can be discerned further investigation is indicated. Perhaps the computerization of the problem is beyond current technology or perhaps some novel combination of techniques can be derived. The watchword here is balance; don't give up too easily but don't be afraid to give up.

One of the most important considerations in this respect is that, as we have repeatedly emphasized, the choice of inference strategy and the choice of knowledge representation are inextricably bound together. This is why in blackboard systems we invariably find a frame or two lying around somewhere, and in production systems it is common to employ backward chaining and/or Bayesian inference. The selection of software tools should carefully balance the two. There is, as yet, no comprehensive theory of this interaction. When it emerges we are sure that it will include some logical features which are not standard and some advance in the theory of handling uncertainty, for the logic of opposites is the least well understood from a formal (and therefore computational) point of view. We can distinguish at least three quite distinct types of human reasoning used for practical problem solving. These are reasoning based on highly specialized domain-specific knowledge, common-sense reasoning based on rules of thumb and naïve physics and the like and reasoning from the existence of prior examples or trends. Other types do exist but are beyond current computer technology; a good example is reasoning by geometrical analogy. Specialist knowledge is narrow but deep; the jocular definition of a specialist being someone who knows ultimately 'everything about nothing'. Common sense is the tool of the generalist, who knows 'nothing about everything'. This knowledge is broad but shallow. Most expert systems up to now have dealt with specialist inference techniques and not common-sense reasoning. The role of uncertainty handling methods in computerizing common sense should be recognized. This is also the case with the third type of reasoning where the traditional techniques of statistical analysis, decision analysis and the less traditional methods of fuzzy forecasting, plausible reasoning and pattern recognition all involve the reduction of uncertainty in some way. Considerations of this type are necessary when assessing the suitability of a particular problem or expert for computerization, or the utility of a particular development environment.

The final question we intend to deal with on this score is the extent to which cognitive emulation cf. Slatter, 1985) can provide any benefits or compromise the efficiency of the resultant computer systems. Is it true that because humans reason in this or that way that an efficient computational solution should mimic their approach? Once again this is a largely unsolved problem and the remarks made already apply to it with some force. In some fields, such as computer chess, it is clear that cognitive emulation does have a rôle to play, as other methods tried so far have failed conspicuously. In others, most chiefly those where computers have been successful for decades, such as computation and data processing this is clearly not the case. At the meta-level we have to extend the question of cognitive emulation to what might be loosely described as 'social emulation'. If a blackboard system is a community of cooperating experts, then are our systems to emulate the social interactions among experts in human societies? Clearly, lessons may be, and have been, learnt from such analogies but we have no clear answer to give at this stage.

4.7 CONCLUSION

We have introduced the basic technology of expert systems: knowledge representation and inference. In doing so we have seen that it is very difficult to separate the two but that this has its conveniences. The bridge between the two is often merged into some mechanism for handling uncertainty, such as a Bayesian network or a non-standard logic. This chapter has largely avoided the details of techniques for uncertainty management. The question of reasoning under uncertainty, and the mechanics of so doing will be addressed in Chapter 6. The next chapter looks at a Bayesian inference engine in detail.

4.8 REFERENCES

Anderson, J. R. (1976) *Language, Memory and Thought*, Erlbaum, N.J.

Barr, A. and Feigenbaum, E. (1981) *The Handbook of Artificial Intelligence* (3 vols.), Pitman, London.

Berliner, H. (1981) The B* tree search algorithm: a best-first proof procedure. In B. L. Webber and N. J. Nilsson (eds) *Readings in Artificial Intelligence*, Tioga Publishing Company, California.

Bobrow, D. and Winograd, T. (1977) An overview of KRL, a knowledge representation language. *Cognitive Science*, 1, 3–46.

Brachman, R. J. and Levesque, H. J. (1985) *Readings in Knowledge Representation*. Morgan Kaufmann, Los Altos.

Braithwaite, R. B. (1953) *Scientific Explanation*, Cambridge, University Press, Cambridge.

Buchanan, B. and Shortliffe, E. H. (eds) (1985) *The MYCIN Experiments at Stanford.* Addison-Wesley, Mass.

Charniak, E. and McDermott, D. (1985) *Introduction to Artificial Intelligence.* Addison-Wesley, Mass.

Creative Logic (1987) *Leonardo Reference Manual.* Creative Logic Limited, Uxbridge.

Davis, R. and Lenat, D. B. (1982) *Knowledge Based Systems in Artificial Intelligence.* McGraw-Hill, New York.

Forgy, C. L. (1981) *The OPS5 User's Manual*, Tech Rep CMU-Cs-81-135 Computer Science Dept. Carnegie-Mellon University.

Forsyth, R. (ed.) (1984) *Expert Systems: Principles and Case Studies*, 1st edition, Chapman and Hall, London.

Forsyth, R. (1986) *BEAGLE User Guide*. Warm Boot Limited, Nottingham.

Graham, I. M. and Jones, P. L. K. (1988) *Expert Systems: Knowledge, Uncertainty and Decision.* Chapman and Hall, London.

Haack, S. (1978) *Philosophy of Logics.* Cambridge University Press, Cambridge.

Hayes-Roth, F., Waterman, D. A. and Lenat, D. B. (1983) *Building Expert Systems.* Addison-Wesley, Mass.

Hempel, C. G. (1966) *Philosophy of Natural Science.* Prentice-Hall, NJ.

Holsapple, C. W. and Whinston, A. B. (1986) *Manager's Guide to Expert Systems using Guru.* Dow Jones-Irwin.

Intelligent Environments (1986) *Crystal User Documentation*, Intelligent Environments Limited, London.

McCawley, J. D. (1981) *Everything that Linguists have always wanted to know about Logic (but were ashamed to ask).* Basil Blackwell, Oxford.

McCorduck, P. (1979) *Machines Who Think.* W. H. Freeman & Co., San Francisco.

Marcuse, H. (1955) *Reason and Revolution*, Oxford University Press, Oxford.

Michalski, R. S., Carbonell, J. G. and Mitchell, T. M. (1983) *Machine Learning – an artificial intelligence approach*, Tioga Publishing Company, California.

Minsky, M. L. (1985) A framework for representing knowledge. In Haugeland (ed.), *Mind Design*, MIT Press, Mass.

Minsky, M. L. and Papert, S. (1969) *Perceptrons.* MIT Press, Mass.

Newell, A. and Simon, H. A. (1963) GPS: a program that simulates human thought. In E. A. Feigenbaum and J. A. Feldman (eds), *Computers and Thought*, McGraw-Hill, New York.

Robinson, J. A. (1965) A machine-oriented logic based on the resolution principle, *J. of the ACM*, **12.**

Ross-Ashby, W. (1956) *An Introduction to Cybernetics.* Chapman and Hall, London.

Shortliffe, E. H. (1976) *Computer Based Medical Consultations: MYCIN.* American Elsevier, New York.

Slatter, P. E. (1985) Cognitive emulation in expert system design. *The Knowledge Engineering Review*, **1.**

Webber, B. L. and Nilsson, N. J. (eds) (1981) *Readings in Artificial Intelligence.* Tioga Publishing Company, California.

Weiner, N. (1948) *Cybernetics.* MIT Press, Mass.

Welbank, M. (1983) *A Review of Knowledge Acquisition Techniques for Expert Systems.* Martlesham Consultancy Services, Ipswich.

Winston, P. H. (1984) *Artificial Intelligence* (2nd ed.), Addison-Wesley, Mass.

Winston, P. H. and Horn, B. K. P. (1985) *Lisp* (2nd ed.), Addison-Wesley, Mass.

5

How to build an inferencing engine

CHRIS NAYLOR

There is something about the title of this chapter which seems to contain an implicit clang. The title, in case you hadn't noticed, is 'How to build an inferencing engine' and the clang seems to lie in the apparent disparity between the esoteric smoothness of the phrase 'Inferencing engine' and the rather prosaic dullness of the phrase 'How to build...'.

An inferencing engine would be fine. Talking about such things, we could very well feel that we are at the cutting edge of modern computer thinking. But 'How to build . . .'; that's a different matter altogether. Because we all know that, when we get back to wherever we call home, we're going to have the same old keyboard and screen in front of us and, on the machine, will be loaded the same old computer languages with which we have always worked.

The tools we have aren't bad tools by any means. But they are familiar tools about which there is nothing esoteric at all. And it is with these tools that we are going to have to build our inferencing engine. And suddenly, the esoteric nature of the engine itself begins to lessen. Because with those tools we can write programs, and nothing more – at which point our super-smooth inferencing engine becomes a program, and nothing more.

The end-product of this chapter – if there is an end-product – is an approach which might be used next time you feel like spending a few weeks sweating in front of a keyboard and screen. It is not even a close cousin of the magic wand approach to solving problems. I wish it was but, outside of the funny papers, such approaches just don't exist.

However, having poured out a modicum of cold water, let's go back to the esoteric-sounding bit – the 'inferencing engine' itself. What is it? A simple enough question, but not such a simple answer is available. For just about everything we do can be subsumed under the general heading of 'inferencing'. Clearly, if we had a program which would do our inferencing for us, then we could call such a program an inferencing engine. That would then sound super-smooth and we could use the end-product to impress friends and enemies alike (if only by a description of the same, rather than by its actual workings).

But again: what is inferencing?

Let me give you an example of an inference. I am a large employer and I employ Fred Bloggs and pay him £1 per hour for each hour that he works. Last week he worked 20 hours for me. Therefore, I infer, I shall this Friday pay him £20. That is an inference.

It is also, of course, the essence of a payroll program. And, frankly, anyone who starts to sell their payroll programs as inferencing engines may be, semantically, correct but I would have certain reservations about buying the product from them.

But return to that payroll example again because there are a couple of interesting (if obvious) points to be made about it. The first is that the inference we made (concerning Fred Bloggs' requirement for £20) was exact. The second is that the inference was also made very easily. And, to date, this has tended to be a prime feature of a very great deal of work done in the field of computers. The tasks which they have been set to solve have, in general, been tasks which have exact solutions and, almost by virtue of this, the solution of those tasks has been easy. It is, in a way, the very exactness of the solutions which has enabled programmers to see a way straight through the problem and solve it without too much difficulty.

Now, of course, there will be some groans when I say that all current computer programs produce exact solutions easily. I, too, have at least a limited groan when I think of some of the things with which I have had difficulty in the computer field.

Consider, for instance, numerical analysis. Does that have an exact solution? Is that easy? No, in general it is neither of those things. But at least you can buy a book on numerical analysis, look up an appropriate method, and use that. And, having done so, the book will usually give a pretty thorough analysis of the likely range and type of errors that might be inherent in the system. It may not be exact in the analytical sense, but it is exact in the sense that, using a given method, we would know exactly what order of error was involved.

But now turn to a different sort of problem, the problem of medical diagnosis. Is that exact or easy? It might be. Maybe doctors find it to be both exact and easy – after all, they've spent their lives doing it. But how do they do it? If you were to ask them you would almost certainly get some very woolly answers indeed. It all seems to be a curious mixture of guesses, hunches, direct observations, reported comments, practical experience... You name it and they use it. The whole thing is about as coherent as any witches' brew you care to imagine. And yet, of course, we understand perfectly well what it is that they are doing. We may not understand medicine, and we may not be able to program their activities on to a computer, but we certainly understand the type of thing that a doctor does when faced with a patient. And that is simply because, like the doctor, we are human too. And we work in just the same way in our own various fields of expertise.

Now that the word 'expertise' has crept in, it may be possible to see how the subject of inferencing engines links through to expert systems.

The kind of inference with which we are concerned is not the simple, exact and easy inference. It is the very opposite. The inexact and difficult inferences which, typically, human experts use in all walks of life. It is these which we are trying to build and our problem is that, unlike the payroll problem, we don't really know even what the basic equations are, never mind how to program them to a solution.

Upon reflecting now on what I have just said it seems to me that I could almost stop there with the claim that the subject is so riddled with problems that there is no hope left for those who would wish to proceed. But, in fact, things aren't quite as bad as that and, if they were, those of you who have parted with good money to buy this book would feel, possibly, that the next reasonable thing for you to do would be to lynch me.

So what I propose to do is to describe an inferencing engine (that esoteric phrase once more!) which I have worked on, which seems to give good-ish results on certain types of problems, and which is, really, fairly easy to build.

I think it possible that, in the course of what follows, you may find some of the things I have to say familiar and I hope that you will bear with this because for anyone unfamiliar with some of the ideas to leave them out would possibly be to leave them in the dark. This is particularly true, I think, of the occasions when I shall have to mention certain aspects of statistics.

5.1 THE INFERENCING ENGINE AND THE KNOWLEDGE BASE

In a very great deal of expert systems work there has been a conscious effort to divide the problem into two parts – the inferencing engine and the knowledge base. The idea is that the inferencing engine is the general purpose thinking machine and the knowledge base is that about which the engine shall think.

The former, if you like, is the equivalent of a 'raw' human brain with the in-built capacity to do anything. Whereas the latter is the sum of all human experience in some particular field. Add the two together and you have the equivalent of a human expert. Or so, at any rate, the theory goes.

In many ways, of course, it's a good idea. After all, suppose that you had just such an inferencing engine and that you also had a knowledge base applicable to the field of medical diagnosis. Why waste the engine at such time as you wanted an expert on, say, weather forecasting? Why not simply unplug the medical bit and design and plug in the meteorological bit? Well, the reason 'why not' is simply that – as yet – your inferencing engine might not be up to handling knowledge from two such disparate fields. But that doesn't prevent anyone from trying. A much more practical point from my own standpoint is this: even if you were only working on a single problem (such as medical diagnosis) breaking the problem into the two parts – knowledge base and inferencing engine – does make the problem much more tractable. It allows you to spend one day worrying about why the inferencing engine won't work and the next day worrying about what's wrong with the knowledge base. This is, I find, much better than having to spend two days worrying about the both of them as would happen with more conventional techniques. And, if maybe that sounded a bit like a joke, it isn't really so funny.

Obviously, you'll realize that, put like that, it's little more than saying that one has a program and one has data. Life is then made much easier if, for the time being, you forget about the data and, using test data maybe, spend the day getting the program itself to work.

But the fact is that, when working with rather diffuse problems, there is often a great deal of uncertainty about what, exactly, is the program and which is the data. The overlap between the two can be considerable and the trick is to draw the dividing line so that absolutely as much as possible of the problem is defined as data (the knowledge base) rather than as the program (the inferencing engine). A side advantage of doing this is that it enables you to see just to what extent you really can write a general-purpose inferencing engine. After all, if every single bit of 'data' were excluded from the program it really could be general purpose and, with a different knowledge base, it really could be used again for something else.

I think now that in order to help make the discussion a little more concrete I ought to say something about one particular knowledge base. Now, obviously, the knowledge base isn't the inferencing engine which you were promised – but it's what that engine has to drive and the format it comes in will have to be the same format as a knowledge base in some other field if the inferencing engine is to work in another field.

The examples I give, incidentally, will almost all be in the field of medical diagnosis although I think most people will accept that there are many other fields which could be formulated in the same way to be driven by the same engine.

Anyway, there are two basic data formats within this particular knowledge base.

1. The first format holds the knowledge on a particular illness:

Illness name, p, no. of applicable symptoms (j, py, pn)

The first item is the name of the illness. The second item is the prior probability of that illness being present in any member of the population taken at random. In Bayesian language, it is the prior probability of that illness. The third item is the number of symptoms which are applicable to that illness – either as indications of the condition or as contra-indications. After this there are a series of triples – three-element fields – corresponding to each of the applicable symptoms. The first item in the triple is a reference number giving the symptom which is now being considered. The second item in the triple is the probability that this symptom will be observed given that the patient has the illness in question. The third element of the triple is the probability that the symptom will be observed given that the patient does not have this illness.

2. The second type of data is that concerning the symptoms:

Symptom number, symptom name, question to be asked concerning this symptom

There are three fields. The first is the symptom number – and you will recall that this is the reference used in the illness data – the first item in those triples. The second is the name of the symptom. The third field is a question which may be asked of the user of the system in an attempt to determine whether he or she is exhibiting this particular symptom or not.

Anyway, so far so good. That's the knowledge base as it is used. There's nothing sacred about it, but it seems roughly adequate for our purposes. Maybe it would shed a little more light if you were to think of influenza. That's the first field – illness name – completed. Now, what's the probability of any random person having influenza? Let's say it's one in a thousand. That's the second field, p, completed: p = 0.001. Now, how many symptoms indicate or contra-indicate influenza? Lots of course, but, say, fever and runny nose – two symptoms. If the patient has influenza then he certainly has a fever and he probably has a runny nose. If he doesn't have influenza then he may still have a fever, but it's much less likely, and the same goes for noses of the runny variety.

So we finish up with something like this:

INFLUENZA, 0.001, 2, 1, 1, 0.01, 2, 0.9, 0.1

which fairly neatly summarizes what any doctor would tell you about influenza. Or it would do if, for instance, that particular doctor had a rather limited knowledge of his subject.

Corresponding to this we have the following items concerning the symptoms:

1, FEVER, DO YOU HAVE A HIGH TEMPERATURE?
2, RUNNY NOSE, DO YOU HAVE A RUNNY NOSE?

And that is the knowledge base (summarized in Fig. 5.1). Obviously it can be fairly quickly and easily modified to refine the knowledge therein and so, at this stage, that particular problem is dealt with.

Illness name, prior probability, number of symptoms, (j, py, pn)
Symptom number, symptom name, question to be asked
e.g.:
INFLUENZA, 0.001, 2, 1, 1, 0.01, 2, 0.9, 0.1
with 2 associated symptoms:
1, FEVER, DO YOU HAVE A HIGH TEMPERATURE?
2, RUNNY NOSE, DO YOU HAVE A RUNNY NOSE?
  So: the prior probability of anyone having influenza is 0.001.
  There are two symptoms associated with influenza.
  The first symptom is FEVER. The probability of FEVER given
  INFLUENZA is 1.
The probability of FEVER if INFLUENZA is *not* present is 0.01.
The second symptom is RUNNY NOSE.
The probability of RUNNY NOSE given INFLUENZA is 0.9.
The probability of RUNNY NOSE if INFLUENZA is *not* present is 0.1.

Fig. 5.1 The format of the knowledge base

The real problem now remains – how are we going to drive this thing? What does the inferencing engine look like?

And, at this stage, I am going to divide the problem into two parts. The first part will be concerned with the inference itself; and the second part with the engine within which the inferences fit. If it sounds a little odd to draw this distinction then bear with me because by 'inference' what I am really referring to is more-or-less a single calculation. By 'engine' I really mean the system by which we shall determine – or the system shall determine – exactly what order it is to carry out its inferences.

5.2 BAYES'S THEOREM

The whole essence of the approach I have used towards inferencing is Bayes' approach. And, for those of you who didn't already know this, the Reverend Bayes was an 18th century English vicar who spent his life studying statistics. Now, just as a safeguard for myself, I will say that Bayes' approach to inferencing is not the only approach possible. There are others, such as the methods of classical statistics and the more recent methods of pattern matching. I am not going to dwell on these alternative approaches simply because I feel that to do so would widen the topic of this chapter beyond belief. Personally, I have found a Bayesian approach extremely useful and I think that to concentrate on the one method and see it through is likely to give you the maximum benefit from this contribution.

Essentially, Bayes' theories rest on the belief that for everything, no matter how unlikely it is, there is a prior probability that it could be true. It may be a very low probability. It may in fact be zero. But that does not prevent us from calculating as if there were a probability there. Now, given a prior probability about some hypothesis (does the patient have influenza, say, or is the world flat?) there must be some evidence we can call on to adjust our views (beliefs, if you like) on the matter. If there were not then the process would stop right there with the prior probability remaining forever unchanged. But, given relevant evidence, we can modify this prior probability to produce a posterior probability of the same hypothesis given some new evidence.

For those who like to think in terms of equations, it goes like this (see Fig. 5.2). $P(H)$ is the prior probability of some hypothesis. $P(H:E)$ is the posterior probability of the same hypothesis given some item of relevant evidence E. Now, by definition,

$$P(H:E) = \frac{P(H\&E)}{P(E)} \quad \text{and} \quad P(E:H) = \frac{P(E\&H)}{P(H)}$$

So, with a bit of re-arranging, we get:

$$P(H:E) = \frac{P(E:H)P(H)}{P(E)}$$

and the question that then remains is: have we achieved anything useful? Well,

P(H) = the prior probability of H given no Evidence
P(H:E) = the posterior probability of H given evidence E
Now:

$$P(H:E) = \frac{P(H\&E)}{P(E)} \quad \text{and} \quad P(E:H) = \frac{P(E\&H)}{P(H)}$$

So:

$$P(H:E) = \frac{P(E:H)P(H)}{P(E)}$$

And:

$$P(E) = P(E:H)P(H) + P(E:\text{not } H)P(\text{not } H)$$

Relating this to the format of the knowledge base:

$$P(H:E) = \frac{py \cdot p}{py \cdot p + pn(1 - p)}$$

Fig. 5.2 Bayes's theorem

yes. We started off with P(H) and we wanted P(H:E).

Now, think about our patient with influenza (or not with influenza – that is the problem, to find out). We know roughly what the prior probability of influenza for patients in general is – that is P(H). But we want to know the probability for influenza in this patient in particular.

We find that he has a fever (the evidence is there) and we now want to know P(H:E) – the probability of the patient having influenza given that he has a fever. Well, we could make a guess on it, but somehow that isn't really a very easy question to answer. It would be very much easier to answer the opposite question: If the patient has influenza what is the probability that he has a fever? The answer is that a fever is certain – the probability is 1 – and that seems a much better way to proceed. And that is how Bayes's theory allows us to proceed.

We are still left with one other item to clear up – the bottom line in the equation – P(E) the probability of the evidence as a standalone item. In this case, what is the probability of anyone having a fever? Because, obviously, if everybody always had a fever all the time then the fact that this patient has a fever would tell us nothing. Our patient has a fever, but are fevers, in general, rare events?

And the way we can proceed on this is to calculate P(E) as

$$P(E) = P(E:H)P(H) + P(E:\text{not } H)P(\text{not } H)$$

In other words, the probability of a fever occurring in anyone is the probability of a fever occurring in an influenza patient times the probability of anyone having influenza plus the probability of fever occurring in a non-influenza patient times the probability of this person being a non-influenza case.

And now, maybe, you see how this all fits in with the previous definition of our knowledge base. For P(E:H) is the py associated with influenza and P(E:not H) is the pn we had associated with influenza. So we get the formula:

$$P(H:E) = \frac{py \cdot p}{py \cdot p + pn \cdot (1 - p)}$$

This is where the Bayesian neatness now comes into play. For the original value of P(H) that we used was the 'p' (prior probability) that we held in our knowledge base. But, having calculated a new P(H:E) (i.e. having asked about the patient's fever, say) we can now forget the original P(H) and, instead, use this new P(H:E) as a new P(H). So the whole process can be repeated time and time again as new evidence comes in from the keyboard, each time the probability of the illness being shifted up a bit or down a bit using exactly the same Bayesian equation each time with, simply, a different prior probability being used derived from the last posterior probability.

Eventually, having gathered in all of the evidence concerning all of the hypotheses we, or the system, can come to a final conclusion having successfully inferred the correct hypothesis to be true (if nothing goes wrong, that is).

Now that may have sounded good, but there are one or two criticisms of the method which could be made and so I will make a few here and now. The first is the calculation of P(E). The calculation presented here is accurate, but fairly simple. That is, it is accurate if we know P(E:not H) but we might not know this very accurately. Think, by way of illustration, of the probability of someone having a fever given that he does not have influenza. Typically, we would know P(E:H), the probability of a fever given the patient has influenza, very accurately, but not always P(E:not H).

One way around this is to use the fuller formula (see Fig. 5.3):

$$P(E) = \sum_{i=1}^{n} P(E:H_i)P(H_i)$$

of which our previous formula was a subset.

In many ways it is tempting to do this, because what it says is that the probability of E, the evidence, is the probability of E given every single condition with which E might occur multiplied by the probability of that condition. It is very

---

The probability of some item of evidence E

$$P(E) = \sum_{i=1}^{i=n} P(E:H_i)P(H_i)$$

So: as the $P(H_i)$ are continually updated at run time
P(E) could, in theory, be continually updated also.

Fig. 5.3 Formula for probability of evidence

complete. Of course, if our knowledge base held details of each and every single condition with which fever might occur and the current probabilities of those conditions then we would have an exact estimate of $P(E)$ being constantly updated as $P(H_i)$ changes and being always accurate. It would be very nice to work like this. The problem really lies in the fact that our system is liable in some ways to be less than perfect. For instance, Lassa fever causes a fever but if we do not have Lassa fever in the knowledge base then our calculations of $P(E)$ will be that much in error as a result. Similarly for each and every item in which our knowledge base is deficient.

From a practical point of view a rough estimate using $P(E:H)$ and $P(E:\text{not }H)$ is probably good enough and, if it makes you feel uneasy, then you can always console yourself with the thought that, by using the simpler method, we reduce the computational overhead and get answers today, rather than, say, next week.

The second criticism to be made of the method is that it assumes independence of the variables being used. Theoretically, this is quite a serious point. Suppose in our knowledge base we had two symptoms. The first was 'fever' as previously mentioned. The second was 'high temperature'. Now, of course, there would be no point in having both items because they mean the same thing. They are exactly correlated. But, if they did both creep in, what then? We would have included the same evidence twice and therefore, either incremented, or decremented, the probability of influenza more than we should have done and the final posterior probabilities would be wrong.

Now, on a small scale, this sort of trouble is almost bound to occur simply because most symptoms (in medical diagnosis: 'items of evidence' in some other field) will tend to have some correlation one with the other somewhere. And there is no theoretically nice way out of this problem. I say 'theoretically nice' because the problem worries statisticians much more than it worries anyone else. The reason for this is as follows.

If, at the end of the process, we wanted the exact probabilities to be attached to each of the hypotheses under consideration then there are plenty of criticisms which could be made of this method. But if, at the end, we were happy just to have an idea of the relative magnitude of the various probabilities then the problems tend to disappear. As long as the information in the knowledge base is equally erroneous for every item and a similar number of items of evidence are available for each hypothesis then the relative order of the errors which occur tends to be much the same throughout. The last few decimal places may be somewhat shaky, but the overall picture which the system infers appears to be, generally, quite reasonable. Perhaps the point will be made a little more strongly if I just digress into a consideration of the matter of odds. (See Fig. 5.4.)

Now, odds and probabilities are related in a way by the formula:

$$O(H) = \frac{P(H)}{1 - P(H)}$$

So, for a hypothesis with probability 0.5 the odds on that hypothesis are 1 to 1.

$$O(H) = \frac{P(H)}{1 - P(H)}$$

$$O(H:E) = \frac{P(E:H)}{P(E:\text{not }H)} \cdot O(H)$$

$$= \frac{py}{pn} \cdot O(H)$$

So:

$$\ln |O(H:E)| = \ln \left|\frac{py}{pn}\right| + \ln |O(H)|$$

Fig. 5.4 Odds versus probabilities

Now, some workers prefer to do their Bayesian sums using odds rather than probabilities simply because it is computationally easier.

Using odds our earlier formula becomes:

$$O(H:E) = \frac{py}{pn} O(H)$$

In other words, the odds change as a straight linear function of $P(E:H)$ and $P(E: \text{not } H)$ – and, of course, if we took logs and held in our knowledge base log (py/pn) then the calculations would be a matter of simple addition.

Personally, I have objections to the use of odds in this way. The main one being that the end points of the range are at plus and minus infinity rather than the 0 and 1 of probabilities. Infinity being outside the range of most machines, it seems to me that some very valuable information is lost about these end points, for events which occur with probabilities 0 and 1 are very interesting events and can greatly help to solve a problem quickly.

As a further digression it will be apparent that the odds relationship, being a straight line one, means that the probability relationships are not. $P(H:E)$ tends to move asymptotically towards its end points of 0 and 1. (See Fig. 5.5.) It may, given strong evidence, actually get to its end points. But, in the meantime, when it is simply approaching them, it means that the probability change induced by any item of evidence tends to get progressively less, and this helps to ameliorate the effects of possibly correlated items in the knowledge base. Maybe the same question is being asked twice but it will hardly show in the final result if we stick with probabilities and there is a reasonable body of other evidence available to the system as well. The essence of this point is that I, and I think other people, tend to perceive probabilistic events in fairly close accord with probability measures rather than as odds, and that makes the use of probabilities preferable.

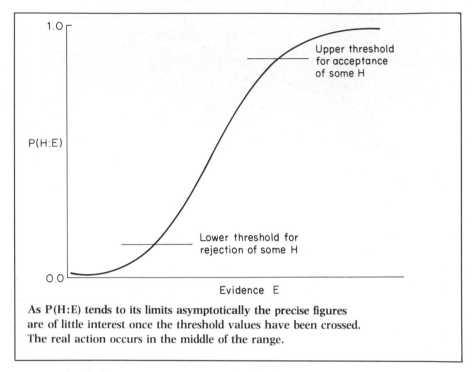

As P(H:E) tends to its limits asymptotically the precise figures are of little interest once the threshold values have been crossed. The real action occurs in the middle of the range.

Fig. 5.5 Thresholds 1

Well, that was a quick skim through Bayes and outlines the inferencing process, but, before we pass on, we should look at the criterion the system uses for making a decision. What we could have the system do, if we wanted, would be to simply print out at the end of each session a listing of all the hypotheses and the probabilities associated now with each one of them. And that would be rather unimaginative.

Typically, what most workers do is to set two thresholds – an upper and a lower. If the probability exceeds the upper threshold that hypothesis is accepted as a likely conclusion to make. If it falls below the lower threshold it is rejected as unlikely. So the system is able to display some fairly intelligent inferencing behaviour. In practice this method of rigidly setting threshold criteria is open to criticism and to show what I mean consider one hypothesis about which certain items of evidence are all instantly available.

Assuming all of these items to be independent, we could, instead of proceeding stepwise as we have done before, just consider the one big calculation to find P(H:all the relevant supportive evidence).

The basic calculation is the same as before but this time we use, instead of P(E:H), P(all supportive evidence:H) which is simply the product of all of the supportive P(E:H) for that hypothesis.

By doing this we obtain the maximum possible posterior probability which that hypothesis could achieve if every single item of evidence went in its favour given what is in the knowledge base at the moment.

Likewise, we can calculate a minimum possible probability for that hypothesis supposing that all the evidence currently in the knowledge base worked against it.

Clearly, these values are unlikely to be the same for all hypotheses. In fact, we might find that for some hypotheses the maximum possible probability attainable might only be, say, 0.5. So, if we set a rigid upper probability threshold of 0.9 and a lower of 0.6 this particular hypothesis would always be rejected as unlikely.

However, suppose the hypothesis was: the patient has lung cancer. Now, you simply cannot accurately diagnose lung cancer via a computer keyboard. You need, at the very least, the addition of X-ray evidence. So what you want to do is to get the system to report on a particular hypothesis if the system thinks that, to the extent of its own internal knowledge, the patient might have lung cancer. That is to say, you want the system to tell you if it is as certain as it can be about the hypothesis given its own internal constraints of having, for instance, no X-ray machine and no eyesight of its own.

The better approach to adopt on threshold criteria is to simply set an upper limit, M1, as maybe 0.9 of the maximum attainable for that hypothesis given the current knowledge base. Similarly, a lower threshold, M2, can be calculated as, maybe, half of this maximum or some multiplier of the minimum value possible. This way both the upper and lower threshold criterion values are specific to each particular hypothesis. (See Fig. 5.6.)

5.3 UNCERTAINTY IN USERS' RESPONSES

Just in case anyone thought that we were getting to the end of the inference itself there is a bit more to come. This concerns uncertainty in the users' responses.

Ideally, when the system requests a certain piece of information, the user can give a straight answer. But it may be that the user is not sure of what answer to give. The example I like occurs in the case of that excellent system Prospector which at some point in its process of mineral exploration asks the user the question: 'Has hornblende been pervasively altered to biotite?' I sympathize with anyone who isn't quite sure about the answer to that one.

The problem can occur in other fields. 'Do you have a bad cough?' can be a pretty subjective question to answer and so it becomes necessary to allow the user to reply on, say, an 11 point scale with + 5 being Yes and − 5 being No, 0 being Don't Know and everything else being somewhere in between.

The calculations then proceed much as before except that $P(H:E)$ is replaced by $P(H:R)$ calculated as:

$$P(H:R) = P(H:E)P(E:R) + P(H:\text{not }E)P(\text{not }E:R)$$

where R is the user's response. In other words, to allow for uncertainty the system

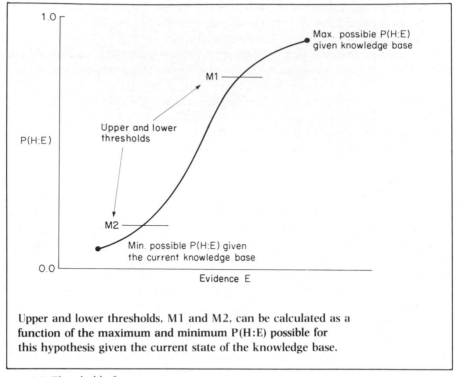

Upper and lower thresholds, M1 and M2, can be calculated as a
function of the maximum and minimum P(H:E) possible for
this hypothesis given the current state of the knowledge base.

Fig. 5.6 Thresholds 2

has to allow for a bit of P(H:E) and a bit of P(H:not E) and the amount of each it
uses depends on the extent to which the user's response supports the presence or
absence of this particular item of evidence. See Fig. 5.7.

Clearly, if the response is nought then P(H:R) = P(H), nothing changes, and for
other responses a system of linear interpolation between P(H:E) and P(H:not E)
allows for uncertainty.

And that, more or less, covers the inferencing system used.

5.4 THE ENGINE

This brings us now to the engine part – the means the system is to use to drive
around amongst the various inferences it might make. The obvious question to
ask is: does it matter? After all, the system could just start at the front of its list of
questions and work through them until it got to the end and then stop.

You could do it that way and, if you did, you could call it forward chaining. A
data-driven strategy, this simply asks a question, or takes what the user gives it,
and then makes what inferences it can from that data, after which it asks another
question, and so on until all of the hypotheses have been resolved one way or the
other.

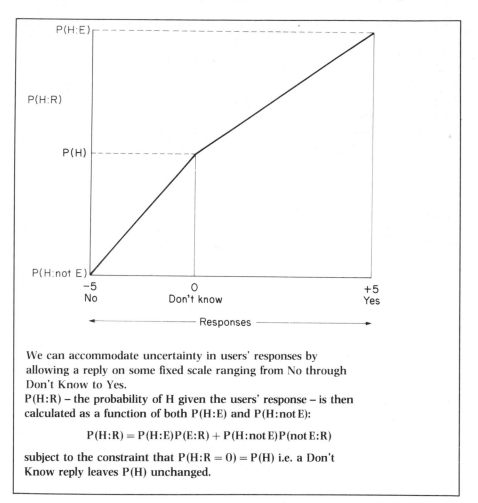

We can accommodate uncertainty in users' responses by allowing a reply on some fixed scale ranging from No through Don't Know to Yes.

P(H:R) – the probability of H given the users' response – is then calculated as a function of both P(H:E) and P(H:not E):

$$P(H:R) = P(H:E)P(E:R) + P(H:not\,E)P(not\,E:R)$$

subject to the constraint that P(H:R = 0) = P(H) i.e. a Don't Know reply leaves P(H) unchanged.

Fig. 5.7 Uncertainty in users' responses

Essentially, there are two problems with this approach. The first is that it can be very wasteful in time. Some items of evidence are obviously going to be much more generally important than others so that to leave them until last simply because, by historical accident, they happened to be at the end of the list would be wasteful.

Consider two questions: 1. Do you feel generally ill? 2. Do you have clubbed fingers? Now the first question is obviously a good question to ask very early on in a medical diagnosis session because a No answer would instantly rule out a very large slab of illnesses whereas a Yes answer would raise the probabilities of many others. The second question, however, can often be used as an indication of certain lung complaints, but, even at that, it is by no means a very certain indication and its absence would rule out very few, if any, items at all.

The second problem with forward chaining is that, to the user, it can seem a bit purposeless. Just a series of questions being fired out at random until the system either stops or gives up.

Of course, if the first problem were solved (that of asking 'good' questions first) then probably the second problem would tend to be solved also because the user might well perceive that the system was at least trying to help.

The second method often used is that of backward chaining. What the system does here is to select a hypothesis from its knowledge base. Having done so, it then looks backwards, as it were, in order to try to see what items of evidence it needs in order to resolve that hypothesis one way or the other and so it asks the user for these items.

Such a system obviously looks a lot more purposeful in its behaviour because it can always say just what it has 'on its mind' by way of a current theory, the current theory being the hypothesis it is currently trying to resolve. But, in its basic form, it has serious disadvantages. Primarily these stem from the problem of deciding in which order it shall consider the various hypotheses open to it and then in which order it shall try to obtain the relevant evidence for these hypotheses.

Suppose the first illness in the knowledge base is acne rosacea. Backward chaining as ever, the system decides to purposefully resolve that hypothesis first. Looking at the 'evidence' for acne rosacea it finds that the condition is often associated with excessive tea drinking. Or, at least, of the various items of evidence associated with the condition excessive tea drinking is the first item in its knowledge base.

So the user switches on his favourite doctor and the first question he or she is asked is: Do you drink a lot of tea? The system is purposeful but to the user it might appear just a trifle obsessive. It reminds me of a medical officer from whom I once suffered who was convinced that the world was divided into two parts – those who had glandular fever and those who did not.

5.5 THE RULE VALUE APPROACH

The approach to this general problem – which is really the problem of which question to ask next – that I have developed is a Rule Value approach, which it has been suggested could also be called 'sideways chaining'. It uses neither forward nor backward chaining, both of which tend to concentrate on the hypotheses, but, rather, it concentrates on the evidence. Essentially, for each item of evidence it assigns a value – the value of this rule in the process of inferencing – and asks that question with the highest value first.

Intuitively, the method seems reasonable, because the system simply asks questions which seem kind of important to it, continually modifying its ideas of what questions are important as the answers come in. This, it seems likely, is something like the way human experts behave.

The problem is, of course, how to define an important question. And the

$$RV = \sum_{i=1}^{i=n} \left| P(H_i:E) - P(H_i:not\,E) \right|$$

So: the Rule Values are calculated for each item of evidence as the sum of the maximum probability shifts that they can induce in all of the *n* hypotheses to which this evidence is applicable. That question is always asked first which has the highest Rule Value.

Fig. 5.8 Rule Values (or sideways chaining)

answer, in its simplest form, goes like this: we can calculate the value of each item of evidence as the total sum of the maximum probability shifts which it can induce in the whole of the hypotheses currently in the knowledge base. So calculate:

$$RV = \sum_{i=1}^{n} |P(H_i:E) - P(H_i:not\,E)|$$

(See Fig. 5.8.) In this way we develop an RV for each item of evidence in the knowledge base. The system can then search for the maximum RV and request information on that item.

Now, obviously, these Rule Values are not static. As the posterior probabilities, the $P(H_i:E)$, become continually updated they will continually cause the Rule Values to be altered. For instance, if a particular set of hypotheses are 'killed' during questioning then there becomes little scope for their probabilities being changed so, consequently, the items of evidence which would have applied to them become less important, as they are re-calculated, and there is a reducing chance that those questions will now be asked. Conversely, as certain hypotheses become increasingly likely there is an increasing scope for their probabilities to be altered by any relevant remaining items of evidence. So these acquire higher Rule Values and are more likely to be asked next. It is as if the system had a measure of 'attention' in it paying heed to those hypotheses which it had the greatest scope for resolving at any given moment.

Another big advantage of this method is that it is relatively easy to implement – which is not a point to be ignored.

There are, of course, variations on the theme. For instance, we might take RV squared instead of plain RV because, by doing so, we will emphasize those items which produce large shifts in certain hypotheses at the expense of those items which only produce small shifts in a large number of hypotheses. Of course, large shifts are the ones most likely to quickly reject or accept a hypothesis and cut down on the need for further processing.

Yet another variant is to take the sum of squares of RV about its mean value. The purpose of doing this is, again, to try to slice up the problem more cleanly, emphasizing even more those items which can produce a big shift in some hypotheses at the expense of the many small shifts in a large number of hypotheses which might merely cause a large number of hypotheses to wobble up and down around their middle values without coming to any very definite conclusions quickly.

A further refinement to the method is to 'weight' the Rule Values in such a way that those items of evidence which were applicable to hypotheses which were relevant to the last-asked item of evidence receive an increased Rule Value.

The purpose of this is to try to avoid 'jitter' in the system. Suppose our system is running and there are two 'kinds' of hypothesis currently being considered, say Group A and Group B. The highest Rule Value is found and a question is asked and it so happens that this item of evidence is mainly applicable to Group A hypotheses. However, the next question to be asked, with the next highest Rule Value, is, by a small margin, mainly applicable to Group B hypotheses. Then the next question is Group A, and then Group B and so on.

It all occurs by chance and the differences in Rule Values which cause this jitter might be very small. But, to the user, it could appear that the system was jumping around the subject in a very odd fashion. What is needed is to slug the system with a bit of inertia to try to make it stay on the point for a while and to give it some greater sense of 'attention'.

The extent to which these refinements are worthwhile in practice, of course, depends on how much programming effort one wants to put into it and what sort of processor overhead you're willing to put up with. Basically, a simple Rule Value approach works well and is not too slow.

A very real difficulty lies in the problem of evaluating each approach, because in practice how would you assess a question-asking sequence as either good or bad? A horrendous sequence can be spotted very quickly by almost anyone. But a sequence which is good enough compared with one that, theoretically, might be better would be hard to evaluate.

This problem – of evaluating the running of such a system – is not at all trivial. If you have an expert inferencing system with 100 different items of evidence it could gather, all measured on an 11 point scale, then there are 1100 different ways it could be driven by the user.

For each of these 1100 ways there are 100! (factorial) different ways of ordering the question-asking process. With numbers of that order, one's computer cannot even calculate how many different ways the thing might be made to run, let alone evaluate them all. And yet such a system fits quite comfortably inside an Apple II or a Sinclair Spectrum.

So, in essence, you dream up a method you like and see, roughly, what it does. And if it doesn't actually explode in your face then it's probably OK.

5.6 COMING TO A CONCLUSION

Essentially, the system is running, it is asking good questions and it is updating its hypotheses according to the answers it gets. It can carry on until it has no more questions to ask and then stop, but it can also come to a conclusion. It can say, 'This is what I think is the case, and maybe you should consider these other items too...'

The first item to consider is the Most Likely Outcome. At its simplest this might just be that outcome with the highest probability. But remember what I said about the minimum and maximum probabilities for each hypothesis depending on the information currently in the knowledge base.

Essentially, for each hypothesis we have five quantities each of which is a probability and each of which offers considerable scope for confusion. However, they are these (see Fig. 5.9):

1. P(H), which is the current estimated probability of that hypothesis being true.
2. P(Max), which is the current maximum probability that this particular hypothesis could attain if all the remaining evidence went in its favour.
3. P(Min), which is the current minimum probability which a particular hypothesis could attain if all of the remaining evidence worked against it.
4. M1, which is the upper threshold criterion for accepting a particular hypothesis calculated as a proportion of P(Max) before any evidence had been accumulated at all.
5. M2, which is the lower threshold criterion for rejecting a particular hypothesis calculated as a proportion either of P(Max) or P(Min) before any evidence had been collected at all.

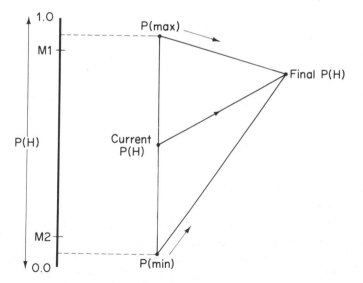

Fig. 5.9 Minima, maxima and conclusions

Now, the most likely outcome has been found if there is some hypothesis for which P(Min) is greater than P(Max) for any other hypothesis. In other words, even if all of the evidence has not yet been gathered in, it may still be possible to say which outcome is the most likely if no other outcome can conceivably overturn this particular hypothesis. This may well help to cut the session a little shorter than it might otherwise have been.

The next category of conclusion is that of Likely Conclusions. These are hypotheses which have P (Min) greater than M1, i.e. their minimum attainable probability is greater than the upper threshold.

The next category is Uncertain Conclusions. These are items for which P(Min) is less than M1 but for which P(Max) is greater than M2. In other words, they have not exceeded the upper threshold (although with more evidence they might) but they are still likely to exceed the lower threshold so they should still be considered. These items are prime candidates for the system to extend its questioning session in an attempt to resolve uncertainty.

At the bottom of the list we get No Inferences Possible – except, of course, for the obvious inference that none of the hypotheses are true. In this case the greatest P(Max) is less than M2, the lower threshold. In general, some uncertainty still exists in the system whenever P(Max) is not equal to P(Min) and equal to P(H). But whether it is worth resolving this uncertainty depends on the extent to which the various hypotheses may be made to cross the two thresholds M1 and M2 and this can be seen by examining P(Min) and P(Max) against M1 and M2.

I will now come to my own conclusion simply by giving a general overview of the process I have described so far:

1. For each hypothesis establish a prior probability. This is done by scanning the knowledge base and extracting the variable p for each hypothesis (see Fig. 5.1). This is held as P(H) to be later updated.
2. For each item of evidence establish a Rule Value. This is done by scanning the knowledge base to extract the variables (j, py, pn) where j is the 'evidence number' and py, pn are, respectively, P(E:H) and P(E: not H) for this item of evidence, j. Then calculate RV for each item of evidence as in Fig. 5.8.
3. Of all the RVs find the greatest RV to identify that item of evidence which can induce the greatest probability shift in all the hypotheses under consideration.
4. Interrogate the user on that item of evidence using the question stored in the knowledge base. The user's response may be on a scale from -5 to $+5$ and is the variable R.
5. Given R, recalculate all hypotheses which referenced that item of evidence in their knowledge base to find P(H:R) (see Fig. 5.7).
6. Recalculate the Rule Values for all items of evidence to allow for the change in probabilities that have taken place given the last response.
7. Calculate the minimum and maximum values which each hypothesis may yet attain (see Fig. 5.9).

8. Find the greatest of the possible minima of these hypotheses.
9. Check to see if any hypothesis has a maximum possible value which exceeds this maximum of the minima. If there is such a maximum exceeding the greatest minimum then go back to 3. and ask another question. If there is not then there is a most likely outcome and this is it.
10. Send the system into a summary routine during which it announces, possibly with a fanfare of trumpets, the exact details of all of the inferences it has made.

Finally, never ever tell the end user what was involved in writing this inferencing engine. He'll never believe you if you do tell him because, like most people, he thinks that inferencing is easy. And, of course, he's right (as long as you don't have to use a computer, that is).

5.7 APPENDIX: AN EXAMPLE KNOWLEDGE BASE

Suppose that you wanted an expert system that could act as your own personal car mechanic. This example is of a knowledge base, a very small knowledge base, designed to offer expertise in the field of car mechanics using the methods described so far:

FLAT BATTERY
    0.1, 5, 1, 0, 0.99, 2, 0.7, 0.05, 4, 0.2, 0.5, 5, 0, 0.99, 6, 1, 0.01
NO PETROL, 0.05, 2, 2, 1, 0.01, 6, 0.9, 0.02
DAMP IN IGNITION, 0.01, 3, 3, 0.9, 0.1, 4, 0.25, 0.05, 6, 0.9, 0.02
DIRTY SPARK PLUGS, 0.01, 2, 4, 0.01, 0.5, 6, 0.9, 0.02

1, LIGHTS WORKING, ARE THE LIGHTS WORKING?
2, PETROL GAUGE LOW, IS THE PETROL GAUGE READING LOW?
3, VEHICLE EXPOSED TO DAMP, HAS THE VEHICLE BEEN PARKED IN DAMP CONDITIONS?
4, VEHICLE RECENTLY SERVICED, HAS THE VEHICLE BEEN RECENTLY SERVICED?
5, STARTER MOTOR TURNING, IS THE STARTER MOTOR TURNING?
6, CAR WON'T START, WILL THE CAR NOT START?

Just skimming briefly through all this, the first group of items are the hypotheses – for instance, the hypothesis that there is a flat battery. The second group of items are the items of evidence; for instance, the evidence that the lights are working.

As I am not a brilliant car mechanic the probabilities may be a little adrift from the exact truth but, despite that, consider the first hypothesis – that the car has a flat battery. The prior probability of this on any given car, knowing nothing further about the situation is, we'll say, 0.1, i.e. every tenth car is normally reckoned to have a flat battery.

There are, we reckon, five different items of evidence that could be used to establish whether or not the car did, in fact, have a flat battery. The first of these is item 1 (lights working). If the battery is flat then the probability of observing that the lights are working is 0. If, on the other hand, the battery is not flat then P(E:not H), the probability of observing that the lights are working is, say, 0.99 (i.e. almost certainly they will be working, except in the event that a bulb or fuse has blown).

The second item of evidence is 2: petrol gauge low. Since the petrol gauge is electrically operated, this could also be relevant. It isn't quite so important, because it doesn't take much electricity to run a petrol gauge. So we reckon that the probability of observing a low petrol gauge reading if the battery is flat is 0.7 and the probability of observing a low petrol gauge reading if the battery is not flat is 0.05. (We could have a low reading for some other reason, such as a lack of petrol!) Note that this probability corresponds to the prior probability of the hypothesis 'no petrol' since that is the only other reason we can think of for the petrol gauge reading low. And so on through the list of applicable items of evidence. The car is less likely to have a flat battery if it has been recently serviced; it is totally unlikely to have a flat battery if the starter motor is turning; and the car definitely won't start if the battery is flat (probability 1) although it might not start even if the battery isn't flat (probability 0.01, say).

The next hypothesis, that there is no petrol, is influenced by the items of evidence: petrol gauge low, and car won't start. Similarly, the hypothesis 'damp in ignition', is influenced by the evidence: vehicle exposed to damp, car recently serviced, and, car won't start. Dirty spark plugs are influenced by the evidence: vehicle recently serviced, and, car won't start (the former contra-indicating dirty spark plugs, the latter giving a positive indication). These probabilities may be judged from experience or may be built up in a more exact and rigorous fashion, but the final proof is to run the thing to see what it does.

Consider Fig. 5.8 and the equation given there for working out Rule Values. If we look at the Rule Values using that equation on this example knowledge base we get the following values:

Evidence	Rule Value
Lights working	0.9174
Petrol gauge low	1.4151
Vehicle exposed to damp	0.0822
Vehicle recently serviced	0.1376
Starter motor turning	0.9174
Car won't start	2.3807

Every time the system is run, the first question it will always ask is: Will the car not start? After that it adjusts its Rule Values according to how you reply. But a glance at the table of Rule Values shows that, after 'car won't start', this particular expert is most interested in the matter of whether or not the petrol gauge is reading low and whether or not the starter motor will turn, all of which seems eminently sensible.

Just out of interest, if you give a definite Yes reply to the question 'Will the car not start?', the system then recalculates its Rule Values to give:

Evidence	Rule Value
Lights working	0.9991
Petrol gauge low	1.2135
Vehicle exposed to damp	0.7554
Vehicle recently serviced	0.8153
Starter motor turning	0.9991
Car won't start	0

So the next question it asks concerns the petrol gauge. But note how all of the remaining Rule Values have shot up in value on hearing the news that your car won't start. Suddenly, the expert car mechanic has started to take an interest in a large number of things that didn't really interest it before.

If, on the other hand, you had replied No to the question 'Will the car not start?' (i.e. it's working OK) then all of the Rule Values plummet. The expert car mechanic discounts all of the four hypotheses it was considering, concludes that there's nothing wrong with the car, and asks you no more questions.

6

Uncertainty management in expert systems

PETER JONES

6.1 THE ROLE OF UNCERTAINTY

It is an unusual luxury to be able to say 'I am 100% confident that the decision I have just reached is the correct decision'. Anyone who makes decisions in the real world is conscious that this is a fact of existence.

The building of an expert system entails the development of a model of some facet of the real world, and the uncertainty associated with the real world must in some way be represented in the model. This incontrovertibly poses a problem for the developer of the system.

There is a school of thought which says that the development of any kind of expert system is sufficiently difficult in any case that the sensible builder of a system ignores the entire issue of uncertainty, and simply builds a deterministic model. This is an approximation to reality, of course, but then surely any model is only an approximation, whose limitations must be understood by the user?

This rather misses the point. Expert systems can be classified into those where, indeed, the approximation of suggesting certainty in a conclusion is acceptable, because one and only one decision can be taken at the decision time, and the purpose of the system itself is to guide the direction of the decision in a normative way.

An example of this class of system might be in an equipment proposal by a vendor in response to an invitation to tender. The person who raised the request for a procurement document clearly expects a precise bid from the vendor; if the vendor doesn't know which set of equipment to recommend, who does?

However, other kinds of advice-giving systems will be expected by the end user to hedge their advice with some degree of reserve. For example, if one approached an insurance consultant for advice as to the 'best' self-employed pension scheme to adopt, one might be a little suspicious if the response were along the lines of the absolute statement 'Go for Company X'. Common sense tells us that part of the decision is based on the value of the insurance fund in 20, 30 or 40 years' time. No one knows what that will be. All that can be done is to look at the previous history of the company over the last few years, and extrapolate, adding to the extrapolation the expert's knowledge of the current policies adopted by the

company, the calibre of the company manageme
company's portfolio policies and track record, and
user of the system will expect an answer of the
Company B and Company C are all worthwhile; and
65 and 60 out of a hundred'.

What is this rating? Is it a score, a probability, a
something else? The interpretation of this 'index of
managing uncertainty in an expert system.

6.2 SOURCES AND KINDS OF UNCERTAINTY

There is no good objective model of the way in which a human being reaches
a conclusion in the presence of uncertainty, and therefore it must be clear that
any method used to attempt to emulate a human response through mechanistic
means is at best a projection of some facet of the imagined objective model.

Many ways have been proposed and used with varying degrees of success in the
attempts to emulate rational decision making under uncertainty. These include
Certainty Factors (as used in the notable MYCIN system), Bayesian inference
networks (as used in the equally famous Prospector system), Dempster-Schafer
mass weighting methods, and fuzzy sets.

Some of these are described in detail elsewhere in this volume, notably the use
of Bayes theorem. Here we will concentrate on fuzzy sets theory and
approximate reasoning, and try to identify the areas of applicability as well as
describing the fundamental mechanics of this relatively new tool.

The concept of 'uncertainty' deserves more scrutiny. It can arise from at least
the following sources:

1. lack of data
2. inconsistency of data
3. imprecision in measurement
4. imprecision in concept
5. lack of a theory

all of which present different problems in reaching a conclusion.

Very frequently, one could arrive at a confident conclusion if all the facts were
available; but when all the facts are not available and a decision must still be
made, how should one reason in this presence of only partial, incomplete facts?
Bayes theorem offers a way of accumulating such evidence as may be available,
and using it to modulate the prior expectation of each of a set of possibilities – the
more evidence available (as long as each piece of evidence remains independent of
the others), the greater the probability which can be attached to various of the
hypotheses.

The other side of this coin, in a sense, is the embarrassment of data which allows
one to reach conflicting conclusions due to the inconsistency of the data
available. Here one is faced with the problem of maintaining multiple parallel

s of reasoning – a situation where the use of the Certainty Factor
something to offer.

data as are gathered cannot be measured to arbitrary precision, and this is
classical problem of experimental error, for which the tools of the statistician
re available. However, there is a more insidious facet of imprecision, relating to
the concept which is being discussed – and a 'concept' may not even have an
underlying metric. This is an area in which fuzzy set theory has a contribution to
make.

6.3 FUZZY SETS

The concept of a **fuzzy set** was introduced by Lotfi Zadeh (1965). Zadeh was
working in the field of control engineering, and recognized that many problems
which a human being could solve were not amenable to the standard PID control
systems used by the process control engineer. This led Zadeh to enunciate his
principle of incompatibility which states that 'As the complexity of a system
increases, our ability to make precise and yet significant statements about its
behaviour diminishes until a threshold is reached beyond which precision and
significance (or relevance) become almost mutually exclusive characteristics.'

In the 23 years of its existence, fuzzy set theory has been applied in many areas
including engineering, business, psychology, mathematics and semiology. Fuzzy
control systems are in use in applications as diverse as cement kiln control and
passenger train control. This does not stop purists from claiming that fuzzy set
theory is 'bad mathematics' or 'not rigorous', particularly in the context of its
application to knowledge engineering. These objections are principally based on
the concept of 'truth' as a distinguished object admitting only of two values. But it
has been recognized for many years that two-valued, or classical logic, deals with
an abstraction. Bertrand Russell noted in 1923 that 'All traditional logic
habitually assumes that precise symbols are being employed. It is therefore not
applicable to this terrestrial life, but only to an imagined celestial existence.'

Some of these recognized shortcomings of classical two-valued logic in
representing human understanding of the real world can be addressed using
Zadeh's tools of fuzzy sets and approximate reasoning.

6.3.1 Basic concepts of fuzzy sets

Classically, a **set** is defined by its members. Thus we can recognize the set of all
clocks, or the set of all people living in Steeple Bumstead who were born before
1940. All members of the set exhibit a common property, which is the ticket of
admission to the set, and equally is the set's defining property.

Set theory and formal logic are dual representations of the same information.
When we say that something is a member of a set, we can equally well say that it
is true that this thing has a property. The property is, of course, the defining
feature of the set. If the property is not exhibited, the 'something' is not a member

of the set, and the logical proposition that it possesses the property is not true.

This is the law of the excluded middle; for any 'thing' it is either true or untrue that it possesses any given property, and equally and equivalently it is either true or untrue that it is a member of the set defined by that property.

Fuzzy sets and fuzzy logic simply repeal this law. Any object may be a member of a set 'to some degree'; and a logical proposition may hold true 'to some degree'. The philosophical implications of this axiom have exercised logicians since the concept was first introduced. Some hold that truth is a distinguished concept, which may only entertain the value true and false, and that to speak of partial degrees of truth is, self-evidently, a nonsense. This view is strongly expressed by Hayes (1985) and Haack (1978) and held but not expressed quite so cogently by others in the field of knowledge engineering.

On a less formal basis, however, introspection suggests that we communicate with other people very frequently by making qualitative statements, some of which are vague because we simply do not have the precise datum to hand (as when we describe a person as tall, although that person has a measurable height which we could ascertain) or because the datum is not measurable on any scale (as when we describe a person as 'good looking', for which no metric exists). In this case, 'tall' and 'good looking' are **fuzzy sets**. A fuzzy set can be regarded as the label applied to a linguistically expressed concept which has no precise boundary; and such concepts, with all their associated vagueness, are one of the important channels by which we mediate and exchange ideas, information and understanding. As a simple 'thought experiment', you might imagine being shown a photograph of a group of half-a-dozen or so people. If someone says 'I am now going to refer to the tall, good-looking person in the photo', somehow there is an expectation that most people will correctly identify the person referred to. The use of the fuzzy concept has transferred information and understanding.

How may we represent these fuzzy sets numerically, so that they may be processed on a digital computer? Consider Fig. 6.1, which illustrates the set of

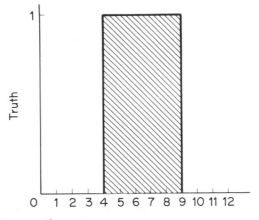

Fig. 6.1 The set $\{x : 4 < x < 9\}$; a crisp set

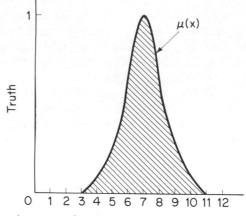

Fig. 6.2 The fuzzy set {x:x near 7}; a fuzzy set

numbers between 4 and 9: this is a **truth diagram**, where the y-axis is scaled from 0 (meaning false) to 1 (meaning true).

The block indicates that in the range 4 to 9, it is true that the numbers lie within the set.

Now consider Fig. 6.2, which illustrates the numbers which are near seven. This is a fuzzy set, and instead of the truth function switching between 0 and 1, it takes on any value in the interval. We refer to the truth function as the degree of membership of the set, or sometimes as the compatibility function of the element with the set. It is normally represented by the Greek letter mu, and we write $\mu(x)$ to represent the membership of some object to the set X.

Now that we have a numerical representation for a fuzzy set, we need to define the set theoretic operations of **intersection, union,** and **complementation,** along with their logical counterparts of **conjunction, disjunction,** and **complementation.**

6.3.2 Intersection and union

An object lies in the intersection of two sets A and B if it possesses the defining property of both sets. In logic terms of conjunction, it holds that A is true AND B is true. Figure 6.3 illustrates the arithmetic employed in fuzzy logic and fuzzy sets. The intersection of two fuzzy sets A and B is defined as the minimum value of the corresponding membership values for all points in the sets. Informally, we are saying that the truth of the joint propositions can be no more true than the smaller of the two truths forming it, or

$\mu(A\ AND\ B) = \min(\mu(A), \mu(B))$

Thus in Fig. 6.3 we have two fuzzy sets: 'numbers near 10' and 'small numbers'. The number 8 has a grade of membership of 0.8 in the first set, and 0.2

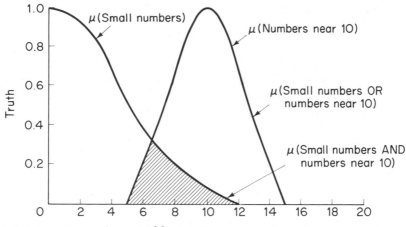

Fig. 6.3 Intersection and union of fuzzy sets

in the second. Thus the grade of membership of the combined set 'small numbers AND numbers near 10' is min $(0.2, 0.8) = 0.2$.

The union of two sets consists of objects which are in one set OR another. For fuzzy sets, the grade of membership is defined as the greater of the degree of membership in either of the two elementary sets. Again informally, we are saying that the degree of truth of a fuzzy joint proposition is as great as the larger of the degrees of truth of the elementary propositions. Once again referring to Fig. 6.3, we see that the truth of the proposition that 8 is in the set 'small numbers OR numbers near 10' is max $(0.2, 0.8) = 0.8$, or

$$\mu(\text{A OR B}) = \max(\mu(\text{A}), \mu(\text{B}))$$

6.3.3 Negation

The complement of a set is simply the set of all things NOT within the set. For fuzzy sets, where an object may be partly in the set, the degree of truth of the membership to the complement of the set is defined as $(1 - \text{membership})$:

$$\mu(\text{NOT A}) = 1 - \mu(\text{A})$$

The definitions given above are the most commonly used operators in fuzzy sets, and were shown by Bellman and Giertz (Dubois and Prade, 1980) to be derivable from a set of plausible axioms. However these are not the only definitions available for representing intersection and union. Others include the probabilistic sum and difference:

$$\mu(\text{A AND B}) = \mu(\text{A}) \times \mu(\text{B})$$

$$\mu(\text{A OR B}) = \mu(\text{A}) + \mu(\text{B}) - \mu(\text{A}) \times \mu(\text{B})$$

and the bold intersection and union:

$$\mu(A \text{ AND } B) = \max(0, \mu(A) + \mu(B) - 1)$$

$$\mu(A \text{ OR } B) = \min(1, \mu(A) + \mu(B))$$

There is not the space in this chapter to explore all the various definitions which have been proposed, but the interested reader is referred to Zimmermann (1986), Graham and Jones (1988) or Dubois and Prade (1980) for a fuller discussion of the definitions and their merits and demerits in various applications.

6.3.4 Implication

The utilization of fuzzy sets in mechanized reasoning depends on the introduction of a definition of fuzzy implication: A IMPLIES B. In Chapter 4, the mechanisms of inference including *modus ponens* and *modus tollens* were introduced and defined. *Modus ponens* allows us to reason that if A implies B, and A is found to be true, then B can be inferred to be true. By extension, in the fuzzy world, if A implies B, and A is known to be true to some degree, then we can infer that B may be true to no greater degree than A.

Thus if we have the statement about traffic on the outer London ring-road (M25):

'If the time is around 5.30 pm, then the M25 will be busy'

and we are told that the time is 6.00 pm, how do we deduce the degree of business on the M25? Figures 6.4 and 6.5 illustrate the fuzzy sets 'around 5.30 pm' and 'busy'. At 6.00 pm, the truth of the proposition that 'the time is around 5.30' is 0.67. The truth of the proposition that 'the M25 will be busy' is thus presented by the fuzzy set shown in Fig. 6.6: the original fuzzy set, truncated at the level of 0.67. In other words, the implication opera⹀ or is represented by taking the truth of the antecedent proposition, and truncating the fuzzy set representing the consequent proposition to the value of the antecedent. Notice particularly that

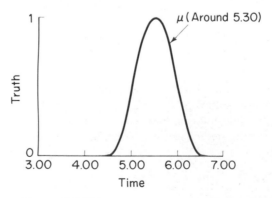

Fig. 6.4 The fuzzy set 'around 5.30'

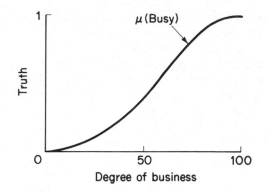

Fig. 6.5 The fuzzy set 'busy'

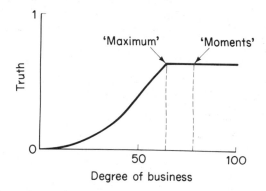

Fig. 6.6 The possibility of the M25 being busy at 6.00 pm

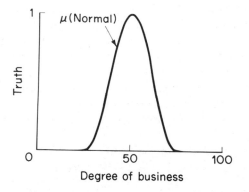

Fig. 6.7 The fuzzy set 'normal'

the truth-bearing object is exactly this fuzzy set. For this to be used in a decision making process such as 'Shall I take the motorway or the back roads', we have to defuzzify or scalarize this consequent fuzzy set in some way. In other words, it is necessary to represent a complex object by approximating it using one, two or more scalar parameters. These are most often defined as being a characteristic point on the x-axis of the set, and a characteristic truth value. There are a number of options available for this process, and the one which is selected depends principally on the application to which the system is directed. All the methods are pragmatic; there is no underlying theory in terms of their definition or of their selection.

One method is to select the point on the x-axis at which the consequent fuzzy set attains its maximum truth value. This is the maximum method. Another is to weight the consequent fuzzy set, and take the point on the x-axis which runs through the centre of gravity. This is the moments method. In general, the maximum method is the more suitable in applications which are directed towards discrete decisions, and the moments method is the more appropriate in applications involving continuous control.

In the current case, the maximum method is appropriate, because we are making the discrete decision as to whether to use the M25 or to give it a miss. This introduces another slight complexity, because the effect of truncating a fuzzy set to the extent of an antecedent truth value is, in the general case, to introduce a plateau – a range having the same truth value. Operationally, it is the practice to take the mid-point of the plateau as characterizing the set, if the plateau has both a left and a right edge within the domain of the set; and to take the inner point of the plateau if only one edge is available. Thus the defuzzification of the consequent fuzzy set in this example leads to the conclusion that the most possible value for business is 60, with a truth of 0.67.

Now supposing we have further information, expressed as

'If the day is Saturday then the M25 will be normal'

We can evaluate the proposition that the 'day is Saturday' to be either true or false (unless of course we are in a condition where we shouldn't be driving at all, in which case everything is fuzzy in a way not covered in this book). So the contribution to the consequent fuzzy set describing the state of the M25 will be either the full fuzzy set representing 'normal' as shown in Fig. 6.7, or the null fuzzy set. These two possibilities are shown in Fig. 6.8.

Notice that the operation of combining the contributions of two fuzzy rules is one of union. The maximum of the two sets is taken as the representative point in the combined set. This reflects the linking of the various rules by an implied ELSE statement.

We now have the basis for a tiny expert system, which will advise us on whether to take the M25 or not. The rules are

If the day is Saturday then the M25 is normal

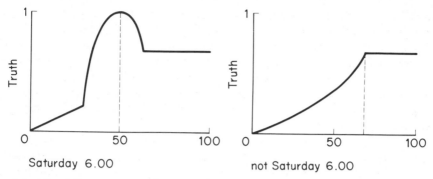

Fig. 6.8 Alternative outcomes of a two-rule set

If the time is around 5.30 pm then the M25 is busy

These rules will cause the variable 'M25' to be returned with a numeric value between 0 and 100 (the domain of the fuzzy sets normal and busy), and an associated truth value which may also be regarded as a confidence factor. A couple of further rules are required to transform this value into a decision statement. These might be:

If M25 is greater than 55 then route is 'not the M25'
If M25 is less than 55 then route is 'take the M25'

and if the system we are using allows us to set up a directive such as

Determine route

then we have constructed a goal-seeking expert system which will backwards chain from the goal statement, through the required value of the variable 'M25' and the fuzzy sets 'busy', 'normal' and 'around 5.30' to the data day and time.

Looking again at Fig. 6.8, we see that if the data values returned are 'Saturday' and '6.00', the truth-bearing object representing the variable 'M25' will exhibit a maximum at 50, contributed by the fuzzy set 'normal'. If the data values returned are 'Not Saturday' and '6.00', the maximum lies at 60, although with a smaller degree of truth.

6.3.5 Issues in knowledge representation

This simple model immediately raises two issues. Firstly, what knowledge is being represented, and in what form? Clearly, the fuzzy rules express useful 'rules of thumb' derived from real world experience. Their evaluation depends intimately on the definitions provided for the fuzzy sets 'around 5.30 pm', 'busy' and 'normal'. Who shall define these fuzzy sets, and on what basis?

In the case in question, statistics will be available in terms of number of vehicles per hour through the day, and the fuzzy sets could be expressed based on reasonably valid statistical data. In other cases, such data may not be available, and the fuzzy sets will represent a genuine piece of knowledge derived by the expert from personal experience. The issue of this definition of the fuzzy sets is clearly an important one, since the sets are the major method of encoding knowledge. In any case, the definition of 'busy' is a subjective one. How much excess traffic or stop–start driving is a given person willing to put up with? This leads us to the concept of fuzzy sets as **possibility distributions** as opposed to **probability distributions**.

A probability distribution expresses information about the likelihood associated with a given outcome from a well-specified set of alternatives. Normalization applies – in other words the total of all the probabilities must, by definition, be unity.

A possibility distribution on the other hand can be thought of as expressing the degree of ease with which one of a set of outcomes may occur.

One of the classic examples illustrating the difference between these two representations is the question 'How many eggs did I eat for breakfast this morning?'. The probability distribution has quite high values for zero, one and two, with the probability for any higher number tailing away very quickly. However, the possibility distribution would remain quite high up to say six eggs, and remain non-zero for an even larger number, reflecting the fact that one could, for a bet say, eat six eggs without undue difficulty.

6.3.6 Fuzzy quantifiers, usuality and dispositions

Zadeh has introduced the concept of usuality as a method of expressing a subjective judgement on a bi-modal probability distribution. Anecdotally, I may say that 'Usually, it takes twenty minutes to drive from Uxbridge to Chertsey on the M25; but if there is an accident on the motorway, it can take more than an hour'. This information could be expressed statistically, when it might look like Fig. 6.9. Note that this diagram is a probability distribution, not a fuzzy set. There

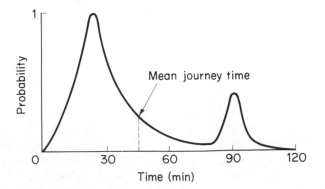

Fig. 6.9 A probability distribution for journey time

will be a mean and a standard deviation for the time taken for the journey, but this is a case where these data are not much help in making a decision. Either I leave in time to make an appointment assuming the traffic is normal; or I leave enough time to get there even if it is jammed up badly. Leaving enough time for the average journey will get me there too early most of the time, but still make me late when there is an accident. In practice, my decision will be based on the data that

'Usually the journey takes twenty minutes'
'Occasionally the journey takes ninety minutes'

and I will make my decision based (presumably) on the importance of making the appointment on time.

Usually and occasionally are **fuzzy quantifiers**. The classical pair of quantification operators of universal quantification (for all, or $\forall$) and existential quantification (for some, or $\exists$, which actually means 'for at least one') can be extended in fuzzy logic to incorporate an open set of quantifiers such as for most, for a few, for nearly all.... Arithmetically, fuzzy quantifiers are developed on a test score counting basis, and are represented by a number in the range zero to one: a simple proportion of the population.

If we know that Q_1 As are B, and Q_2 Bs are C, how many As are C? The answer is that $Q_1 \times Q_2$ As are C – a multiplication of the quantification constants. So if we are told that 'Most As are B' and that 'Most Bs are C' then the proportion of As that are C is 'most $\times$ most'. If the quantifier 'most' is represented (in the given universe of discourse) by 0.9, the possibilistic interpretation of the proportion of As that are C is 0.81. Notice that the interpretation of this proportion is explicitly possibilistic, not probabilistic. It is easy, for example, to construct an example where both propositions are true, but no As are C. Consider the set A { A: the letters a to e}; the set C{ C: the letters f to z} and the set B {B: b, c, d, e, g, h, i, j, k, l, m, n, o, p, q, r, s, t, u, v, w, x, y, z}. It is clear that most As are B, and that most Bs are C, whilst in this pathological case, A and C are disjoint. The point about usuality is that we don't expect to find pathological cases such as the above, and commonly, in expressions, ignore their existence. Zadeh (1984) terms this a disposition. Thus when we say 'It takes twenty minutes to drive from Uxbridge to Chertsey', there is an implicit but unstated quantification operator, understood by both parties to the dialogue, that 'It mostly takes twenty minutes to drive from Uxbridge to Chertsey'. In normal discourse, we subconsciously restore the existence of the implied quantifier – what Zadeh calls dispositional restoration.

The issue of apprehending the existence of these implied quantifiers is bound up in many ways with the much larger and largely unsolved issue generally termed the **frame problem** in artificial intelligence: how is it that participants in a dialogue intuitively develop or possess a shared frame of reference, implicitly and without preamble, which permits unambiguous discourse? Further exploration of this important topic is out of place here, but the interested reader is referred to Brown (1987).

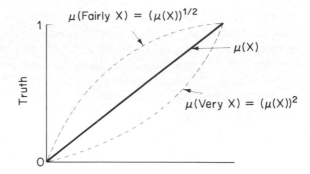

Fig. 6.10 Power hedges

6.3.7 Hedges

If we identify a fuzzy set with a label attached to some linguistic concept, such as 'tall', 'busy' or whatever, we see that the fuzzy set plays the role of a qualifier. In setting up an expert system to tackle some domain, the first thing to do is to establish the term set of fuzzy sets or qualifiers which adequately covers the spaces of the domain. For example, if we were talking about weather temperatures, the term set {freezing, cold, temperate, warm, hot}, with their appropriate definitions, might be a first approximation to an adequate term set. The question is, what granularity of representation do we need in the term set? Too few, and the system will be inadequately descriptive. Too many, and the associated rule sets will become cumbersome. One desirable facility would clearly be to extend the utility of the term set by defining an analogue of the adverb: an operator to qualify a qualifier. Then we could represent concepts such as 'fairly cold', 'extremely hot' or 'very warm' by extension from our primitive term set.

'Fairly', 'very', 'extremely' and similar words are called **hedges**. They are represented as arithmetic functions applied to a fuzzy set to generate a new set. Since the grade of membership of a fuzzy set falls in the interval [0, 1], power factors are a simple and convenient way of carrying out this sort of transformation. Figure 6.10 illustrates how 'very' and 'fairly' can be represented using the operators of raising to the power two, and taking the square root respectively.

Using the hedges and conjunctions at our disposal, we can now experiment with building up a fuzzy set to represent a complete phrase. Starting with the set 'busy' first defined in Fig. 6.5, let us generate the set 'fairly busy but not very busy'. First we generate the set 'fairly busy' by taking the square root of 'busy'; then the set 'very busy' by squaring 'busy'; then the set 'not very busy' by negating the set 'very busy'. Finally we take the intersection of these two sets (representing 'but' by the conjunction 'and') producing the final set shown in Fig. 6.11. We should note that it is possible to proceed in the reverse way, and represent some generated fuzzy set by a process of linguistic approximation as an English phrase. This method, suggested by Eshragh and Mamdani (1979), is elegant but has not seen much practical application to date.

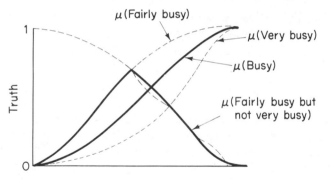

Fig. 6.11 Linguistic approximation

One point to be clear about is that we are simply using fuzzy sets here to map linguistically expressed concepts into numeric arrays. This should not be confused with natural language understanding, which requires different techniques altogether.

6.3.8 Practical applications of fuzzy sets

The principal systems available for developing fuzzy set based systems are REVEAL from ICL (Small, 1984; Small, Pinkerton and Meyer, 1986), FRIL (Fuzzy Relational Inference Language) from Equipu A.I.R. (Baldwin, 1987; and 1988), and Leonardo from Creative Logic.

REVEAL is essentially a decision support system with the ability to embody approximate knowledge as a set of 'policies' within an overall application. The user is allowed to generate a vocabulary of fuzzy sets, and then use these in preparing sets of fuzzy rules. These rules are evaluated much as described in this chapter, and cause the values of one or more system variables to be established, for further usage in the decision support component of the system.

FRIL is an interesting language which extends the concept of logic programming, as exemplified in Prolog, by permitting inference under uncertainty and incompleteness. Both facts and rules may have uncertainties associated with them. These uncertainties are represented probabilistically, but instead of being point valued probabilities, an interval valued probability may be given. This is essentially an approximation to full usage of fuzzy sets, which reduces the computational overhead which explicit fuzzy set evaluations can introduce. Thus the common-sense rule of thumb

'IF someone is tall THEN they probably wear large shoes'

can be thought of as the conditional probability

P(X wears large shoes | X is tall) = high

where high represents the qualifier probably in the original rule. Rather than restricting the value of high to a point value such as 0.90, it can be represented as a support pair [0.80 0.95], meaning that its value lies in the interval 0.80 to 0.95, which in FRIL notation is represented as

((wears_large_shoes X) (tall X)): (0.8 0.95)

6.4 SUMMARY

In the absence of an agreed objective model of how the human mind encompasses and deals with uncertainty in the real world, it is inevitable that no single method of mechanizing the process of reasoning with uncertainty will be suitable for all application types. When building expert systems which need to manage uncertainty, the important step is to try and identify the cause and nature of the uncertainty being handled, and then to pick from the range of tools available the method most sympathetic to the case at hand.

Fuzzy set theory offers a tool which recognizes the imprecision with which we label and discuss many concepts, and thus offers a way of dealing with linguistically defined objects. It thus offers a way of developing rules which have the expressive power to represent vagueness in a very natural way.

6.5 REFERENCES

Baldwin, J. F. (1987) Evidential support logic programming, *Fuzzy Sets and Systems*, **24**, 1–26.

Baldwin, J. F. and Monk, M. R. M. (1988) *Evidence Theory, Fuzzy Logic and Logic Programming*, Information Technology Research Centre Internal Report ITRC 109, University of Bristol.

Brachman, R. J. and Levesque, H. J. (eds.) (1985) *Readings in Knowledge Representation*, Morgan Kaufmann, Los Altos, CA.

Brown, F. M. (ed) (1987) *The Frame Problem in Artificial Intelligence*, Morgan Kaufmann, Los Altos, CA.

Dubois, D. and Prade, H. (1980) *Fuzzy Sets and Systems: Theory and Applications*, Academic Press, New York.

Eshragh, F. and Mamdani, E. H. (1979) A general approach to linguistic approximation, *Int. J. Man-Machine Studies*, **11**.

Goodman, I. R. and Nguyen, H. T. (1985) *Uncertainty Models for Knowledge-Based Systems*, North-Holland, Amsterdam.

Graham, I. M. and Jones, P. L. K. (1988) *Expert Systems: Knowledge, Uncertainty and Decision*, Chapman and Hall, London.

Haack, S. (1978) *Philosophy of Logics*, Cambridge.

Hayes, P. J. (1985) The logic of frames. In Brachman and Levesque (eds), *Readings in Knowledge Representation*, Morgan Kaufmann, Los Altos, CA.

Prade, H. and Negoita, C. V. (1986) *Fuzzy Logic in Knowledge Engineering*, Verlag TUV Rheinland.

Small, M. (ed.) (1984) *Knowledge Engineering and Decision Support*, International Computers Ltd, Bracknell, UK.

Small, M., Pinkerton, A. and Meyer, I. (1986) Practical Applications Involving Uncertainty, *Future Generations Computer Systems*, **2**.

Zadeh, L. A. (1965) *Fuzzy Sets, Information and Control,* **8.**

Zadeh, L. A. (1984) A computational theory of dispositions, *Proc. Conf. the Assoc. Computational Linguistics.*

Zimmermann, H-J. (1986) *Fuzzy Set Theory and its Applications,* Kluwer-Nijhoff, Dordrecht.

Zimmermann, H-J. (1987) *Fuzzy Sets, Decision Making and Expert Systems,* Kluwer Academic Publishers, Dordrecht.

Representation

7

From data to knowledge

RICHARD FORSYTH

An expert system contains two central components – the **inference engine** and the **knowledge base**. This chapter is concerned with the second of those two components. It introduces the important AI topic of **knowledge representation** by considering the question: what is a knowledge base and how does it differ from a conventional database?

'Knowledge', in the full sense of the word, requires a knower. Information that resides in a book is not knowledge unless and until someone reads and understands that book. Digital computers, therefore, know nothing; they merely store and manipulate information. Thus the very term 'knowledge base' carries a presumptuous philosophical claim. Strictly speaking, it is a misuse of language.

Linguistic misuse, however, is one of the ways in which people adapt to changing circumstances. Yesterday's error can become tomorrow's standard usage; sometimes mistakes are a symptom of creative energy at work. What we want to know in this case is to what extent expert system designers are justified in stretching the word 'knowledge' to cover what is – in the last analysis – a string of binary digits in a computer's memory.

The central motivation behind the technology of expert systems is to represent and deploy human know-how, with the aid of a computer. If we use the less contentious term 'know-how programming', rather than 'knowledge-based programming', it is perhaps easier to appreciate why the pioneers of the new methodology felt they were dealing with information structures sufficiently different from traditional databases to warrant a new name. (Brachman and Levesque, 1985.)

7.1 REPLICATING REALITY

Any non-trivial program attempts in some way to model the world outside the computer. This applies to conventional data-processing applications such as payroll and stock control as well as to more obvious simulation systems. In AI programming it applies more strongly than almost anywhere else. AI programs, including expert systems, are usually centred on a 'micro-world' which explicitly captures the properties and relationships of certain parts of the external world.

One way to gain appreciation of the problems of representation is to start with a data structure that no one would want to call 'knowledge' and to see how it has to

be extended in order to approximate the subtlety of human know-how.
Consider the humble BASIC statement

DIM   H(100)

which instructs a standard BASIC interpreter to create a data structure consisting of 101 cells, each of which is capable of holding a single floating-point number. It is just about the simplest data structure you can have. It could be used as a rudimentary model of an aspect of the world (e.g. to represent the age of up to 101 horses) but it has virtually no in-built organization. It is emphatically not a knowledge base, even when it contains the values you intend it to contain.

The BASIC array has four salient properties as a representational tool. It is:

1. static
2. flat
3. homogeneous
4. passive.

In calling it static, we draw attention to the fact that it has exactly 101 elements, no more and no less. Its size is fixed when it is created, and it will not grow or shrink during the computation (unless you have a peculiar version of the BASIC programming language).

It is flat in so far as it contains no substructures. The contents of each cell are (ignoring bit-fiddling tricks for the sake of argument) atomic: they are not meant to be further subdivided. The programmer cannot, for instance, write something like

H(19) = DIM A(20)

to assign an entire array as the value of element number 19 in H.

This example also illustrates the third feature listed above: it is a homogeneous structure in as much as all its elements have the same data-type. They must all be floating-point numbers. BASIC does not provide arrays which can store, let us say, an integer in one cell, a floating-point number in the next cell, a sub-array in the next cell and a character string in the one after that. (This facility is in fact available in some quite old-fashioned languages, e.g. Snobol4 and the dBase III command language.)

Finally, it is a passive repository for information. It simply stores data, with no computational attachment. New values are computed by removal of the old value, followed by processing (elsewhere, in the CPU), followed by replacement in the array. This is the only way to do it; and many of us are so conditioned by the Von Neumann machine and the outlook that it fosters that we tend to imagine there is no other way of working.

The one-dimensional array, then, can be taken as the classic example of what we don't mean when we speak of knowledge representation. It is widespread, handy and taken for granted. Its limitations, however, quickly become apparent when we attempt to model some of the complexities of human expertise. Indeed it is not far from the truth to say that the art of knowledge representation consists in finding ways to remove the four restrictions outlined above. The knowledge engineer, to do any kind of justice to the richness of human know-how, demands structures that are:

1. flexible
2. layered
3. heterogeneous
4. active.

Let us take each of these four attributes in turn.

7.1.1 Flexibility

Human know-how increases (learning) and diminishes (forgetting) with time. Any attempt to represent it that is not dynamic, therefore, is asking for trouble. As a very minimum, knowledge structures must be extensible. This was recognized very early, in the design of the AI programming language LISP, which was based on the concept of list structures which can be extended, truncated and combined as desired.

More recently the distinction between database and knowledge base has arisen. In a database, one creates simple 1-level entities, called records, which relate to individual objects or events and are composed of several fields (i.e. attributes). Typically the number of fields is small and fixed. The operation of adding or deleting a field is possible, but it can be quite time-consuming – because the default assumption behind database design is that all objects (records) are normally measured on all attributes (fields). Records with missing values are anomalies.

In contrast, the guiding assumption behind knowledge-base design is that the number of fields (more often known as **slots** or **facets**) is not known in advance, may change at any time and is, in principle, unlimited. New slots are frequently created 'on the fly' as a computation unfolds, and it is most unusual for an object to have all its potential slots actually filled. This is simply a different attitude to data than that manifested by the database fraternity (despite the fact that the more commonly used knowledge representations look rather like relational databases).

7.1.2 Hierarchy

Knowledge engineers also require their representational schemes to be multi-layered. The one-dimensional array has no sub-structure; but it is normal for knowledge representations to have many layers. Often the layering is based, at least in part, on a **sub sumption hierarchy** where objects point to subordinate and superordinate types. Thus, in a zoological knowledge base, the mammal entry would point upwards to vertebrates and downwards to dolphins, hamsters,

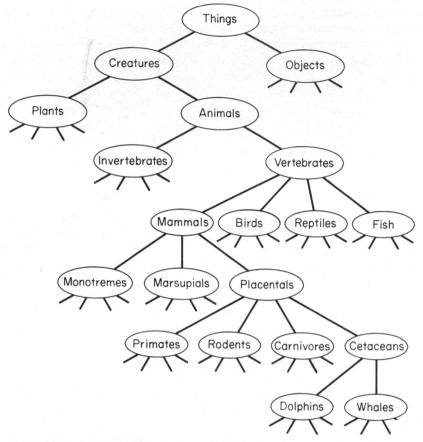

Fig. 7.1 Inheritance hierarchy

horses and sloths (among other species), as shown in Fig. 7.1.

Such **inheritance hierarchies**, based on class-membership and the superset/subset relationship, are found at the heart of the new wave of **object-oriented** languages, such as SmallTalk-80 and its imitators. Object-oriented representations are ideal for taxonomic trees, and convenient in programming by specializing high-level generic functions for specific tasks. AI programmers, being the sort of people they are, tend to go beyond the boundaries of the class-inclusion relationship and create 'tangled hierarchies' where the levels are not clearly separated.

7.1.3 Heterogeneity

It is also characteristic of knowledge representations that they contain a wide variety of data-types. When we define a field called AGE in a traditional database, we are normally required to specify that the values for this field are of a particular type – non-negative integers, for instance. We may also be able to specify a permitted range, such as 0 to 42. (We are talking about horses again.)

In an equine knowledge base, on the other hand, there might well be a slot called AGE, but it would not necessarily contain only numbers. In one case it could hold a figure (e.g. 9), while in another it might refer to a procedure, such as the one sketched below in an imaginary programming language.

```
Compute-Age (h)
     if colour-of-teeth (h) = white then AGE = [0..2]
     if colour-of-teeth (h) = yellow then AGE = [2..7]
     if colour-of-teeth (h) = brown then AGE = [4..20]
     if colour-of-teeth (h) = black then AGE = [16..35]
     if absent (teeth (h)) then AGE = [0, 22..42]
end-compute.
```

Thus the value in the age slot may be an integer, a range or a procedure call.

In general, representation schemes for knowledge engineering are not 'strongly typed' because it may be necessary for a single slot to be filled by numbers, strings, pointers, procedures or other kinds of value on different occasions. Consequently it is important that data objects are 'self-describing': it should be possible to interrogate an item, e.g. by calling a system function, to find out what sort of data it currently contains.

7.1.4 Activity

The idea that a slot can contain a routine or procedure brings us to the final distinguishing feature of knowledge representations – activity versus passivity.

A knowledge base contains both procedural and declarative elements: it is not restricted to encoding facts. Objects in a knowledge base may have rules or 'methods' associated with them. These methods determine their relations with other objects in the system.

There is also the possibility of data-driven processing, employing what have become known as 'demons'. A **demon** is a procedure that is attached to a data object. Whenever that object is accessed, the demon checks to see the result of the access and, if its activating conditions are satisfied, performs an appropriate processing function. Demons can be implemented on sequential hardware; but obviously they will be especially well suited by the next generation of highly-parallel computers. For that reason the 'demonic' style of programming can be expected to become more prominent in future.

7.2 ALTERNATIVE REPRESENTATIONS

Once a certain level of organized interrelatedness is reached in a data structure, it does after all make sense to talk about representing 'knowledge'. As we have seen, the particular demands of AI programming have forced knowledge engineers to come a long way from the simple one-dimensional array that we took as our starting point, even though all representations implemented on a Von Neumann computer are ultimately mapped on to a storage structure that is essentially a one-dimensional array.

But we are still only groping towards adequate methods of representing human know-how in a computer. There is no agreed best way of representing knowledge. In fact, there are several approaches, grouped into two main streams – **symbolist** and **connectionist**. (See also Chapter 8 of this volume.) These are sometimes presented as antitheses, though it is likely that complex projects in the future will rely on finding ways to harmonize both major paradigms successfully within a single system. The competent knowledge engineer should at least be aware of the highlights of both approaches.

The 'classical' or mainstream approach to knowledge representation in AI has been inspired, historically speaking, by the insights of mathematical logicians (from Boole through Russell to Carnap and Church). It is based on the notion of a correspondence between discrete, identifiable (and arbitrary) tokens in the computer and external objects, events or relationships. Such tokens symbolize the objects, events and relationships. They are manipulated by following rules of deduction to arrive at new conclusions, also represented symbolically. We might characterize this viewpoint as asserting, albeit implicitly, that thinking is the same thing as reasoning. (See Newell and Simon, 1972.)

An alternative viewpoint was proposed by a number of cyberneticians in the early days of AI (the 1940s and 1950s) which identified cognition with perception. This school of thought was more influenced by discoveries in biology (mainly neurophysiology) than in philosophy; but, for reasons we have not space to go into here, it fell from grace, and has only recently become respectable within AI again, under the banner of 'connectionism'. (See also McCulloch, 1965; Minsky and Papert, 1969.) We will discuss both styles of knowledge representation briefly, beginning with the symbolist approach.

7.2.1 Symbolic systems

All symbolic representations are grounded in logic, and most symbolic implementations could (at least in theory) be mapped into logic; but for practical reasons symbolic representations come in four broad flavours, each with its own distinctive pros and cons:

1. predicate logic
2. production rules
3. semantic networks
4. frame-based systems.

We have been talking so far in rather general terms, so let us bring the discussion down to earth by looking at a simple example. Simple examples are always somewhat misleading, since the acid test of a representation is whether it can cope with complexity. Nevertheless, there is not room to delve into a complex example, and this small one does at least illustrate how the four main symbolic representations can be put to use.

Below, in English, are a few simple pieces of racing lore which might (just might) serve as a small part of a prototype expert system for lovers of the turf.

Blakeney's male offspring tend to mature late.
Pontevecchio Notte is a three-year-old colt, trained by GA Pritchard-Gordon at Newmarket.
The sire of Pontevecchio Notte is Blakeney and his dam is Oula-Ka Fu-Fu.
Pontevecchio Notte won three of his five races as a two-year-old collecting £6956 in prize-money.
The sire of Blakeney was Heathersett.
The sire of Oula-Ka Fu-Fu was Run the Gauntlet.

This rather stilted paragraph is hardly world-shattering news (it will be out of date by the time you read it); and would not seem to pose any great conceptual difficulties. Certainly it doesn't begin to scratch the surface of what a follower of racing picks up in the way of knowledge by idly scanning the pages of the racing press during the course of a mis-spent youth.

Yet once we begin to start formalizing these innocuous assertions, the magnitude of the task of representing human know-how becomes alarmingly clear. The difficulty of translating natural language into a formal representation lies not so much in what is said as in what is left unsaid. Every statement is the apex of a pyramid of meaning built on the broad base of what we usually call 'common sense' – i.e. a knowledge base about the world which is never spelt out but only implied.

Let us begin with first-order predicate logic, arguably the fundamental symbolic representation scheme. Most of the above information can be captured in the following 'Pidgin Prolog' notation. First the facts:

```
sire (pontevecchio_notte, blakeney).
dam (pontevecchio_notte, oula_ka_fu_fu).
sire (oula_ka_fu_fu, run_the_gauntlet).
sire (blakeney, heathersett).
age (pontevecchio_notte, 3).
colt (pontevecchio_notte).
trainer (pontevecchio_notte, pritchard_gordon_ga).
prizemoney_won (pontevecchio_notte, 2, 6956).
```

Next, a few rules:

```
racehorse (X):—colt (X).
racehorse (X):—filly (X).

better (Y1, Y2, H):—
    racehorse (H),
    prizemoney_won (H, Y1, X),
```

```
        prizemoney_won (H, Y2, XX),
        Y2 = Y1 + 1,
        greaterthan (XX, X).
better (2, 3, H):—colt (H), sire (H, blakeney).
```

The facts should be more or less self-explanatory. We have followed (nearly) the Edinburgh syntax of Prolog (see, for example, Bratko, 1986). The underscore in a symbol like

prizemoney_won

is needed because a space would break it into two separate identifiers. Initial upper case is used to indicate variables, so constants, even names like Blakeney, have to begin with lower-case letters.

The rules can be read by interpreting ':—' as 'if'. The first two rules are relatively trivial; but of course with a computer everything has to be spelt out. They merely say that a racehorse is a filly or a colt. (We are ignoring geldings for the moment.)

The second pair of rules try to say something about whether a racehorse is better in one year than the next. Everything has to be operationalized, and readers may disagree with my operationalization, but the first rule boils down to saying: a racehorse is better in one year than the previous one if it wins more prize-money in the succeeding year. The purpose of that rule is to lay the groundwork for the final rule which attempts to encapsulate the gist of the assertion that Blakeney's male offspring tend to mature late. Actually it says that they are better as three-year-olds than two-year-olds.

Armed with this ammunition, one could reasonably expect a Prolog-style inference engine to deduce that any given horse was better in its three-year-old career than its two-year-old career in two distinct ways: 1. by comparing prize-money won, if known; or 2. by seeing if it was a colt sired by Blakeney. It would not be beyond the wit of a competent Prolog programmer (which I am not) to make it deduce the fact that Pontevecchio Notte will win more prize-money this season than last; in other words, to make a forecast.

Now this all seems rather long-winded, as indeed it is. If we want to represent knowledge in terms of logical relations manipulated by a standard inference mechanism, we have to enter a large number of simple and boring facts and rules. And there is always the danger of leaving out the obvious, just because we find it too obvious to need stating.

If we move on to the most closely related alternative representation, production-rule format, the rules become even more verbose.

IF Horse is Pontevecchio Notte
THEN Trainer is GA Pritchard-Gordon.

IF Trainer is GA Pritchard-Gordon
THEN Location is Newmarket.

IF Horse is Pontevecchio Notte

THEN Sire is Blakeney.

IF Horse is a Colt AND
    Sire is Blakeney
THEN Development is Late-Maturing.

IF Development is Late-Maturing
THEN Prizemoney-won-at-2 is less than
    Prizemoney-won-at-3.

It is simply too tedious to list even the fragmentary 'knowledge base' listed earlier, since production rules are not very good at representing facts. To put it another way: it is not worth making a rule for singular propositions, only for generalizations. Production rule systems, in practice, do not only use production rules to represent knowledge. There is in addition something called the 'working memory' which uses some other formalism entirely. There may be other kinds of structure too. For example, the Prospector system (Gashnig, 1982) is a rule-based expert system which has a semantic network in the background to supply geological knowledge. So most real expert systems that employ production rules also employ alternative representation in the background – very often in the form of semantic nets and/or frames.

A semantic net consists of **nodes** (roughly speaking: nouns) linked by **arcs** (roughly speaking: verbs and adjectives). It is particularly suited to representing linguistic information, i.e. to encoding sentences. In the computer, semantic nets are held in the form of property lists or object–attribute–value triples, but they are most easily understood in visual terms, as two-dimensional diagrams. Some of the sentences describing our old friend Pontevecchio Notte are shown in diagrammatic form as Fig. 7.2.

Finally, we can recode the knowledge in a frame-like notation.

```
(Item H592
(Printname "Pontevecchio Notte")
(Type Colt)
(Age 3)
(Prizemoney-won (Yo 2 6956)
                (Yo 3 Unknown))
(Sire H221)
(Dam H703)
(Trainer GAPG)
)

(Item H703
(Type Mare)
(Printname "Oula-Ka Fu-Fu")
(Sire H991)
....
)
```

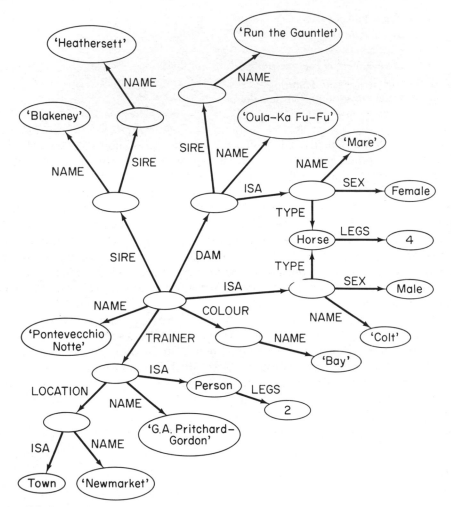

Fig. 7.2 Semantic net

```
(Item GAPG
(Type Person)
(Printname "GA Pritchard-Gordon")
(Location L775)
(Strikerate 13.2%)
....
)

(Item L775
(Printname "Newmarket")
(Type Place)
(County Suffolk)
....
)
```

Without going into too much detail, it is worth noting two features of this (partial) translation from English into Frame-ish: 1. the type/token distinction; 2. the tangledness of the hierarchy.

The distinction of type from token is fundamental. (See also the next chapter.) It is the distinction between an individual entity and the class to which it belongs. For example the horse H592 and its superclass 'Colt'. It is essential to both cognitive and computational economy that information should only be stored in the appropriate place. Generally speaking, this means that individual objects only need to be associated with the slots that distinguish them from the prototype of their class. Information about horses in general need not be held with every instance of type Horse. This permits the inheritance of default values. Thus, in the absence of information to the contrary, every horse will inherit the number 4 as the value of its Number-of-Legs slot from the prototype horse record. This is a great simplification, although it can be a mixed blessing in exceptional cases. There is psychological evidence, however, that prototype-based reasoning plays a large part in human thinking. (When it goes wrong we call it 'prejudice' or 'stereotyping'; but it clearly saves a lot of time.)

As we have seen, even a few simple facts ramify very rapidly. A knowledge base can become very densely interconnected. Explicitly drawing out all the connections is tiresome, but it is an essential part of the encoding process. Again, this is a lifelike feature: we talk about

a list of facts
 versus
a body of knowledge

and this itself suggests that a person's knowledge is an interrelated system of multiple interlocking parts. Every fact links to others in many directions. The facts themselves are not the knowledge, however they are represented. What matters is how they relate to each other. This emphasis on connectivity is the final distinguishing mark of knowledge bases, compared to conventional data structures.

7.2.2 Connectionist architectures

Connectionist approaches to knowledge representation are, if anything, even more committed to the principle of richness of interconnectivity than symbolic ones. Nothing is stored in a single location: all knowledge is implicit in the pattern of the system's interconnections. (Hinton and Anderson, 1981.)

The chief difference between connectionist and symbolist representations is that the connectionists are quite happy to deal with black boxes whereas the symbolists insist that knowledge has to be explicit and, ideally, comprehensible to an outsider looking into the system.

Connectionism springs from two main sources: 1. an engineering source, rooted in dissatisfaction with today's serial computing engines; and 2. a biological source, rooted in a belief that the nervous system is a good guide for designing intelligent systems.

The drawbacks of conventional computer architectures have been known for a long time. John Von Neumann himself (credited as the designer of the modern digital computer) was well aware of the deficiencies of serial machines, and proposed various ways of employing large numbers of processing elements simultaneously (Von Neumann, 1958).

Today, in the age of array processors, floating-point accelerators, database controller chips and ULAs (all of which exhibit at least a degree of parallelism), there are signs that the Von Neumann design is reaching the end of its natural lifespan.

'With the advent of the microprocessor and the ever-advancing technology of integrated circuits, it is becoming increasingly obvious that we need to break away from the straight-jacket of the conventional approach to computing. The principles on which it has been based are becoming less and less realistic in the light of present-day knowledge.'
(Sharp, 1985.)

In AI, this dissatisfaction with the Von Neumann model has been felt especially keenly. Many AI workers believe that a genuine breakthrough towards machine intelligence can only be achieved by utilizing radically new computer architectures. This was one of the themes of the Japanese Fifth Generation Computer Initiative (JIPDEC, 1981). Naturally enough, AI workers are also fascinated by the human brain, and some of them have been bold enough to try to simulate it. Simulating the brain as a way of designing intelligent systems found favour in the early days of computing, as with the Perceptron (Rosenblatt, 1962); but the task proved too hard. Recently there has been a revival of interest in this approach, partly because we now have much more powerful hardware at our disposal.

Of course there is no evidence to suggest that electronic neural nets are replicas of the neural networks in our brains; but they do follow the same general principles and exhibit similar qualities. One brain-like quality is the emergence in large neural nets of properties that do not seem to be present in the units of which they are composed. Another is the fact that such machines cannot be programmed: they can only be trained. Thus learning returns to the forefront of AI after an absence of several decades.

In designing a neural net, whether built in hardware or simulated in software, two major aspects must be considered. One is the overall pattern of interconnections among the components making up the net. The other is the operational performance of each individual neuron. An artificial neuron must be capable of five important functions (Weber, 1988):

1. Input: the neuron must respond to the output values of other neurons connected to it.
2. Weightings: the neuron will typically assign a weight by which each of its inputs is multiplied, positive for excitatory inputs and negative for inhibitory ones.

3. Summation: the neuron summarizes the information it is receiving at any given instant by adding up the weighted sum of all its inputs.
4. Threshold: a nerve cell fires (i.e. sends out a message) only when its inputs exceed a threshold value. If the input sum falls below the neuron's threshold, no firing occurs.
5. Transfer function: in the binary nerve cell first proposed by McCulloch and Pitts (McCulloch, 1965) the output is 1 if the input sum achieves the threshold or else 0 if it does not. But more complex transfer functions are possible. (Alternatively, more complex functions may be built by linking groups of cells.)

Various ways of carrying out these five central functions give rise to a variety of different neurologically inspired systems. We shall briefly consider two of them – the Boltzmann Machine and WISARD.

A team at Carnegie-Mellon University (Hinton, 1985) has designed a machine which they call the Boltzmann Machine after Ludwig Boltzmann, a pioneer of statistical thermodynamics, since it works on statistical principles.

The Boltzmann Machine is composed of a network of many computing elements, all working in parallel. It can be simulated on a conventional computer, but the ultimate aim is to use it as a blueprint for a novel form of computing device.

The elements in the network are threshold units which produce binary outputs (0 or 1) by summing their inputs and firing if the sum exceeds a certain quantity. An important point is that the thresholds are not fixed: they 'jitter'. The larger the input, the more likely is the unit to fire, but the response is probabilistic, not deterministic. This is illustrated in Fig. 7.3.

All processing units are of the same type, but connections between them vary in strength. Connection strengths are symmetric, so the link from A to B has the same weight as that from B to A. This is not like the real nervous system, but it makes proving theorems about the behaviour of such nets feasible.

The network itself may be as complex as desired. Frequently it will have many

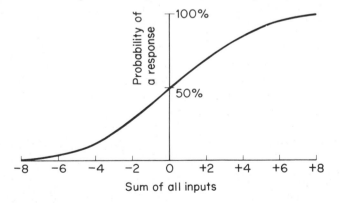

Fig. 7.3 Neural element response curve

Intermediate nodes

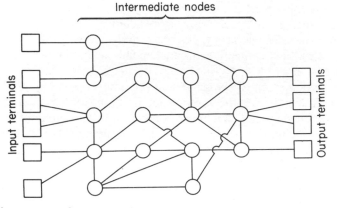

Input terminals

Output terminals

Fig. 7.4 Boltzmann Machine network layout

layers. It may also contain internal feedback loops (unlike Rosenblatt's Perceptron). An example is depicted in Fig. 7.4.

The system can be trained to acquire new input–output relationships by adjusting the connection weights in the following way.

1. Phase 1:
    (a) Clamp the training pattern to the input units and the desired response pattern to the output units.
    (b) Allow the network to settle to equilibrium.
    (c) Increment the weights linking any two elements that are simultaneously active by a small amount.
2. Phase 2:
    (a) Remove the output connections but leave the inputs connected (that is: take away the teacher).
    (b) Let the network stabilize again.
    (c) Decrement the weights between any pair of elements that are active together by a small amount.

The learning process consists of alternating these two phases repeatedly until the input–output behaviour in phase two (unsupervised mode) reaches some criterion of success. The procedure is known as 'simulated annealing' by analogy with the hardening of hot metal as it cools. Hot metal has plenty of random motion among its molecules. As it gets cooler, they settle into more and more fixed positions.

The idea behind simulated annealing is to 'shake' the system (by introducing randomness) in the early stages, but to let it become increasingly deterministic later on. This helps to avoid the problem of getting stuck at a local optimum.

Boltzmann machines can be taught a wide range of behaviour, but when simulated on serial hardware are very slow. However similar systems in the same spirit have been successful in such areas as vision, speech recognition and robotics. One of these is NETalk, a self-optimizing net built at Princeton University. This takes text as its input and drives a speech synthesizer to produce its output. Initialized with random connection weights it babbles incoherently. After a period of training by matching text strings with phonemic patterns it adjusts its connections till it can chatter quite intelligibly (Sejnowski and Rosenberg, 1986). This one has to be heard to be believed.

Another innovative design with a neurological flavour is the WISARD system (Aleksander and Burnett, 1984). This was devised at Brunel University and Imperial College as a visual pattern recognizer.

The interesting point about WISARD is that it is a highly parallel machine which is not a multi-processor system. In fact it has no processors at all, only memory. It works by examining a TV image made up of 512×512 pixels, which are sampled in groups of eight. The groupings, or octets, are randomly assigned. Each one can be in one of 256 states, depending on the pattern of 0s and 1s which feeds into it. In effect each octet is a primitive feature detector, and the state it is currently in says something about the picture being presented.

Every octet is connected to a bank of 256 RAM locations, which allows the system to use a form of content-addressing. The state of a detector is used as an address (between 0 and 255 inclusive) which points into its own RAM bank. During training, the bit to which it points is set when the image it is required to recognize is present; if some other image is being shown, that bit is left at zero. All 32 768 detectors point to particular locations within their own RAM banks. After the training phase, when a new image is shown to the system, the contents of these are read out and added up. A high total indicates that many detectors were in the same state as when they saw a positive training instance. A low total indicates that few of them are, and hence that the image is unlikely to be a positive example.

WISARD effectively computes a 'fingerprint' or 'signature' of what it sees and compares this with past experience. It needs a large memory (one megabyte) but these days that is not excessive. It is highly resistant to noise, i.e. random distortions of the image. For example, it has been taught to recognize a bearded face and then respond correctly to the same face in a different orientation with the beard shaved off.

This is an impressive feat for a computer. It is the sort of thing people are good at but computers, programmed algorithmically, have been conspicuously bad at. WISARD is a fast, practical visual recognition system, with numerous practical applications. It is not, however, a general-purpose machine.

And, like other connectionist systems, it only acquires inscrutable knowledge. With all such systems the 'knowledge' is represented in ways that are unintelligible to the human observer. You simply cannot look inside at the connection weights and see what the system knows any more than someone could write your biography by opening up your skull. That is the chief reason why there has been a forking of the paths in AI, with connectionists taking one route and symbolists another. The question of whether know-how must be explicit to be of value is a matter of heated scientific debate.

7.3 CONCLUDING REMARKS

The danger inherent in the return of neural networks to fashion is that, as in so many backlashes, the reaction may be overdone – sweeping away the gain in system perspicuity for which the expert system movement has laboured long and hard. It is not hard to imagine, for example, a weather predictor, built along connectionist lines, that performs better than any human forecaster (whether aided and abetted by a Cray-XMP atmospheric model or not) but which adds nothing at all to our understanding of meteorology.

The issue of the day in knowledge representation is whether connectionist or symbolist methods are going to prove more effective. Undoubtedly the future will reveal a 'middle way'; that is to say: connectionist techniques will prove better for some tasks (mostly perceptual), symbolist techniques will prove superior for other tasks (mostly intellectual), while the best systems will combine both approaches at appropriate levels.

My own opinion is that the burden of proof should rest with the connectionists. In other words, connectionist representations should only be used where symbolic systems have failed, and even then only as subordinate modules in an overall system whose high-level reasoning is as transparent as it can be made.

To put it anthropomorphically, the intuitive component is important but it should be governed by the rational component. That is, after all, roughly how we judge sanity in human beings. It is unsafe to build irrational systems, however clever they are.

Of course it is highly predictable that inscrutable, opaque and irrational systems will be designed and built with the neural-net methodology, just as they have been with previous methods (see Ennals, 1986); but that is no reason to encourage such practices.

7.4 REFERENCES

Aleksander, I. and Burnett, P. (1984) *Re-Inventing Man.* Penguin Books, Middx.

Brachman, R. J. and Levesque, H. J. (1985) *Readings in Knowledge Representation*: Morgan Kaufmann, Los Altos, CA.

Bratko, I. (1986) *Prolog Programming for Artificial Intelligence.* Addison-Wesley Publishing, Wokingham and Massachusetts.

Ennals, R. (1986) *Star Wars: A Question of Initiative.* John Wiley & Sons, Chichester, England.

Gashnig, J. (1982) PROSPECTOR: an expert system for mineral exploration: in D. Michie (ed.) *Introductory Readings in Expert Systems* Gordon & Breach, New York.

Hinton, G. (1985) Learning in parallel networks, *Byte,* **10**.

Hinton, G. and Anderson, J. (eds) (1981) *Parallel Model of Associative Memory.* Erlbaum, New Jersey.

JIPDEC (1981) *Preliminary Report on Study & Research on Fifth Generation Computers.* Japan Information Processing Development Centre, Tokyo.

McCulloch, W. (1965) *Embodiments of Mind.* MIT Press, Mass.

Minsky, M. and Papert, S. (1969) *PERCEPTRONS: An Introduction to Computational Geometry.* MIT Press, Mass.

Newell, A. and Simon, H. (1972) *Human Problem Solving.* Prentice-Hall, New Jersey.

Rosenblatt, F. (1962) *Principles of Neurodynamics.* Spartan Books, London.

Sejnowski, T. J. and Rosenberg, C. R. (1986) *A Parallel Network That Learns to Read Aloud.* Technical Report, Johns Hopkins University Press, Baltimore.

Sharp, J. (1985) *Data-Flow Computing.* Ellis Horwood Ltd., Chichester.

Von Neumann, J. (1958) *The Computer and the Brain.* Yale University Press, New Haven.

Weber, J. (1988) A window into the brain. *Personal Computer World,* **11,** 3.

8

Knowledge representation in man and machine

NIGEL SHADBOLT

This chapter will consider the fundamental topic of knowledge representation. We will sketch the systems of representation proposed within AI and cognitive science, discussing their strengths and weaknesses.

The problem of knowledge representation is at first glance an easy one to understand:

> 'It simply has to do with writing down, in some language or communication medium, descriptions or pictures that correspond in some salient way to the world or a state of the world.'   (Brachman and Levesque, 1985)

But how is this enterprise to be carried out when building machines to encapsulate knowledge? What do we know of the processes and means by which humans represent knowledge?

Until very recently most work in cognitive science (that subject characterized by an intersection of interests between AI, psychology, philosophy and linguistics) reflected common underlying assumptions about these questions.

The first of these was the assumption that mental activity and intelligence can be explained in terms of symbols manipulated by an information processing system. These symbols are taken to represent objects, events, relations between objects, relations between events and so on. This assumption occurs throughout cognitive science (Newell and Simon, 1972; Dennett, 1979; Fodor, 1981; Pylyshyn, 1984). It has become known as the 'Physical Symbol System (PSS) Hypothesis'. Moreover, the representations posited by the PSS Hypothesis are regarded as 'causally indispensable'. They are regarded as essential in explanations of intelligent behaviour. '...one of the main things cognisers have in common, is that they act on the basis of representations'. (Pylyshyn, 1984.)

A second important assumption underlying work in cognitive science we will call the 'Levels Hypothesis'. In any adequate explanation of an intelligent process there are always a number of levels. When building models of the mind, constructing robots or whatever we have to be clear about the descriptive level of our program or theory.

The best account of the levels required in cognitive science is contained in the work of David Marr (1982). Consider the problem of explaining how one recognizes the word following the full stop of this sentence. In any theory of word recognition we would want to specify the goal of the computation, why it is appropriate, and the logic of the strategy by which it can be carried out. Such a description Marr would call a Level 1 account – a computational theory in the sense that it specifies what is being worked out, why it is being worked out and how the goal of the computation can be realized. Another type of account, Level 2, would tell us how the Level 1 computational theory can be implemented. In particular, what is the representation for the input and output, and what is the algorithm for the transformation of raw sensory data to this representation? This is the level of representation and algorithm. Finally, there exists a Level 3 account that has to do with hardware implementation. It describes how the components of Level 2 can be physically realized in a device.

Each of these levels has a role in any complete account of a cognitive process. Each of these levels has its own components and vocabulary. We have to be careful in AI and cognitive science to know the level at which we are operating.

Philosophers such as Dennett point out that providing explanations and theories of intelligent agents (whether humans or robots) is particularly tricky since each of Marr's levels has a real existence in the system. However, the best level of description for complex goal-directed systems is in terms of goals and knowledge states – that is, the computational level. This is the right level at which explanations of behaviour and activity should be couched. This applies to artificial knowledge-based systems as well as the natural variety. We would no more think of explaining a modern chess program in terms of its base voltage states than we would think of taking EEG readings and trying to predict from these descriptions what a person might say or do next.

8.1 KNOWLEDGE REPRESENTATION LANGUAGES

Behind all of these assumptions lies the idea of a representation language – a formal way to model the world, its objects and relations. A language which in turn is manipulated and used as the basis for thought. As we examine the various representational systems we will discuss their form and structure, their strengths and weaknesses.

8.2 SEMANTIC NETWORKS

Semantic nets are intuitive and simple to understand. They represent relations between items in a domain. The items are represented as nodes, and they are connected by arcs labelled with the particular relation linking the two nodes.

From the net shown in Fig. 8.1 we can retrieve simple items of information such as 'Issigonis is the designer of the Mini'. We can also deduce facts such as 'the Mini is a vehicle'.

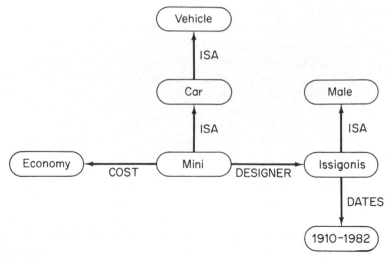

Fig. 8.1 A semantic network

The net serves as data which only becomes knowledge in association with a reasoning capability. Reasoning takes the form of traversing arcs in the net to identify complex relationships between the nodes. There are various techniques involved in this searching, many of them having their roots in graph theory – a branch of mathematics which provides the terminology, and some of the methods, for semantic nets. A common way of retrieving data from nets is the 'intersection search'. Imagine that one has a network representing the structure of a physical system, say a computer. Suppose we want to discover the ways in which two components are related. A search can be made by 'activating' all the arcs connected to one component and all the arcs connected to another. The nodes connected by these arcs can themselves be activated, and so on. Eventually all the paths between the components should be found, and we will have found all the relations encoded in the net that link these two elements.

One specialized type of net structure is the hierarchical network. This is called a tree in graph theory. In a tree no arc leaving a node can feed back either directly or indirectly to that node. The net shown in Fig. 8.2 is a tree – the links are 'is a' links and inheritance is possible. Inheritance allows properties true of a node to be passed on to subordinate nodes.

This type of tree structure simplifies information retrieval. One can restrict the search to a 'monotonic' form, i.e. one need only search upwards or downwards in the net to find out the properties of nodes.

The introduction and use of nets as one of the first AI knowledge representation devices owes a lot to psychology. Nets (often called 'associative nets') have a long history in psychology. Anderson and Bower (1973), Lindsay (1973), and Brachman (1979) all provide accounts of the early work in psychology that postulated nets as the foundation for knowledge representation in human

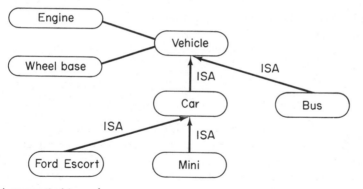

Fig. 8.2 A semantic hierarchy

cognition. Nets assumed this status in psychology because of an obvious feature of human memory. In memory a high number of connections exist between the different pieces of information that are represented in it. Memory presents an organization very suggestive of a network.

The work of Quillian (1966, 1967), Collins and Quillian (1969), Collins and Loftus (1975) investigated the idea that human memory really was implemented as a semantic network. Current psychological theory allocates a role for such representations but does not put all the burden of explanation on them.

Similarly, within AI although semantic nets offer a straightforward way of representing knowledge they are rarely used as the sole means of representation in modern systems. There are a number of reasons for this, all of which have to do with problems of expressive and inferential adequacy.

One problem with semantic nets is the difficulty of picking the right set of semantic primitives at the outset. There tends to be an early commitment to a particular range of nodes and links. Later on it is difficult to introduce new primitives into the formalism.

A second problem is the difficulty of expressing quantificational knowledge succinctly. The knowledge contained in the following propositions is not easy to represent in basic networks.

Some micros have hard disc drives
All the directors approved all the figures

Intensional concepts are also hard to express in nets. Representing the content of the propositions below is problematic.

John believed that Mary knew Bill
John does not know that George Orwell was Eric Blair

Whilst proposals have been made that aim to overcome these expressive restrictions (Hendrix, 1979) it is clear that the rather impoverished representational primitives used in nets do not make for efficient systems in large and complex domains. This gave rise to 'the possibility of organisations of conceptual knowledge into units more structured than simple nodes and links or predicates and propositions.' (Brachman, 1979.)

This brings us on to consider the next major class of representational formalism.

8.3 FRAMES AND SCRIPTS

One can conceive of frame systems (Minsky, 1975) and scripts (Schank and Abelson, 1977) as extensions to semantic nets. Nodes are replaced by more structured groupings of information which we call frames. In many frame systems the frames are organized in a hierarchical manner. Frames are thus able to represent class/subclass dependencies. The internal structure of frames themselves is usually some version of a slot and filler notation representing properties and their values.

The expressive power of simple frame systems resides in two features of the representation.

Firstly, each frame is a fairly detailed description of what an object is. This can contain not just declarative properties and values – frames can also embody procedural knowledge. This is done by procedural attachments to slots; that is, depending on the state of a particular slot, procedures can be called to execute necessary computations.

A second expressive feature of frames is that information can be transferred between them, for example, using an inheritance link. Using such a link the frames lower in a hierarchy can inherit values in their slots (even slots themselves) from a superordinate frame. This is used as a form of default reasoning – unless one has information to the contrary, a slot may be filled with a default filler.

Frames then are descriptions and the descriptions in frames are called slots. The simplest type of slot is a simple attribute-value pair. The following is an example:

{name "nigel shadbolt"}

Since frames are often organized into hierarchies we store information about what class a frame is an instance or subclass of. Thus we might have a frame which represents an individual that looks like the following:

{instance_of "employee"}
{name "nigel shadbolt"}
{age 30}
{job "chief bottle washer"}
{salary 6000}

This frame is an instance of a class "employee" which is also represented as a frame.

{instance_of "person"}
{name "employee"}

{nationality "british"}
{age (restrict (> 16))}
{nat – ins – contrib ← ((salary/100)*6)}

There are a number of points to make about this simple representation of ours. In the frame that has the **name** slot "employee", that is itself an instance of another frame called "person", we have a slot called **nationality**. Now this slot is not represented explicitly in the frame with the **name** "nigel shadbolt". Nevertheless, instances of the "employee" frame will inherit this slot implicitly. This slot could have been represented explicitly on the lower level frame but this would normally only be done to overwrite what we can regard as a default value for the **nationality** slot, in this case the value "british".

The "employee" frame illustrates another important type of value for a slot. This type of value is known as a "restriction". In our example it is on the **age** slot. Restrictions reflect the fact that often we do not know the particular value for a slot – what we have is knowledge that it must fall within a certain range or else be restricted in some other way. In this case the restriction states that the value for **age** must be greater than 16. In fact, this knowledge has been overwritten in the particular case of the frame "nigel shadbolt".

A third type of slot value we have already mentioned is 'procedural attachment'. The slot **nat – ins – contrib** (national insurance contribution) has associated with it a procedure to work out a value for the slot if it is needed. This simply takes the value of the slot **salary**, divides it by 100 and multiplies the result by 6.

Procedures, restrictions and ordinary values can all be inherited by subordinate frames in hierarchical systems. In different frame notations different conventions are used and sometimes different distinctions drawn. For example, some systems distinguish two classes of slot for generic frames – **own** and **member** slots. This accords with the epistemological intuition that some properties can only be predicated of classes and others of instances. Thus we might have organized the "employee" frame in the following way:

own _ slots
        {instance _ of "person"}
        {name "employee"}
member _ slots
            {nationality "british"}
            {age (restrict(> 16))}
            {nat – ins – contrib ← ((salary/100)*6)}

Frames are not just used to describe objects in the world or classes of objects. They are also used to describe actions or classes of action, events or prototypical courses of events. Putting this sort of information into frames is perhaps most often associated with the work of Schank (1975). He called the resulting structures scripts.

Reasoning in frame-based systems is supported by two mechanisms, i.e. matching and inheritance. To reason we must first select existing frames to match a current situation – the matching phase. These frames may allow us to go beyond the given information of the current situation. But we also want to use generic information held in our frame system to supplement any particular frame(s) selected as a match with the current situation – this is the inheritance phase. Different frame systems vary as to the emphasis they place on these two aspects of reasoning. In fact, in many modern systems the matching phase has been minimized and inheritance is the primary vehicle for reasoning.

To some extent frames and scripts have their roots in psychological theorizing – notably in the work of Bartlett (1932), Franks and Bransford (1972), and Rosch (1973). Minsky himself argues that the apparent speed and power of mental operations suggests structured chunks of knowledge in which the declarative and procedural aspects of knowledge are tightly connected.

It was Bartlett who introduced the precursor to the frame, he called his structure the 'schema'. He was trying to explain the fact that when we perceive any object or situation our perception is influenced by our expectations. Bartlett further claimed that recall was a reconstructive process, memories were not reliably filed away and then simply withdrawn on demand, rather the outline was stored and much of what was recalled was reconstructed on the basis of expectations about what must have happened. The role of expectation and reconstruction is taken as fundamental in all modern theories of cognitive psychology. Frame-based representations are one of the most powerful methods for explaining and modelling these processes.

It is not just in cognitive simulation that frame systems play a key role. Frame systems are now used widely for non-emulative problems. A number of frame-based representations have been extensively used in AI. KRL (Bobrow and Winograd, 1977), KL-ONE (Brachman and Schmolze, 1984), NETL (Fahlman, 1979) were all influential and led in turn to the development of object-oriented languages (e.g. LOOPS (Bobrow and Stefik, 1983); SMALLTALK (Goldberg and Robson, 1983)).

For psychologists and programmers alike the advantages of frame-based systems seem mostly to be what Brachman (1979) calls 'epistemological'. These advantages have to do with the range and type of knowledge structuring methods placed at our disposal. The organization of knowledge around objects and the use of inheritance seems very natural. Inheritance, in particular, allows us to represent and use default knowledge.

The disadvantages have to do with what Brachman calls the 'logical' properties of the systems. These notions are concerned with formal ideas which have to do with the provision of a precise account of the meanings of all the elements in a representational system. We shall not dwell on these issues here since we consider such formal properties in our section on logics. If frame systems suffer they do so by comparison with what logic-based representations offer.

The systems to which we now turn offer very different methods of representation and reasoning. We move from systems which organize knowledge around objects to those which represent knowledge as rules.

8.4 PRODUCTION SYSTEMS

The simplest class of architectures which use rule-based approaches to represent knowledge are called production systems. These systems have interested cognitive scientists as explanations of human behaviour (Anderson, 1983; Young, 1979). They are also the most commonly implemented architecture for expert systems shells.

A production system has three basic components: 1. a rule base; 2. a working memory (sometimes called a context); and 3. an inference engine.

The rule base consists of a set of production rules. These rules have the following form:

IF ⟨ condition ⟩ THEN ⟨ action ⟩

Rules may have multiple conditions or actions. Rules are independent, they do not receive or pass information directly to other rules.

The working memory is a representation of the current state of the world. It usually contains initial information about the problem/world and also contains any information that the system derives in the course of a consultation.

The inference engine is that part of the system which actually runs the production rules. It checks to see if a rule can apply given the contents of working memory.

An important aspect of the inference engine's job is conflict resolution. This is the name given to the process of deciding how to deal with competing rules. The inference engine works entirely by pattern directed invocation. It is this invocation via working memory that confers independence on the production rules themselves.

To illustrate these various concepts we will consider a tiny production system example. We have a rule base consisting of the following rules:

Rule 1	IF	a person has a risk of heart attack
	AND	a person has had a previous heart attack
	THEN	give that person digitalis
Rule 2	IF	a person has left quadratic pain
	AND	a person has high blood pressure
	THEN	that person has a risk of heart attack
Rule 3	IF	a person has raised intraocular pressure
	THEN	that person has high blood pressure

We are not concerned with the verisimilitude of the rule set nor the details of the grammar of the production rules. It is intuitively clear what the meaning of these rules is. Now consider the following list of facts which we have labelled A – I.

Fact A	Smith has raised intraocular pressure
Fact B	Smith has had a previous heart attack
Fact C	Smith has left quadratic pain
Fact D	Smith has high blood pressure
Fact E	Smith is a heavy smoker
Fact F	Smith has a risk of heart attack
Fact G	Jones is an asthmatic
Fact H	Jones is a heavy smoker
Fact I	Give Smith digitalis

Suppose that our working memory contains the following facts at the beginning of a run; A, B, C, E, G and H. Also suppose that the system is running in a mode which we call 'forward chaining' – sometimes known as data-driven. This means the left-hand side of rules will be matched against the contents of working memory to see if any new fact can be added to the working memory. The basic inference engine works on a recognize/act cycle and we will assume it operates the most basic of conflict resolution strategies – 'textual order' and 'refractoriness'. This means the inference engine looks through the set of rules from first to last – the moment it finds a rule all of whose left-hand side is satisfied it puts the action into effect (asserts a fact in our case), the interpreter then returns to the top of the rule set and proceeds through again ignoring any rules that have already fired.

The sequence of changes to our working memory is shown in Fig. 8.3. In the first cycle only Rule 3 can fire. This is because fact A is present in the working memory. As a result of Rule 3 firing fact D is added to the working memory. During the next cycle Rule 2 fires and fact F is added. Finally, in the next cycle Rule 1 fires and fact I is asserted.

Now there is another global control mode for such an architecture. We could run it in a 'backwards chaining' manner or in so called goal directed mode. In this case we start off with an action/fact/hypothesis we want to try to establish. The inference engine now matches the right-hand sides of rules. It then sets up as new goals the left-hand sides of any rules which have fired.

We have glossed over some points of detail, for example, the method of substituting constants for variables when matching rules. Nevertheless, our small example allows us to illustrate some of the major features of production system programs.

Production systems derive much of their power from the types of control we can exercise over the ways rules are matched and selected. We have already looked at the two major types of global control – forward and backward chaining. We will now consider what Jackson (1986) calls methods of 'local control'.

Earlier we referred to the term conflict set to describe a set of rules that are potentially able to fire in any single cycle of the interpreter's operation. It is the job of the interpreter to decide which of this set of rules to fire – and this is called conflict resolution. In our small example there was never more than one rule able to fire at any one time. Local control concerns methods of selecting which rules to

Rule base

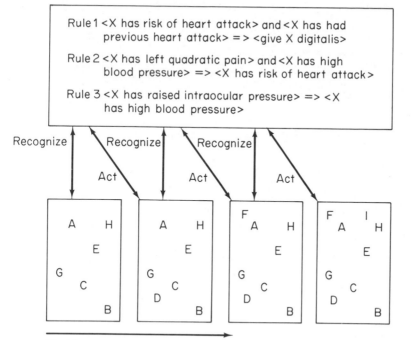

Working memory states through time

Fig. 8.3 A sequence of recognize/act cycles in a production system

fire if the conflict set is larger than one and what to do after firing that rule.

We have already described two such methods. The first of these was a heuristic of local control called 'textual order'. This takes the first rule in the rule base that matches the contents of working memory. There is an additional control decision to be made with this heuristic – whether to go back to the beginning of the rule base on the next interpreter cycle or to carry on from the position immediately below the rule that has just fired. The second heuristic we mentioned was called 'refractoriness'; this has an inhibitory effect on rules that have already fired. It does not allow the same rule to be applied twice on the same data. This heuristic prevents looping of those rules that do not delete or modify any of their own conditions or the data in working memory.

A further heuristic that is widely used is 'recency'. Rules are preferred that match against the most recently added or modified working memory elements. The effect is to pursue the 'leading edge' of computation and to give quick response to changes in the problem data.

A final heuristic we will describe is 'specificity'. This heuristic can be realized in a number of ways depending on how one reads the instruction to prefer the most specific rule in a conflict set. It might mean select the rule with most left-hand conditions or right-hand actions. It might amount to choosing the rule whose

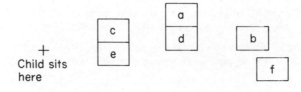

Initial position of blocks (aerial view)

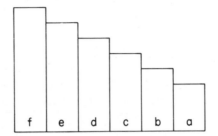

Final positions of blocks (side view)

Fig. 8.4 The seriation task

conditions or actions have the most specific restrictions on the range of values that variable can take.

The net effect of these and other local rules of control which we have not described, is to place a great deal of power in the hands of the system designers. It allows them to 'fine-tune' the performance of a program.

As mentioned at the beginning of this section, production systems have been extensively researched as models of human cognition and problem solving. Young's work in this area demonstrates the approach particularly well (Young, 1976).

Young looked at a phenomenon known as 'seriation'. In seriation children are asked to take a pile of blocks and order them by size (see Fig. 8.4).

The task was used by Piaget (1952) to explore various aspects of the cognitive development of children. Piaget found that a child's performance on this task progressed through three stages:

1. Stage 1: child cannot do it and the blocks end up in an arbitary sequence.
2. Stage 2: child eventually succeeds, but only after repeated re-arrangements.
3. Stage 3: child performs the task smoothly choosing correct block in order, one at a time.

What Young did was to try to faithfully model the behaviour that children showed at these various stages using a production rule formalism. His systems had rules of selection (choice of block to deal with), evaluation (whether to accept the block as a suitable addition to the line), and placement (where in the growing line the block should go). The combination of these three components determined the nature and quality of the child's seriation ability: the characteristic techniques, kinds of problems he can and cannot do, and the typical form of his errors.

What is particularly striking about Young's simulations is the 'cognitive modularity' of his production systems. Two production systems differing only by the addition of one or two rules can display many of the developmental phenomena described by Piaget. For example, the addition of a new rule can cause the system to display new behaviour similar to that of an older child more advanced in seriation skills.

Quite apart from their utility in psychological modelling the following advantages are claimed for production systems as a means of building knowledge-based systems (Davis and King, 1977).

One alleged advantage is that the form and manner used to represent and manipulate knowledge is both 'natural' and 'plausible'. It is claimed that experts' behaviour, for example, resides in heuristic rules of thumb. When interviewing experts these heuristics are explicitly articulated in production-like formulations.

A further property of production systems is their 'modularity'. This is an advantage not just in simulating stagelike cognitive development but also in building and maintaining knowledge-based applications. There is modularity throughout a production system architecture. Firstly, in partitioning permanent knowledge (in the rule base) from transient or temporary knowledge (in the working memory). Another aspect of modularity, which we have repeatedly stressed, is the structural independence of the rules. There is also modular decoupling of the interpreter from the knowledge base. This means that control knowledge is separated from domain level knowledge. The overall modularity of these systems and their components helps in the construction, debugging and maintenance of knowledge-based applications (Hayes-Roth, Waterman and Lenat, 1978).

Exponents of production systems make a virtue out of necessity when they argue that the 'restricted syntax' of production rules is an advantage. This makes it feasible to write programs to check the consistency of rule bases – do rules have circular dependencies? Are expressions in the rules typed consistently? And so on. It also allows for the possibility of the automatic generation of rules using machine learning and knowledge acquisition methods (Quinlan, 1979; Boose, 1985).

A further advantage resides in the nature of the problem-solving process of production systems. Minimal changes to the working memory can lead to a rapid response by the system as new rules fire and change the focus of the problem. But since the whole of the working memory is open to inspection a breadth-first style of problem solving is also available – not committing to one hypothesis too early in the problem-solving process.

A final advantage and something we have not mentioned so far is the ability of a production system to present useful records of its own problem-solving process.

These are usually annotated records of the chain of rule invocations used to derive or support a conclusion. This gives us a facility for explanation (how) and justification (why). In most systems these facilities can be used interactively so that if a system is asking the user to provide additional information in the course of a consultation the user can ask 'why' the information is needed. The system will look at its local goal (right-hand side of rule invoked) and produce in some readable form a justification. By repeatedly asking 'why' the user can ascend the system's goal hierarchy. On completion of any run the user can ask 'how' a result, fact, hypothesis was derived. The system will produce an explanation in terms of the immediate rule that led to the result. Again the user can trace up the tree of rule firings that generated the result. Research on explanation facilities continues and significantly more powerful facilities than those described here are now available (Clancey, 1983a; Hughes, 1986).

Production system architectures are not without their drawbacks. One of the most commonly cited is an efficiency problem and has to do with determining the conflict set. In very large rule bases the way in which rules are searched and the ease with which those that are potentially applicable can be assembled into a conflict set can become a huge computational overhead. Various optimization methods have been proposed for this problem (Forgy, 1982). But the problem still remains, if the conflict set is large, of applying the local control heuristic (conflict-resolution rule) as efficiently as possible. Davis (1980) discusses interesting methods that alleviate this aspect of the efficiency problems associated with production systems.

One way of overcoming some of the problems of large knowledge bases is to partition the system into smaller subsystems. This approach has produced so-called 'blackboard' systems (Nii and Aiello, 1979; Hayes-Roth, 1984). In such architectures the rule base is divided into different knowledge sources, each of which encapsulates those pieces of knowledge that are relevant to a particular part of the larger problem the system is trying to solve. Knowledge sources communicate with each other via a global blackboard. Knowledge sources can look at the blackboard to find information that might be relevant to them and when they derive new conclusions these in turn are placed on the blackboard for the use of other knowledge sources. The blackboard itself is often partitioned so that knowledge sources can read and write only to specified parts. This type of architecture solves some problems but reintroduces new bottlenecks. Most of these systems are run on serial machines and so queues form of knowledge sources wishing to interrogate the blackboard. The advent of parallel hardware may help this problem – we could imagine separate knowledge sources being assigned to separate processors. It is argued that blackboard systems are well placed to take advantage of these new developments in hardware design.

A final problem for production systems is the issue of their 'restricted syntax'. Although this can be regarded as an advantage for self-modifying and learning systems, it nevertheless places severe constraints on the kinds of knowledge that can be expressed.

As an example consider what is called disjunctive knowledge – knowledge that an object may have one value or another, that a condition may lead to one action or another. Disjunctive knowledge in the conditional parts of rules can be expressed though not very efficiently. Thus if we wanted to express the knowledge that:

```
IF     X has high blood pressure
AND    (X has left quadratic pain OR X has pain in left arm)
THEN   X has risk of heart attack
```

we could write

```
IF     X has high blood pressure
AND    X has left quadratic pain
THEN   X has risk of heart attack

IF     X has high blood pressure
AND    X has pain in left arm
THEN   X has risk of heart attack
```

But it is not possible to express disjunctive knowledge in the right-hand side of rules. Suppose we want to express the knowledge that 'if X has raised intraocular pressure then X has high blood pressure or X has glaucoma'. We cannot perform the same trick as above since this would commit us to too much.

The restrictions of expressive adequacy have led researchers to consider significantly more complex rule-based representations. They turned to the calculi of logic.

8.5 THE LANGUAGES OF LOGIC

There are, in fact, a large number of logics which have been developed and used over the years. Logic was until recently the preserve of philosophers and mathematicians. Now it is a powerful tool in the AI practitioner's repertoire of techniques. We shall discuss the major generic types of logic and we start with the simplest – the propositional calculus. First we need to define some terms.

The purpose of all logics is to provide a method of representing information about the world and reasoning with it. The discussion of any logic used in an AI context must make reference to three components: the syntax, the semantics and the proof theory. The syntax of a logical language dictates what the 'grammatical' expressions of the language are. The semantics defines under what conditions a sentence of the logic is true – this is a precise specification of the meanings of the syntactically correct expressions of the language. The proof theory of a logic is particularly critical when we consider using the logic as a computational method of representing knowledge. We can regard a proof theory as an abstract specification of a computer program for finding the valid consequences of a set of sentences. The proof theory consists of a set of axioms and a set of inference rules. Axioms are sentences that can always be assumed and inference rules are rules that take as input one or more sentences and return as output another sentence.

The syntax for the propositional calculus is very simple. In the propositional calculus statements (or 'propositions') are labelled and manipulated as indivisible elements. So, for example, the statement 'the book is on the table' may be labelled proposition P, while the statement 'the cup is on the table' may be labelled Q. We can now combine these statements using connectives to obtain further statements of the language (called well formed formulas or wffs). The connectives provided by this calculus are

~   not
&   and
∨   or
⇒   implies
= = equivalence

The connectives are used on wffs and are guaranteed to produce more wffs. Thus the following two compound propositions are well formed in our language.

(P & Q)

$(P \vee Q) \Rightarrow \sim (\sim P \& \sim Q)$

Of course, well-formedness has no bearing on the truth or falsity of the propositional content of these statements – it is only a syntactic property.

In any real problem domain, one starts by adopting a logic and then asserting a set of axioms representing what one knows about the world. The assignment of meaning to expressions in the propositional calculus is straightforward and the proof theory is then employed to try to prove new statements about the world. So, the logic not only gives you a way of representing facts (in its notational syntax) but also a way of reasoning (in its proof theory).

As a logic the propositional calculus has three formal properties which are attractive to those wanting to represent knowledge and reason with it: completeness, soundness and decidability. Completeness means any statement that is implied by the logic given its axioms and rules of inference can be derived (a theorem); soundness means that it is not possible to prove a theorem and to prove its negation (contradictions cannot arise); decidability means that there is always a way of proving whether a statement is a theorem or not.

The propositional calculus has some real limitations. One of these is the expressive independence of its statements. Within propositional logic the statements 'the book is on the table', 'the cup is on the table', and 'Issigonis was a Greek' all have the same status. But we may want to capture generalizations over and relations between propositions. This is one reason why in AI the predicate calculus is favoured over its propositional.

In the predicate calculus, we represent facts as a combination of predicate and argument.

on (book, table)
on (cup, table)
Greek (Issigonis)

and so forth. This allows us to construct general statements with variables:

on(X, table)

that is, X is on the table. Where X may take on, or 'instantiate to', any object which is on the table. The use of variables extends the representational possibilities open to us. Thus we may want to say that whatever value X has, then some predicate on X implies some other predicate on X. Alternatively, we might want to posit some predicate which only holds for one value of X. These kinds of statements are formed using quantifiers: for example, $\forall$ and $\exists$. The first means 'for every...' and the second 'there exists a...'. The following are now legitimate statements in our language

$(\forall x)(on(x, table) \Rightarrow \sim heavy(x))$

$(\exists y)(logician(y))$

The first reads, 'for every value of X, if X is on the table, then X is not heavy'. The second states there is some value of Y for which the statement 'Y is a logician' holds.

This use of variables and quantifiers is called first-order predicate logic. Such logics are now one of the primary representational tools of AI. The reasoning process over facts represented in this way is equivalent to attempting a proof of some statement from the axioms representing what is known (as in the above statement) and from the ordinary proof capabilities in the logic.

An example of a proof in first-order logic is shown below to give a flavour of this type of representation and reasoning. For more detailed and thorough expositions of the first-order calculus and associated proof methods the reader is referred to Mates (1965) and Tennant (1978). The proof below has been worked by hand using some of the common laws of inference of the predicate calculus. We have numbered consecutive lines in the proof. Below each logical statement we have provided an English interpretation of what the statement in logic is taken to represent. This would be determined in detail by the semantics we would provide for our language. To the right of the logical statement is an annotation which shows how the statement was derived. Thus the sixth statement 'Ga$\Rightarrow$Ha' is derived from statement 2, using the rule of inference annotated US (the rule of universal specification).

1. $(\forall x)(Fx \Rightarrow Gx)$ Premise
   if x is a metal commodity then x is volatile

2. $(\forall x)(Gx \Rightarrow Hx)$ Premise
   if x is volatile then x is bad long term investment

3. Fa   Premise
   Tin is a metal commodity

4. Fa ⇒ Ga   1 US
   Tin is a metal commodity implies tin is volatile

5. Ga   3, 4 T
   Tin is volatile

6. Ga ⇒ Ha   2 US
   Tin is volatile implies tin is bad long term investment

7. Ha   5, 6 T
   Tin is bad long term investment

8. Fa ⇒ Ha   3, 7 C
   Tin is metal commodity implies tin is bad long term investment

9. (∀x) (Fx ⇒ Hx)   8, UG
   x is metal commodity implies x is bad long term investment

There is a problem with this more general first-order logic. It can be shown that predicate calculus does not have the property of 'decidability'. It is no longer possible to prove whether any wff is true or false. This is a real problem with the calculus but it is tolerated because of the expressive and inferential power of predicate logic.

The question arises as to how logics of this sort are computationally implemented. The problem is to come up with an efficient proof strategy which can run on a computer. The standard strategy is called resolution (Robinson, 1965) and is a way of combining many of the inference rules in standard logic. To use resolution, one first converts all axioms into their simplest form. All statements in the logics discussed so far can be expressed using only the connectives ∼ (not) and ∨ (or). This is called conjunctive normal form of CNF. One then takes these CNF statements together with the negation of the statement one is trying to prove and a search is made for a contradiction in this set of statements. If a contradiction arises with the negation of the statement, then the actual statement must be true. This is a particular use of a standard mathematical technique – proof by contradiction.

The advent of the programming language Prolog (Clocksin and Mellish, 1981; Bratko, 1986) which uses resolution has made the use of logic as a knowledge representation device even more attractive. The idea behind this language is that it should look like, and behave like, predicate logic itself. In fact Prolog is a subset of first-order predicate logic, called the Horn clause subset. If logic really is a good tool for representing and discovering (deducing) facts about the world, then it is helpful to be able to code the information directly in this language. This is the appeal of languages like Prolog.

There are two advantages when it comes to using logic for knowledge representation in AI.

Logics have clear semantics (Hayes, 1977). The semantics is important because it allows you to determine exactly the meanings of the expressions in the language. The semantics can also be used to prove the soundness of any inference procedures chosen.

A second advantage resides in the expressive power of logics (Moore, 1982; Brachman and Levesque, 1985). An interesting feature here is that classic predicate calculus, according to Brachman and Levesque 'determines not so much what can be said, but what can be left unsaid'. This feature means we can express incomplete knowledge about situations. Thus we might know that 'something on the table is Bill's but not which particular object'.

$(\exists x)(on(x, table) \quad \& \quad owns(Bill, x))$

We can also express disjunctive knowledge easily – it is straightforward to represent the proposition we met earlier 'if someone has raised intraocular pressure then that person has high blood pressure or glaucoma'.

$(\forall x)(raised\_iop(x) \Rightarrow (high\_bp(x) \vee glaucoma(x))$

But the classic logics we have described are not all powerful and some of their particular shortcomings have led directly to work on advanced types of logic. Before considering these alternative logics a word about the standing of classical logic and its associated processes in psychology.

What standing do the methods of logic have in human problem solving? Rips and Marcus (1977) conducted research on these questions using basic laws of inference from classical logic. The inference schemas shown below are two of the most common in logic. The first is known as *modus ponens* and an illustration of this form of inference in a concrete situation is shown alongside its abstract formulation. The second is called *modus tollens*. Whilst we might not have complete faith in the premise of the concrete example that illustrates this rule, we must note that it is not the business of logic to decide whether our premises are true only to tell us what the valid inferences are if they were true.

Form 1

1.	$A \Rightarrow B$	Premise	if a man murders then he goes to jail
2.	A	Premise	a man murders
3.	B	1, 2 *modus ponens*	he goes to jail

Form 2

1.	$A \Rightarrow B$	Premise	if a man murders then he goes to jail
2.	$\sim B$	Premise	he does not go to jail
3.	$\sim 1A$	1, 2 *modus tollens*	he has not murdered

The argument forms shown below were also used in the experiment by Rips and Marcus. However, in both cases there are no valid conclusions to be drawn from them. Using these four forms the experimenters presented examples of arguments conforming to them. In the case of forms 3 and 4 they provided what were in fact non-valid conclusions.

Form 3
    1. $A \Rightarrow B$ Premise   if a man murders then he goes to jail
    2. $\sim A$ Premise   he does not murder
    3. No valid conclusions

Form 4
    1. $A \Rightarrow B$ Premise   if a man murders then he goes to jail
    2. B Premise   he goes to jail
    3. No valid conclusions

In the case of form 1 (*modus ponens*) all the subjects performed correctly. On all the other forms errors were made. On form 3 where the experimenters had placed a conclusion of the form $\sim B$ (for example, he does not go to jail) then 16% of subjects said this conclusion cloud never be true. The fact is that it is actually undecidable from the premises supplied. Again in form 4 where Rips and Marcus provided a conclusion of the form A, 23% of subjects thought such a conclusion always true. Again it is not 'decidable' from the premises, we cannot logically say it is always true though it might sometimes be true. Finally in form 2 the valid conclusion here $\sim A$ is always true. However 39% of subjects though this conclusion to hold only sometimes.

There have been many explanations for this data but what is interesting is that virtually all the research in this area shows that at a fundamental level the basic laws of logic and associated proof strategies are difficult for people to apprehend and follow (Wason, 1961; Johnson-Laird, 1983; Sanford, 1985).

8.6 ADVANCED LOGICS

Psychological reality notwithstanding, deduction in predicate logic does not always provide a convenient way of describing situations which we would like to see represented.

Non-monotonic logic (McDermott and Doyle, 1980) is an extension to the predicate calculus which allows statements to change their truth values in the process of reasoning. In traditional logic a proposition is either true or false. However, there are various situations in which we might want to retract a fact. This is the case for example in default reasoning. We might want to assert some fact to be true, not only when we can prove it, but when there is no information to the contrary. So, we might want to have a logical statement of the form

$(\forall x)(\text{bird }(x) \Rightarrow \text{can\_fly }(x))$

This says that for anything that is a bird then that thing can fly. Now this statement is not actually true in the real world – an ostrich can't fly. Nonetheless, this generalization is likely to be useful, we would like to retain it in some way.

Non-monotonic logic allows us to do this. It allows us to make statements of the form:

If X is a bird

and there is no proof that X cannot fly
then assert the fact that X can fly

From this kind of rule, we assert by default that any bird can fly. Only when there is proof that a particular bird 'a' can't fly will the fact can_fly (a) be false.

AI systems often involve many steps in the proof of theorems. In non-monotonic reasoning it may only become apparent several steps into a particular reasoning cycle that the default is inapplicable. That is to say, can_fly(a) may be true at the start of the reasoning process, and only later does evidence appear to the contrary. In this case, the fact must be negated. In monotonic logic truths can only be added to what we already know – the number of truths changes monotonically (upwards not downwards).

By contrast, non-monotonic logic provides ways of retracting statements. This facility is clearly going to be useful. A simple way of representing changing beliefs is necessary for models of human problem solving. In fact the idea has been used in several AI programs, most notably in Doyle's truth maintenance system (Doyle, 1979). This system is designed as an 'add-on' to support other reasoning systems. The idea is that the truth maintenance system (TMS) will look for inconsistencies amongst the statements produced by the reasoning program. When inconsistencies are detected they are eradicated by changing the beliefs in the most efficient way.

There are, however, problems with non-monotonic logic (Charniak and McDermott, 1985). Nevertheless, it is clearly an attractive extension and a lot of effort is going into producing computationally tractable systems which use it.

Another extension to the predicate logic is modal logic. These logics allow us to maintain what is sometimes referred to as a 'two-tier' semantic theory. Many logics have extensional semantics, the meaning of terms and expressions in the language are defined simply as objects, sets of objects, and truth values. However, for over a hundred years there has been a view that argued for a more complex set of semantic values. The German logician Frege was the first to articulate this distinction in terms of logic. He posited two sorts of semantic value – reference (straightforward extension) and what he called sense (nowadays called intension). The need for such a distinction was, in part, derived from semantic facts such as the following:

1. The morning star is the evening star
2. John believes the morning star is the morning star
3. John believes the morning star is the evening star

4. The number of planets is nine
5. Necessarily nine is nine
6. Necessarily the number of planets is nine

Under a simple extensional semantics all that the terms in these sentences could refer to, all they could mean, were the objects they denoted. Thus the terms 'morning star' and 'evening star' both denote the same thing, the planet Venus.

They are denotationally equivalent. Now in ordinary logics we have a general principle called the 'substitutability of identicals'. This means that in an extensional logic given propositions 1 and 2 then proposition 3 is a logical consequence. Similarly, given 4 and 5 then 6 can be inferred. But obviously these are not always appropriate inferences. The problem as Frege saw it was that our semantic theory was too impoverished. There is a genuine difference, he argued, in the meanings of the two terms 'morning star' and 'evening star' that goes beyond their denotation. Many such substitution conundrums exist, all involve what are called opaque contexts. The verbs 'know', 'believes' and sentential modifiers such as 'possibly' and 'necessarily' are all opaque contexts. One response to these problems was the introduction of a technical solution that associates intensions with complex functions. This is done using the machinery of possible world semantics (Kripke, 1963). Logics that rely on possible world semantics are called modal logics. There are formal problems associated with these logics but they do allow us to represent and reason with sentences containing opaque contexts.

There are a number of other exotic logics which we have not discussed and for a good survey of these systems and the intuitions behind them the reader is referred to Haack (1978).

8.7 CONNECTIONISM AND NEURAL NETWORKS

All of the knowledge representation methods discussed so far embody common and deep assumptions about the nature of representations. The first of these has to do with a mode of theorizing which Rumelhart refers to as the 'functionalist fallacy'.

The dominant paradigm over the past 25 years in cognitive science has been the attempt to understand intelligence at a functional level. On this view questions about the hardware which supports cognitive processing are secondary. This line has seemed plausible because results from theoretical computing show us that only a minimal architecture is required to simulate a Universal Turing Machine – these are abstract machines capable of computing anything that is computable. One of the challenges of connectionism has been the claim that architecture does matter. It argues, in fact, that hardware might be the most significant constraint in any theory of cognitive behaviour. In the parallel distributed processing (PDP) view, championed by Rumelhart and McClelland, one generates brain-like architectures and then constructs cognitive models which are constrained by these architectures.

Rumelhart argues that a second reason why we have failed to move beyond a narrow class of ways of thinking about knowledge is the 'tyranny of notation' that our traditional formalisms have produced. These formalisms appear intuitively natural – it seems obvious from them that knowledge is structured into discrete chunks, organized and modified in certain fixed ways. This has, however, prevented us from considering radical alternatives.

To illustrate the basic ideas of connectionism and the PDP group we will consider a simple distributed model. First we need to define some terms.

All PDP models consist of a set of processing units. In building a PDP model one must specify what these units represent. PDP models have units representing features, letters, words and so on. Units are abstract elements over which meaningful patterns may be defined. In PDP models all processing is carried out by the units – there is no control or executive program. Units receive input and as a function of these inputs compute an output. The system is inherently parallel because many units can carry out their computations at the same time.

Activity at any time in the model is represented as a vector or matrix with as many elements as units in the model, this defines the activation state of the model. It is the pattern of activity throughout the entire vector at any time that captures what the system is representing at any time *t*.

Units are connected to one another. The pattern of connectivity constitutes what the system knows and determines how it will respond to any input. Each connection is taken to have a strength or weight. The contribution of inputs to a connected unit is usually taken to be the sum of these weights though there are more complex patterns of connectivity possible. Weights may be either positive or negative corresponding to excitatory or inhibitory inputs.

We need a 'propagation rule' that takes the output of units and combines these values with the connectivity matrix to produce a net input for each unit. Propagation rules are usually straightforward – for excitatory inputs the weighted sum of the excitatory inputs to the units. More complex propagation rules are possible for more complex patterns of input.

An 'activation rule' works out the new activation level due to the combined inputs at a particular unit. Sometimes the rule can insist that the input exceed a certain threshold before any contribution to a new state of activation can be made.

In a network, learning may occur due to three processes: development of new connections, loss of existing connections, modification to the weights of existing connections. Most of the work to date has investigated the last of these means of learning.

To illustrate how knowledge representation works in such networks we will give a relatively informal presentation of a simple PDP model – a pattern associator. Pattern associators are models in which a pattern of activation over one set of units can cause a pattern of activation over another set of units without any intervening units to represent either pattern as a whole.

The basic architecture for this model is shown in Fig. 8.5. There are four units in each of two pools. The first pool, the A units, will be the pool in which patterns corresponding to the sight of various objects might be represented. The second pool, the B units, will be in the pool in which the pattern corresponding to the names of the objects will be represented.

Let us assume that alternative patterns of activation on the A units are produced upon viewing one face, say the author's, and another face, say the

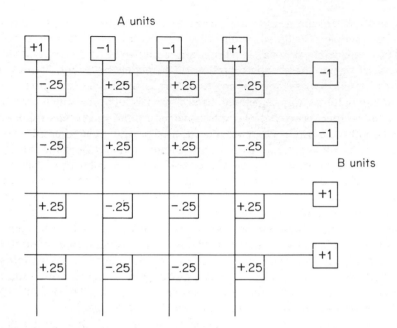

Fig. 8.5 A simple pattern associator

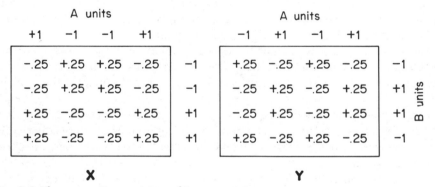

Fig. 8.6 The connection matrices of two associators

editor's. Moreover different patterns of activation are produced on the B units on hearing the names of the same objects. Fig. 8.6 shows these patterns together with sets of interconnections (connectivity vectors) necessary to allow the A member of each pair to reproduce the B member.

In this model we will assume the following behaviour for our individual units. Units take on positive or negative activation values with 0 representing an intermediate neutral activation. The weights on the interconnections can be positive or negative real numbers. The effect of an A unit on a B unit will be the product of A's activation value and its synaptic connection (weight) to the B unit.

The activation of each unit is set to the sum of the excitatory and inhibitory effects operating on it.

We now create on the A units the following pattern $(+1 -1 -1 +1)$ shown in Fig. 8.5. Suppose that this pattern of activation is produced on the A units in the presence of the author's face. How are we to set the connections between the A units and the B units so as to invoke the pattern $(-1 -1 +1 +1)$ on the B units – this pattern represents the author's name? What we have to do is arrange that each A unit excites each B unit which has a positive activation in the name pattern and inhibit each B unit which has a negative activation in the name pattern. This can be done using a propagation rule which sets the weight of a connection between an A unit and a B unit to a value proportional to the product of the activation of the two units. The weights in matrices **X** and **Y** produce exactly what we want.

Even with this simple model some powerful connectionist properties emerge. Firstly, the nets do not need a perfect copy of the input to produce the correct output. Thus if the author's face is somewhat obscured it may still be enough to reinstate the pattern on the B units corresponding to the author's name. It may be somewhat less in strength than $(-1 -1 +1 +1)$, perhaps $(-0.89 -0.89 +0.75 +0.75)$. Similar effects are produced if units are removed or if some set of connections are destroyed. The point in this case is that the pattern retrieval of the model degrades gracefully under both incomplete input and also damage.

In our example we set the weights so as to get the effect we wanted. But these nets can teach themselves the right set of interconnections through the experience of being presented with the paired stimuli of face and name. What we need are learning rules that adjust the weights of interconnections as learning occurs. A simple rule of the form: 'change the weight of the connection between a unit A and B in proportion to the product of their simultaneous activation' is sufficient to train a blank copy of our network to produce the pattern of the name of the author when his face is shown and *vice versa*. The A and B patterns are presented together and the connections between the units are modulated according to our learning rule. The size of the change made on every trial is a parameter we would set. If it was set high we would produce an incautious learner; if the parameter was set low our learner would be slow but sure.

Our network is also capable of learning multiple patterns in the same set of connections. We could train our net to learn to associate the editor's face with his name. We can teach the same pattern associator a number of different associations.

This simple model illustrates fundamental properties of connectionist theories. Representations are regarded as a pattern of activation over units. Secondly, experience is recorded as changes in the weights of a net. Patterns of activation come and go; what remains are traces when they have passed. A trace is bound to be distributed over many different connections, and each connection is implicated in many different associations. The traces of different experiences are therefore superimposed in the same set of weights. The model regards the retrieval of a representation as a partial reinstatement of a network state, using a cue which might only be a fragment of the original input.

What this amounts to is the view that knowledge is stored in the inter-connections between units. But the knowledge is not stored in the connections of a special unit reserved for that pattern; it is distributed over the connections among a large number of processing units. This is the concept at the heart of the connectionist enterprise.

Connectionism is regarded by many as neurologically inspired. Indeed some theorists claim that they are trying to replace the computer metaphor with a brain metaphor as a model of the mind. On what evidence can we propose connectionism as an appropriate architecture of the mind?

Consider the following simple fact about brain hardware. Neurons are slow compared to the components of modern computers – milliseconds as opposed to nanoseconds. This makes the components of our machines a factor of 10^6 faster than the basic elements in the brain. However, it is immediately obvious that complex cognitive abilities – the recognition of a face, memory retrieval, speech processing – take in the order of a second or so. To explain such behaviour with components as slow as neurons Feldman (1985) has proposed the '100-step program' constraint. Most complex cognitive behaviours cannot have more than 100 linear steps, and since some of these processes appear to involve massive constraint satisfaction the operation of such processes must be organized in a parallel manner.

At one stage it was thought that the degree of 'fan-in' and 'fan-out' of neurons (inputs in and outputs out to other neurons) was fairly modest. This might have presented problems for the sorts of highly interconnected network proposed by PDP. It now appears that most neurons have a lower fan limit of 1000. This type of component connectivity makes the brain hardware look even less like our basic digital hardware.

Neurons do communicate through inhibition and excitation in the sorts of ways proposed in connectionist models. Moreover, at a single synapse (the connection of one neuron to another) both excitatory and inhibitory neuro-transmitters can be released. Previously it was thought that at any junction only one neuro-transmitter (either excitatory or inhibitory) was involved. This view, known as Dale's Principle, has been overturned only in the last decade.

A further feature of connectionism which finds support in neurology is the principle of graceful degradation. In most progressive neurological disorders and in evidence from lesion work what is observed is a gradual decrement in mental operation as more and more units (neurons) are lost or impaired. Simulated nets seem to show this same gradual deterioration of performance (McClelland and Rumelhart, 1985). In neurology we do not see the complete collapse of performance that might be expected if mental processes were supported by components with particular functions that were dependent on one another.

In PDP models the knowledge is in the connections and not in the unit states.

There is storage in units but it is of a simple and very short-term nature. Long-term storage is in the connections. In PDP models almost all the knowledge is implicit in the structure of the device that carries out a task rather than explicit in the states of the units themselves. A number of psychological theorists find this aspect of connectionism particularly attractive (for example, Norman, 1985).

There are a number of problems with the connectionist approach and it is certainly not without its critics. Most of the criticism comes from those who see the connectionist endeavour as too low level, throwing aside the advantages of structured representation. The following list is by no means exhaustive but serves to point out the sorts of criticisms levelled at connectionist models.

One obvious feature of connectionist models is the absence of explicit control. This is anathema to many AI workers who are making substantial efforts to make explicit the knowledge suitable to guide problem solving (Clancey, 1983b; Davis, 1980).

Connectionist systems seem to embody no concept of a traditional formal semantics. Certainly nothing like the model theoretic semantics of logic is available.

A further worry is that connectionist models require the decomposition of problems into sets of primitive features which are then represented in units. The idea of semantic theories based on collections of primitive features has a long history in cognitive science (Katz, 1971). But it is not obvious how problems that do not admit to decomposition into sets of semantic atoms are to be represented in connectionist units.

There has been a persistent worry that many of the impressive results from connectionist models, particularly in the area of learning, owe their success to the judicious selection of constants in the complex learning rules. The use of such 'fiddle factors' is hotly debated in the literature and the interested reader might like to look at Pinker and Prince (1988).

Finally, it is alleged that PDP and connectionism loses the clear insights of Marr's levels (Broadbent, 1985; Fodor and Pylyshyn, 1988). It is asserted that connectionist theories do little more than provide Level 3 accounts – implementation level theories. Critics argue that understanding can only come from having Level 1 and 2 descriptions in addition to Level 3 accounts. Rumelhart and McClelland (1985) would retort that their models in fact provide Level 2 models, models of how input and output to key processes are represented, how algorithms work to transform and connect input and output. They argue that this is the level at which, in practice, most cognitive scientists work. It is at this level that mechanisms get built that are sufficient to solve problems.

Despite criticisms the fact remains that connectionism lays down real challenges to those interested in the foundations of knowledge and cognition. In this chapter we have tried to convey the wide range of approaches that workers in the fields of AI, expert systems and cognitive psychology take to the problems of knowledge and its embodiment in systems both natural and artificial.

168   *Knowledge representation*

8.8 REFERENCES

Anderson, J. R. (1983) *The Architecture of Cognition.* Harvard University Press, Cambridge, Mass.

Anderson, J. and Bower, G. (1973) *Human Associative Memory.* Holt, New York.

Bartlett, F. (1932) *Remembering.* Cambridge University Press, Cambridge.

Bobrow, D. G. and Stefik, M. (1983) *The Loops Manual.* Xerox Corporation.

Bobrow, D. G. and Winograd, T. (1977) An overview of KRL, a knowledge representation language. *Cognitive Science,* **1,** 3–46.

Boose, J. A. (1985) Knowledge acquisition program for expert systems based on personal construct theory. *International Journal of Man-machine Studies,* **23,** 495–525.

Brachman, R. (1979) On the epistemological status of semantic networks. In R. Brachman and H. Levesque (eds), *Readings in Knowledge Representation,* Morgan Kaufmann, CA.

Brachman, R. and Levesque, H. (eds) (1985) *Readings in Knowledge Representation.* Morgan Kaufmann, Los Altos, CA.

Brachman, R. and Schmolze, J. (1984) An overview of the KL-ONE knowledge representation system. *Cognitive Science,* **9,** 171–216.

Bratko, I. (1986) *Prolog Programming for Artificial Intelligence.* Addison-Wesley, Wokingham, England.

Broadbent, D. (1985) A question of levels: comments on McClelland and Rumelhart. *Journal of Experimental Psychology: General,* **114,** 189–92.

Charniak, E. and McDermott, D. (1985) *Introduction to Artificial Intelligence.* Addison-Wesley, Mass.

Clancey, W. (1983a) The epistemology of rule-based expert systems: A framework for explanation. In R. Brachman and H. Levesque (eds) *Readings in Knowledge Representation,* Morgan Kaufmann, CA.

Clancey, W. (1983b) The advantages of abstract control knowledge in expert systems, *3rd National Conference on Artificial Intelligence,* 74–8.

Clocksin, W. and Mellish, C. (1981) *Programming in PROLOG.* Springer-Verlag, New York.

Collins, A. and Loftus, E. (1975) A spreading activation theory of semantic processing. *Psychological Review,* **82,** 407–28.

Collins, A. M. and Quillian, M. R. (1969) Retrieval time from semantic memory. *Journal of Verbal Learning and Verbal Behaviour,* **8,** 240–47.

Davis, R. (1980) Meta-rules: Reasoning about control. *Artificial Intelligence,* **15,** 179–222.

Davis, R. and King, J. (1977) An overview of production systems. In E. Elcock and D. Michie (eds) *Machine Intelligence 8,* Ellis Horwood, Chichester.

Dennett, D. C. (1979) *Brainstorms: Philosophical Essays on Mind and Psychology.* Harvester Press, Hassocks.

Doyle, J. (1979) A truth maintenance system. *Artificial Intelligence,* **12,** 231–72.

Fahlman, S. (1979) *NETL: A System for Representing and Using Real-world Knowledge.* MIT Press, Cambridge, Mass.

Feldman, J. A. (1985) Connectionist models and their applications: introduction. *Cognitive Science,* **6,** 205–54.

Fodor, J. A. (1981) *Representations: Philosophical Essays on the Foundations of Cognitive Science.* Harvester Press, Hassocks.

Fodor, J. A. and Pylyshyn, Z. W. (1988) Connectionism and cognitive architecture: a critical analysis. *Cognition,* **28,** 3–71.

Forgy, C. (1982) RETE: a fast algorithm for the many pattern/many object pattern match problem. *Artificial Intelligence*, **19**, 17–37.

Franks, J. J. and Bransford, J. D. (1972) The acquisition of abstract ideas. *Journal of Verbal Learning and Verbal Behaviour*, **11**, 311–15.

Goldberg, A. and Robson, D. (1983) *Smalltalk-80: The Language and its Implementation*. Addison-Wesley, Reading, Mass.

Haack, S. (1978) *Philosophy of Logics*. Cambridge University Press, Cambridge.

Hayes, P. (1977) The logic of frames. In R. Brachman and H. Levesque (eds) *Readings in Knowledge Representation*. Morgan Kaufmann, CA.

Hayes-Roth, B. (1984) *A Blackboard Model of Control*. Report No HPP-83-38. Computer Science Dept, Stanford University.

Hayes-Roth, F., Waterman, D., Lenat, D. (1978) Principles of pattern-directed inference systems. In Waterman and Hayes-Roth (1978).

Hendrix, G. (1975) Extending the utility of semantic networks through partitioning. *IJCAI-4*, 115–21.

Hendrix, G. (1979) Encoding knowledge in partitioned networks. In Findler, N. V. (ed.) (1979) *Associative Networks: Representation and Use of Knowledge by Computer*. Academic Press, New York.

Hughes, S. (1986) Question classification in rule-based systems. In M. Bramer (ed.) *Research and Development in Expert Systems III*. Cambridge University Press, Cambridge.

Jackson, P. (1986) *Introduction to Expert Systems*. Addison-Wesley, Wokingham, England.

Johnson-Laird, P. N. (1983) *Mental Models*. Cambridge University Press, Cambridge.

Katz, J. J. (1971) Semantic theory. In D. D. Steinberg and L. A. Jakobovits (eds) *Semantics* Cambridge University Press, Cambridge.

Kripke, S. (1963) Semantical considerations on modal logics. *Acta Philosophica Fennica*, **16**, 83–94.

Lindsay, R. (1973) In defense of *ad hoc* systems. In R. C. Schank and K. M. Colby (eds) *Computer Models of Thought and Language*. Freeman, San Francisco.

McClelland, J. L. and Rumelhart, D. E. (1985) *Parallel Distributed Processing: Explorations in the Microstructure of Cognition Vol 2: Psychological and Biological Models*. MIT Press, Cambridge, Mass.

McDermott, D. and Doyle, J. (1980) Non-monotonic logic I. *Artificial Intelligence*, **13**, 41–72.

Marr, D. (1982) *Vision*. W. H. Freeman, San Francisco.

Mates, B. (1965) *Elementary Logic*. Oxford University Press, Oxford.

Minsky, M. (1975) Frame-system theory. In P. N. Johnson-Laird and P. Wason (eds), *Thinking: Readings in Cognitive Science*, Cambridge University Press, Cambridge.

Moore, R. (1982) The role of logic in knowledge representation and commonsense reasoning. *AAAI-82*, 428–33. Also in Brachman and Levesque (1985).

Newell, A. and Simon, H. A. (1972) *Human Problem Solving*. Prentice-Hall, Englewood Cliffs, N.J.

Nii, P. and Aiello, N. (1979) AGE: A knowledge-based program for building knowledge-based programs. *IJCAI-6*, 645–55.

Norman, D. A. (1985) Reflections on cognition and parallel distributed processing. In J. L. McClelland and D. E. Rumelhart (eds) *Parallel Distributed Processing: Explorations in the Microstructure of Cognition Vol 2: Psychological and Biological Models*. MIT Press, Cambridge, Mass.

Piaget, J. (1952) *The Child's Conception of Number*. Humanities Press, New York.

Pinker, S. and Prince, A. (1988) On language and connectionism: analysis of a parallel distributed processing model of language acquisition. *Cognition*, **28**, 73–193.

Pylyshyn, Z. W. (1984) *Computation and Cognition: Toward a Foundation for Cognitive Science*. MIT Press, Cambridge, Mass.

Quillian, R. (1966) Semantic memory. Unpublished doctoral dissertation. Carnegie Institute of Technology.

Quillian, R. (1967) Word concepts: A theory and simulation of some basic semantic capabilities. *Behavioral Science*, **12**, 410–30.

Quinlan, J. R. (1979) Learning efficient classification procedures and their application to chess end games. In D. Michie (ed.) *Expert Systems in the Micro-Electronic Age*, Edinburgh University Press, Edinburgh.

Rips, L. J. and Marcus, S. L. (1977) Supposition and the analysis of conditional sentences. In M. A. Just and P. A. Carpenter (eds) *Cognitive Processes in Comprehension*, Erlbaum, Hillsdale, NJ.

Robinson, J. A. (1965) A machine-oriented logic based on the resolution principle. *Journal of the ACM*, **12**, 23–41.

Rosch, E. (1973) On the internal structure of perceptual and semantic categories. In T. E. Moore (ed) *Cognitive Development and the Acquisition of Language*, Academic Press, New York.

Rumelhart, D. E. and McClelland, J. L. (1985) *Parallel Distributed Processing: Explorations in the Microstructure of Cognition. Vol 1: Foundations*. MIT Press, Cambridge, Mass.

Rumelhart, D. E. and McClelland, J. L. (1985b) Levels indeed! A response to Broadbent. *Journal of Experimental Psychology: General*, **114**.

Sanford, A. J. (1985) *Cognition and Cognitive Psychology*. Weidenfeld and Nicolson, London.

Schank, R. C. (1975) *Conceptual Information Processing*. North-Holland, Amsterdam.

Schank, R. C. and Abelson, R. (1977) *Scripts, Plans, Goals and Understanding*. Lawrence Erlbaum, Hillsdale, NJ.

Tennant, N. (1978) *Natural Logic*. Edinburgh University Press, Edinburgh.

Wason, P. C. (1961) Response to affirmative and negative binary statements. *British Journal of Psychology*, **52**, 273–81.

Young, R. M. (1976) *Seriation by Children: A Production-system Approach*. Birkhauser Verlag.

Young, R. M. (1979) Production systems for modelling human cognition. In D. Michie (ed.), *Expert Systems in the Micro-Electronic Age*. Edinburgh University Press, Edinburgh.

Issues and applications

9

Building an expert system

MASOUD YAZDANI

9.1 INTRODUCTION

Expert or knowledge-based systems have become a small but important sector of the general computing market. Their move from novelty items to potential solutions to practical applications has meant changes to the perception of what they are, and what they can do. The fact that this book has needed a second edition in such a short time reflects the dramatic level of change. My contribution to the first edition (Yazdani, 1984) attempted to describe the basic structure of an expert system for someone who wanted to build his or her first expert system. Here I would like to present the lessons we have learnt by attempting to build the first generation of expert systems. In this way I hope that newcomers can avoid the pitfalls we fell into and got out of.

9.1.1 What are knowledge-based systems?

Thirty years of artificial intelligence (AI) research have shown that a great deal of commonsense knowledge is behind people's intelligent behaviour. The task of building an all-round intelligent artefact is further away than it had, at one point, been hoped. On the other hand, some attention has been focused on the form of behaviour which most appropriately should be called intellectual behaviour. This sort of behaviour requires the sort of knowledge which a professional expert has. Such domains are already well defined and well documented in professional journals. Law, citizens' advice, geological and mechanical expertise are easily separable from the whole wealth of general human knowledge.

The attempt to deal only with a narrow bandwidth of human knowledge reduces the complexity of the task faced by an AI researcher, and enables him to offer a working system to users on a reasonable time scale, while major problems of intelligence remain long-term research objectives. However much the bandwidth is narrowed, there are still going to be numerous problems which need to be tackled:

1. How is the knowledge acquired in the first place?
2. How is it represented?

3. How are the representations implemented on particular hardware?
4. How is the knowledge accessed inside the system?
5. How is the knowledge applied to a particular situation?
6. How is the knowledge modified in the light of experience?
7. How is it maintained (and, in most cases, irrelevant knowledge disposed of)?

The list is endless. However, what has made knowledge engineering a respectable part of computing is that we now have at least some standard answers to most of these questions! In this chapter we shall point out some of these answers.

9.1.2 What is so different about expert systems?

Many sceptical observers have pointed out that all computing packages which do anything interesting, are knowledge-based. They would argue that a compiler 'knows about the language translation', an accounting package 'knows about doing the accounts' and so on. What is so different about an expert system which 'knows about medical diagnosis?'

The most eloquent answer to such people is presented by Brachman and Levesque (1985):

> 'What makes AI Systems knowledge-based is not that it takes knowledge to write them, nor just that they behave as if they had knowledge, but rather that their architectures include *explicit knowledge-bases*: more or less direct symbolic encoding of knowledge in the system'.

AI programs in general, and expert systems in particular, are different to traditional computing packages in the way the programs are organized. A program has traditionally been viewed as procedure and data. Expert systems however 'can all be fairly described as data-base-driven' (Michie, 1980). There are, in fact, three distinct modules to an expert system:

1. facts about features of a particular case
2. rules about a domain of expertise
3. rules for processing the rules in (2) or the 'inference engine'

Figure 9.1 shows a superficial view of how such a system would work. Facts about a particular case are collected via a **user interface** under the direction of the **inference engine** which itself works on the knowledge stored in the **knowledge base**.

9.1.3 What does an expert system look like?

The following formal description was approved by the British Computer Society's Committee of the Specialist Group on Expert Systems when that group was formed in order to specify what an expert system is meant to be:

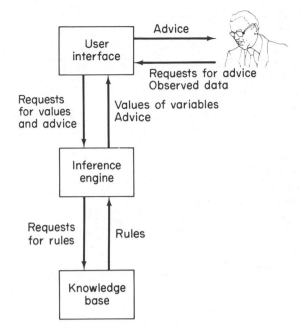

Fig. 9.1 Architecture of an expert system

'An 'Expert System' is regarded as the embodiment within a computer of a knowledge-based component, from an expert skill, in such a form that the system can offer intelligent advice or take an intelligent decision about a processing function. A desirable additional characteristic, which many would consider fundamental, is the capability of the system, on demand, to justify its own line of reasoning in a manner directly intelligible to the enquirer. The style adopted to attain these characteristics is rule-based programming.'

My reason for looking at this outdated definition is that it shows the confusion about the purpose of such systems. The definition mentions 'offer intelligent advice' or 'take intelligent decision' as the role of the system. What has become clear is that each of these two roles would require different ways of looking at the problems:

1. Perspective A – problem-solving systems: 'wise-men' called upon to produce solutions to complex, but essentially well-defined problems in domains such as medicine or for fixing one's car's engine.
2. Perspective B – advice giving systems: supportive environments for people to solve problems for themselves.

These two perspectives in fact can be seen as the two ends of a spectrum as shown below:

Data Processing

E
x   Well-defined problems
p   where clearly defined
e   solutions to problems
r   exist
t

S
y   Problems where
s   our knowledge of
t   what happens and
e   why it happens
m   is less precise
s

Artificial Intelligence

Beyond the two ends of this spectrum are the traditional algorithmic solutions in data processing and the search-oriented solutions of Artificial Intelligence.

In between the problem-solving and advice systems there are a large number of other systems. One such application is where an expert system is devised which is an expert on the workings of another computer package. Such systems are also referred to as 'intelligent front ends'. Using such a system, the user of a complicated statistics package could interact with such an expert and be advised on how to use the system, or even act as an intelligent mediator between the computing package and a naïve user.

Another area of application is in the form of 'coaching systems' which contain the knowledge of a tutor (Sleeman and Brown, 1982). By following the knowledge-based approach we can design diagnostic systems which know how to teach, and who and what they are teaching.

9.1.4 Expert systems architecture

Figure 9.2 shows a second view of how an expert system operates in form of a flow chart. There are two sources of input to the system. The tutor, or the expert, provides the body of knowledge, past medical case histories for example, and the user provides the specific details of the case in hand in reply to questions from the system. The case in hand is then matched against the pool of knowledge in order to find an applicable hypothesis. On the basis of the chosen hypothesis, more questions are asked to prove or disprove it. If most parameters in the hypothesis

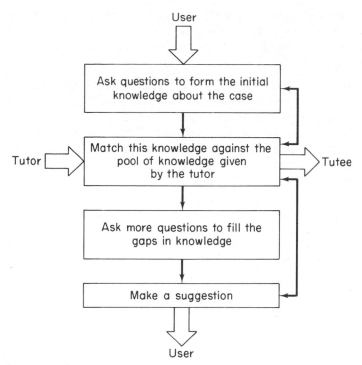

Fig. 9.2 Operation of an expert system

are satisfied then a suggestion is made, otherwise a new hypothesis is chosen.

There are three modes of user interface to an expert system, in contrast to the single mode (getting answers to problems) characteristic of more familiar types of computing:

1. getting answers to problems – user as client
2. improving or increasing the system's knowledge – user as tutor
3. harvesting the knowledge base for human use – user as a pupil looking over the shoulder of the expert system or asking questions of it.

An expert system should at least offer the following features:

1. inference generated requests for data
2. accountability (explanation of behaviour)
3. transparency (tutoring role)

9.1.5 Domains of application

The first choice is to identify the domain of application and see whether the expert system or AI technology is yet advanced enough to tackle it. Currently, any diagnostic application which depends on the knowledge of a very narrow domain is a 'good' application, while anything depending on creative and commonsense reasoning in a wide-ranging domain is a 'bad' one. Some difficult domains are where:

1. Experts do not generally agree with each other at all. Although some techniques have been developed for dealing with multiple experts, when wild disagreements exist it is an indication of problems to come.
2. The strategies in reasoning are complicated. The reasoning strategies which can be modelled with most current tools are simple ones. Any domain which requires sophisticated reasoning from its experts would be demanding too much from the current technology.
3. The knowledge includes temporal relationships. Keeping histories of past activities and drawing conclusions based on past cases are common in human experts. However, such sophistication is beyond the simple tools on offer to most knowledge engineers.
4. Problems take a long time to be solved by people. People have one of the most powerful parallel processing devices yet devised. If such a system takes a long time to do a job what chance has the humble PC or even workstation to deliver results in a finite time!
5. A lot of actions hinge on a lot of conditions. Most expert systems are based on a collection of associations between one condition and one conclusion. In other words each rule is not sensitive to the context within which it resides. A context sensitive situation when a combination of conditions lead to a combination of actions is too much for the current technology.
6. Too many objects and too much reliance on commonsense concepts.

9.1.6 Knowledge acquisition

Not all human experts can code their knowledge into explicit rules accessible to a computer system. Furthermore, some might not even know explicitly what rules they follow. A **knowledge engineer** is a person who bridges this gap and codes the human experts' knowledge into an expert system.

The main bottleneck currently holding back the widespread use of expert systems, is the process by which the knowledge of the human expert is 'extracted' by the knowledge engineers. Originally this process was *ad hoc* and was basically carried out by trial and error. However, a number of methodologies are emerging for this process (see Greenwell, 1988), while the automatic induction of knowledge is on the horizon.

Despite the 'knowledge extraction bottleneck', a simple algorithm based around trial and error methods has led to a number of successful implementations where a three-stage activity takes place:

1. Structuring the domain by finding a good model of the problem-solving process performed by the human expert.

2. Producing a prototype working model, knowing full well that you will not get it right first time, but that it will be easier to correct the specific errors and learn about the nature of the problems in this way.
3. Following the eternal loop of 'testing', 'debugging', and 'refining' the prototype until the system is satisfactory, or until you have learned enough to design a new version.

This rather *ad hoc* methodology has found popularity with some designers (for a more detailed survey, see Wellbank, 1983) for a number of reasons:

1. Human experts find it easier to criticize a working system than say what is needed.
2. Engineers find it easy to give exceptions to rules:
   if A do B, unless C it shouldn't do that because...
3. The prototype keeps human experts interested.
4. In general it is useful to get a system working as soon as possible.

9.1.7 Representations

If a computer program is to perform the task of an expert it needs a large amount of knowledge to carry out complex tasks in a manner comparable to that of humans. Such systems need to be organized in an orderly fashion to avoid complete confusion. In general the knowledge is divided into three kinds.

1. **Factual (declarative) knowledge.** This knowledge represents a particular case and is usually gathered through a dialogue with the user to establish what facts are true at the present time. The way such information is represented is important, as the structure of the representation contains information. We need to choose the structure of the representation with reference to its content.
2. **Procedural knowledge.** This knowledge is usually collected in advance from the domain specialist and forms the core of a knowledge base. This also forms the reasoning part of the system which infers conclusions.
3. **Control knowledge.** The system needs to have a variety of control strategies available to it so that alternatives can be tried out at run-time and failed attempts can be dealt with.

The earliest proposal for knowledge representation in expert systems was that of a **production system**. In this method the program is divided into 3 parts as above, where each part is kept separate and therefore the total system can be easily understood and used.

1. ⇒ database (DB) in working memory
2. ⇒ list of production rules (PR)
3. ⇒ method of choosing which production rule to apply to the current state of the database.

Each production rule is of the form (IF condition THEN action) or possibly (IF condition THEN action1 ELSE action2). Whether a production is applicable is determined by pattern-matching.

The great bulk of the PR list is made up of rules which are invoked by pattern-matching with features of the case-environment and which can be added to, modified, or deleted by the user. A database of this special type is ordinarily called a knowledge base.

The dominance of rule-based programming was such in the early days of expert systems that the British Computer Society definition given earlier makes them a part of the defining characteristics. However, as this technique focuses primarily on the *relationship* between objects it has not been universally popular. Some experts think primarily of *objects* and the properties these objects may have. Such domains are better represented in form of a set of structured data representations (known as frames).

The maturity of expert systems technology is, in fact, reflected in the variety of alternative, and sometimes complementary, knowledge representation techniques available (Richer, 1988) to knowledge engineers. This in turn has made it necessary for the engineer to study the results of the elicitation process to decide on the most appropriate form of representation. This task is usually called **knowledge analysis**.

9.2 TOOLS

Current tools for developing expert systems in the order of their pre-packed sophistication are:

1. expert systems shells (such as Advisor-2, Crystal, Leonardo, Xi-plus etc.)
2. Development environments (ART, KEE, LOOPS, etc.)
3. Symbolic languages (Prolog, LISP)
4. Algorithmic languages (C, FORTRAN, BASIC).

As there are not many off-the-shelf expert systems, anybody wanting to use one in their work needs to construct it for themselves.

1. **Expert system shells** (ESS) are very useful when applicable but in some cases are no use at all. They offer a simple way of representing knowledge and usually have one fixed way of controlling the reasoning process. EESs are usually constructed by taking an existing expert system, such as MYCIN, and generalizing it into a shell such as EMYCIN. These constrain the solutions to a problem by imposing a design methodology best suited to the class of problems to which the original expert system belonged.
2. **Development environments,** such as ART and KEE, provide less ready-made solutions but more possibilities. They offer a variety of methods for representation and control of the reasoning process. They also provide a task-oriented screen editor as well as some partially-working modules in a number of libraries. These systems, however, are only available on large computers or

dedicated AI workstations which cost a reasonable amount of money. Learning to use them is also harder than learning to use shells.

3. **Symbolic languages** such as LISP and Prolog, which are becoming widely available for microcomputers, are the most cost effective entry level for a newcomer who only wants to learn about the issues and who is prepared to learn the language and spend some time programming. However, this route does not provide such a cost effective program generation as 2. above does; nor does it provide such efficient implementation as 4. below.

4. Despite concentrated efforts by some people to argue otherwise, algorithmic languages such as C or BASIC can be used for constructing an expert system. These would act as an implementation language for a production system architecture. The designer needs to be well aware, however, of the internal workings of an inference engine and production system, in order not to end up writing a program which does not exhibit any of the novel characteristics of expert systems. These languages could, however, lead to the most effective implementations on current hardware.

9.3 KNOWLEDGE ENGINEERING

Expert systems are built through a process known as knowledge engineering. I believe that this process can be broken down into at least 12 identifiable sub-processes. I shall present these here and describe them briefly. Many workers in the field might disagree with my choices but, I am sure, would agree that we need to start looking at this branch of engineering, however young it may be, in a more disciplined manner.

1. **Project selection.** Domains which can be clearly formalized are better suited to algorithmic solutions. Domains where no clear agreement can be found on how the task is performed are better suited to search oriented solutions of AI. It is finding the right application somewhere in the middle which would exploit the full potential of the technology.

2. **Feasibility study.** Before starting work, it is imperative to carry out a detailed study of the task, availability of cooperative human experts and management support for the project.

3. **Project planning.** Effective planning is an important aspect of any project. However, planning expert system projects poses some novel problems. Prototyping and cyclic project development are popular solutions to some of these problems.

4. **User identification.** Most early expert systems only considered user's requirements after the development was over. It has become clear (see Collins *et al.*, 1985) that user's expectations, level of understanding and abilities have to be considered well before any serious development starts.

5. **Knowledge elicitation.** Extracting the human expert's knowledge via interviews or knowledge-acquisition tools is the well-known bottleneck in

the overall process. This process should also include collection of test cases to be used as a validation suite in the debugging stage.

6. **Knowledge analysis.** As it is not always possible to represent the knowledge in the simple production rule format, some time should be spent choosing the most suitable formalism, among those available (production rules, frames, semantic networks etc).

7. **Choice of tools.** Having chosen the formalism for knowledge representation, a choice has to be made of the tools suitable for implementation on a particular hardware.

8. **Coding the knowledge.** It is only after all the above work has been carried out that we can look forward to the 'hacking' part, itself an iterative process of code–test–debug against a set of test cases collected earlier plus validation with the experts.

9. **Validation with experts.** The 'debugging' part of the traditional software development takes a new meaning in knowledge engineering as the system needs to be validated against the original specification as well as unspecified expectations of the human expert. The problem which separates knowledge engineering from other forms of engineering is 'the moving target syndrome' of changes in the specification.

10. **Maintenance procedure design.** Having more or less satisfied the human experts that the system is functionally up to scratch one needs to design a policy of how future changes to the system are to be dealt with so as not to reduce the functionality in one part while attempting to improve some other part of the system.

11. **Evaluation with users.** At this point we can return to the actual users of the system and see if it meets with their approval and what changes may be needed to make the system more user friendly.

12. **Maintenance.** While the system is in use many small but important deficiencies are discovered which need to be dealt with in accordance with the pre-set procedures to ensure long-term effectiveness of the substantial investment.

9.4 CONCLUSIONS

We have presented a very brief overview of the steps involved in building an expert system. Obviously not all these steps are covered by most developers as the technology has its roots in the culture of amateur/enthusiasts. The development of projects can be seen in four different forms.

1. **Home-grown applications.** These are produced by an individual with some expertise which can be represented using an inexpensive shell. The expert, knowledge engineer and the user are all one person. Therefore, the usefulness of the system is dependent on the system developer. The system is an effective *aide-mémoire*.

2. **Demonstrator projects.** These are generally toy systems developed to assist the

appreciation of the technology by senior technical and management staff. The knowledge engineer shows off the system to the user. No survival of the system is planned and non-supervised use is not possible. The project usually involves a human expert and one or two knowledge engineers.

3. **Medium-size projects.** These are reasonable size projects including independent prototype and main development phases. The applications are not very ambitious but they need at least two knowledge engineers over two years to complete. Users need to be trained in how to use the system and one knowledge engineer needs to be on call for the system to survive the test of time.

4. **Major systems.** These, involving substantial development costs, time, risk and future maintenance, are still developed in conjunction with major academic laboratories. The R1/XCON system developed jointly by DEC and Carnegie-Mellon University is a good example of this category.

It is important that any newcomers to this game note which type of system they intend to aim for. They should then compare their experience with that in similar projects. There is no point spending one or two years on a small project and then getting depressed when none of the reported results associated with major projects are reached despite considerable effort.

9.5 REFERENCES

Brachman, R. J. and Levesque, H. J. (1985) *Readings in Knowledge Representation.* Morgan Kaufmann, CA.

Clancey, W. J. (1985) Heuristic classification, *Artificial Intelligence,* **27,** 289–350.

Collins, H. M., Green, R. M. and Draper, R. C. (1985) Where's the expertise? In M. Merry (ed.) *Expert Systems 85,* Cambridge University Press, Cambridge, pp. 323–34.

Greenwell, M. (1988) *Knowledge Engineering for Expert Systems.* Ellis Horwood Ltd.

Jackson, P. (1986) *Introduction to Expert Systems.* Addison-Wesley, Mass.

Michie, D. (1980) Expert systems, *Computer Journal,* **23,** 369–77.

Richer, M. (ed.) (1988) *AI Tools and Techniques.* Albex Publishing Corporation.

Sleeman, D. and Brown, J. S. (eds) (1982) *Intelligent Tutoring Systems.* Academic Press, New York.

Wellbank, M. (1983) *A Review of Knowledge Acquisition Techniques for Expert Systems.* Martlesham Consultancy Services, British Telecom Research Labs.

Yazdani, M. (1984) *Knowledge Engineering in PROLOG.* In Richard Forsyth (ed.) *Expert Systems: Principles and Case Studies.* 1st edn, Chapman and Hall, London, pp. 91–111.

10

Debugging knowledge bases

GILLY FURSE

10.1 IMPORTANCE OF GOOD DESIGN

There is one main principle to recall when debugging knowledge bases, and that is the same software engineering principle involved in debugging any piece of software: if the design is right the rest follows. The worst problems follow from inadequate design.

Thus there are two major types of problems which may be encountered: those which stem from problems in the design and those which stem from inconsistency in implementing the design. Although there should apparently be less scope for problems in knowledge-base design when using a shell, this is rather an illusion. Adequate knowledge domain analysis and an appropriate level of conceptualization are equally important with formal knowledge representation design, and on the whole less understood. Hence although there are special issues relating to debugging with particular shells, the general issues are the same.

10.1.1 Debugging conceptual design

This really is part of your knowledge engineering analysis at an earlier stage, but there are a couple of techniques which can be helpful even if employed later than is ideal. One is to use one of the various kinds of object-sort techniques – write the objects or parameters down on index cards and sort them into categories or hierarchies. This is normally used with the expert as a knowledge acquisition technique, but can also be used by the knowledge engineer to show up any gaps in the groupings. You may have, say, characterized people as minors, adults or whatever for the purposes of some bureaucratic system, and forgotten to include the category of pensioners. The card groupings will tend to make these sorts of mistakes fairly obvious.

Another useful technique is a game; it consists of running the system on paper. You need at least a couple of players, and it is better played early on when you have the basic concepts and important objects for the knowledge base, but before you have written too much of it and cannot alter it. Someone plays the inference engine, and someone the knowledge base, and if there are any other important mechanisms like a blackboard, a set of control demons, or a undo and reinference facility then you can allocate those parts too. Someone also has to play the user to answer the questions. The user starts the game by kicking off the system and it runs from there. This can be quite a revealing game and gives quite a strong feel of how the system should work, at the cost of a couple of hours work. It is particularly useful if you have designed the architecture yourself rather than using a shell; it can save a lot of wasted coding. The chief difficulty is persuading players not to cheat – humans will happily infer far more than the current evidence warrants, using their own private knowledge. Ensure strict behaviour of the inference engine and blackboard!

10.1.2 Appropriateness of knowledge representation

Different knowledge representations are closely related together, in terms of a formal description. Like computer languages, each type of representation makes some kinds of work easy and others harder, due to the facilities it emphasizes. Production rule systems and networks are formally very similar, indeed most rule-base types of knowledge base connect the items of the consequent and antecedent parts into a network (or in simpler cases a tree).

In a rule base it is easier to focus on the individual connections: IF a AND b THEN c. When the inference engine runs, and makes an inference chain by also firing the rule IF c AND d THEN e, this inference chain is of course a branch of a tree or network. In cycling through, the rule base is creating the search-tree. When a knowledge base is created explicitly as a network then this search-tree maps more directly on to it and may be easier to follow.

The more complex representations are mostly frame or object-oriented systems. As these are frequently connected in networks they are used when the objects or nodes are both complicated and structured. Broadly speaking, frame-type systems are good for knowledge bases of complicated objects in fairly straightforward relations (including class inheritance), and networks are good for simpler objects for which freer relations are wanted. For instance, in our engine health monitoring system the main kind of object in the knowledge is a 'process', which is something like air compression or fuel pumping. A process is a complex object with various attributes – inputs (atmospheric air), outputs (compressed air), chemical (air, fuel), active engine component (pump, compressor), attribute readings (air pressure, fuel octane). Also for each process there is a set of rules about the process behaviour. This kind of knowledge base is heavily structured and of the object-oriented kind.

It is important to try and get the 'best-fit' representation for your knowledge base. Of course, the process of transforming human expertise into a computable representation inevitably corrupts it in some respects, as people think in many subtle ways not copyable even by expert systems. However, where you have the choice of representation you can choose one whose distortions suit your purpose – which is normally to make the system function as 'naturally' as possible. If you find the knowledge which you are collecting during knowledge engineering is consistently difficult to enter into the knowledge base and you keep making mistakes it may be that you have not got right representation. (Or alternatively that the problem is fundamentally too difficult!) Experiment at an early stage. When you have a page or two of relevant rules or relations you can try these out in different representations or shells. When you have a bookful of them you will not be prepared to do so. So explore the issues of knowledge representation early on.

10.2 THE KNOWLEDGE BASE IMPLEMENTATION

Even when the knowledge base is sound conceptually, and in an appropriate representation, it is easy to make mistakes with setting up the items or rules it contains. There may be simple typographic mistakes – for example, misspelling an item (underscores are a great source of trouble here: 'enginetype' or 'engine_type'?). There are also inconsistencies created by entering differing versions of the same rule, or breaks in the inference chain because a whole set of connections have been omitted. Actual complete logical inconsistencies (which is what most people think of when they think of debugging knowledge base inconsistencies) are in my experience rare and are more often incompletely specified cases (see below). For all of this the practices of consistency checking and testing are at least partial remedies.

10.2.1 Consistency checking

The most classic form of inconsistency is the straight negative. You assert 'a implies b' and then you assert 'a implies not b'.

Frankly I have never seen this, but it probably does occur. A far more common occurrence is incomplete specification: 'a and b implies x' and also: 'a and b implies y'.

Which is true? Well, you might say, it depends... And what it depends on should probably be added as an extra condition to the rules.

10.2.2 Syntax and semantics

Consistency checking comes in two forms: syntactic and semantic. For those without a natural language background here is a short explanation. Syntax is about whether your assertions are well-formed grammatically, semantics is about whether the meaning is sensible. Semantics is far harder to check, because much more difficult, much harder to define, and completely ignored by most computer systems anyway. Computers in general are much more sensitive to syntax than people and much less sensitive to semantics. Here is a badly-formed assertion in English: 'Josie well sleeps not'. Here is a grammatically well-formed assertion: 'colourless green ideas sleep furiously'.

The intended meaning or semantics of the first assertion is clear to us; it is a matter of some debate as to whether the second assertion can be said to mean anything or not.

The syntax versus semantics clash is made more tractable the more you can express your intended semantics as syntax, i.e. the more completely you can formalize meaning (which is what knowledge representation is all about).

10.2.3 Semantics and the meaning of symbols

There is a prevailing view in computing in favour of using meaningful names. In expert systems these meaningful names are the word symbols for the objects being reasoned about, e.g. primary_double_clapper_pump. This combines with the practice of asking intelligent-looking questions, such as

'Is the proposed primary side-winder pump of the double-clapper overrun type?'

and a habit of producing loquacious canned text:

'It is not advisable to use a double-clapper overrun pump in the primary side-winder circuit because on installations over 1000 BThU capacity a sudden peak in water pressure is known to cause the perpetual rotating widget to run counter-clockwise suddenly and cause the pump to malfunction.'

It is fatally easy for users to imagine that this system knows what it is talking about and understands all about large central heating systems. It is even seductive for knowledge engineers to start thinking this too! The system only understands as much as the structure or syntax allows and the meanings we give to the symbol names are our private affair. Meaningful names are important for two reasons: 1. so that the user knows what is being talked about – i.e. the relevant content, and 2. to help us build and debug the system, because abstract symbols get hard to juggle. However, it is important to expose to your view the formal relations between these objects, which may actually be implemented very simply. 'Deep knowledge' is about the extent to which the structure of the objects is being actually built into the system as opposed to merely being reflected in the meaning of their names.

There is a general principle of debugging that you should get as much of the semantics as necessary turned into syntax (i.e. put the meaning into structure) because it makes consistency checking much easier. For instance the objects: 'pump(valves, 2)' and 'pump(valves, 3)' can be related together by a consistency check (and an expert system with a sufficiently powerful Knowledge Representation Language (KRL)) whereas '3_valved_pump' and '2_valved_pump' can only have any connection at all in the mind of the knowledge engineer.

There is of course a cost to implementing structure: it is harder and takes more resources. Hence there is a minimal power principle applicable overall to implementation, which says: only implement as much structure as you need to do the task.

10.2.4 Syntax errors

Syntax errors are probably the most frequent, though the most humble, errors. And one of the most common cause of syntax errors is wrongly-spelled object names. These are exactly the same as typos in program variable names and have exactly the same effect. One difference however is that in many programming languages the typing and declaration requirements mean that such errors are flagged at compile time – e.g. misspelled variable names as 'undeclared variable'. Since the requirements on variables in expert systems knowledge bases are often less stringent than those of compilers, it is possible for such errors to slip through. A symptom of such an error is when you run an example through, for which you are sure that all the appropriate facts and rules are present, but the right questions or path through the knowledge base are not triggered. If it is not, by misspelling you may have completely omitted a rule.

10.2.5 Testing and test cases

To test an expert system it is best to have a set of test cases. You should have assembled these for the knowledge engineering anyway, both for analysis and for definition of the problem cases which the system will solve. It is extremely difficult to test knowledge bases formally (let alone the animated version actually running, which is subject to the inference engine's whims as well) i.e. abstractly. But you need some form of testing, so the most appropriate kind is provided by running test cases; this can be regarded as a form of alpha-testing before parallel running (if you ignore one of the most fundamental rules of commercial computing and start live running of expert systems without parallel running you do so at your peril, and unfortunately at the peril of the reputation of the technology too).

Test cases are useful for other reasons, such as during review of development to prompt the expert for fuller rules by running them through the system. Also, they provide a standard set of benchmarks for the system, so that if it is updated to handle more cases the test cases should be run through to check that none of the existing capabilities of the system have been disturbed by unwary amendments. It is true that when this happens it often points to hidden faults, or things which only work because of the happy coincidence of two errors – but who says that expert system implementers are less prone to error than the rest of the human race?

Be able to describe the test cases in a generic way. For example: as running in real 'real' time (and give times), as giving advice on employee hiring. Specify the characteristics for the classes of problem which can be dealt with. In a PAYE advisory system you might tag a case as 'recently employed'. Then you can summarize the cases which you actually know the system can deal with and can also check for correct performance on expected cases. It is also useful to find or invent some cases you do not expect it to solve and put them in your test set. Then you can monitor what it is supposed to be able to do and how it will fail if it cannot. (This is referred to as the question of 'graceful degradation' – most expert systems degrade very ungracefully.)

10.2.6 Demo Death or your useful destructive friends

You should try your best to bust your system; because if you don't someone else will. Demo Death is what all demonstrators are familiar with – you take your reliable computer/software away from home and boot it up and it goes 'Non-system disk: cannot boot' or the program crashes. Remember Murphy's Law – if it can go wrong it will. Find it yourself first! It's much less embarrassing. Colleagues who can break software are very useful. I once knew someone who could crash almost any software in no seconds flat; even old faithfuls like WordStar, which I used almost daily at the point, and which never crashed on me, fell apart within five minutes of introduction to this man. He was really useful when we produced new software ...

10.2.7 Closed-world assumptions and incompleteness

A closed-world assumption is the assumption that you know all possible effects or causes within the 'world' or domain. The usual error this leads to is the conclusion that when you have eliminated what is impossible, that whatever remains must be the case, however improbable. It is only true it you know everything bearing on the case; otherwise the answer may be something you are ignorant of. The chief point of this for testing expert systems is that you ensure that you are only making closed-world assumptions when you are sure of them. Otherwise if the system cannot find any relevant knowledge or rules have it say so.

Almost all knowledge bases will be incomplete. Very few applications actually require completeness, though some require the system to recognize incompleteness in the form of cases it is not competent to deal with. The concept of 'need to know' is more useful for knowledge bases: do not attempt to ensure that your knowledge base is formally complete, but that it has all the knowledge it needs in order to function.

While considering checking performance there is another way of thinking about assessing performance which is relevant here. This is sometimes described as the 70/100% question. The question is: do you need your system to answer 100% of questions 70% correctly, or do you need it to answer 70% of questions 100% correctly? Strictly this is a question you should address when planning the system, not when debugging it, but given that you have established the answer it is necessary to check by test runs that it is following the strategy it is supposed to.

Example 1: 100/70% – a software diagnosis system. This was intended to help the technical support group of a major software company, so that the more routine problems could be dealt with over the telephone by junior staff.

Essentially, customers rang up and described their problems; at best an immediate solution should be offered, at worst someone else had to ring them back. The system worked from the described symptoms to the causes, and could offer advice about fixing or avoiding the problem (which in fact was its real purpose, rather than diagnosis – a hint about being careful in classifying applications). In principle, with customer support it is a good idea to be able to push the problem one step further and give the impression that you are working on it. Hence for this system it would be beneficial if it could say something useful in 100% of cases, even if it was only 'this does not seem to conform to the standard causes for this kind of problem...'. What it said did not have to be 100% reliable if it was not likely to do much harm, and a real expert was being put on the case shortly. So suggestions about assembler fixes to the user's files were restricted to clearly identifiable corruptions.

Example 2: 70/100% – medical applications. This applies to many medical applications, where the wrong answer may literally be fatal (if anyone takes it seriously). These systems much more frequently have the characteristics that they will only solve a certain percentage of the cases and a great deal of effort is put into making a good knowledge base for the ones they will handle.

Translated into testing, this tells you whether you should test broadly or deeply. The 100/70% type systems need broad testing to check they are covering the ground. The 70/100% systems need deep testing to check the case handling is correct in detail. For the latter, for instance, you may need sets of tests which are closely related around major issues in the domain. In practice this difference is less visible in small systems, but it should be considered in planning your testing.

10.3 UNCERTAINTY

One approach to the 70/100% requirement is to reduce the stress on the 100% correctness by introducing uncertainty handling of some kind. This is also often done because we require to have some idea of the correctness of the solution. (Uncertainty is of course a measurement of certainty of correctness, not of correctness itself.) This is not the place for a large excursion into uncertainty, which is a subject all of its own, but a point about testing is in order here.

Systems with uncertainty fall into two useful categories for this purpose; the first are strict Bayesian types where the factors are probabilities and are derived from actual statistical evidence. Real examples of these systems are few and far between and can be fairly easily identified. The famous Prospector is one of them. It is operating in a domain where there actually exists some statistical evidence about whether molybdenum might be found in conjunction with shale and Vishnu schist. These domains are clear, well-bounded, usually highly technical, and almost inevitably in domains where sophisticated measurement techniques are applied (otherwise where would the statistics come from?). Hence in knowledge-engineering these systems it is important to check that the probability values entered are as correct as can be, and not to disbelieve the results without checking. Because given correct evidence the system may come up with surprising results but they may still be correct. This sort of system has characteristics of 'synthetic' systems which, like planning and design systems, have known elements out of which they build new combinations.

The other kind of system with uncertainty does not have statistical probabilities but what we can properly call uncertainty. These systems have what are called **modal logics** and deal with human judgements of belief. There are various kinds including negative or screening beliefs. The classic type is MYCIN. These systems are usually an 'analytic' type in which the system's task is to identify the correct or possible answer out of the set of known answers. In knowledge-engineering terms it is usually the case that the expert could identify the answers in various conditions and that the uncertainty factors are a way of weighing evidence to get a more sophisticated emulation of the expert's range of solutions. In most cases of these kinds of systems the testing is completely backwards from the Prospector type described above. The proper answers to the test cases are already known and the implementers basically play around with the uncertainty factors until the system gives the 'correct' answers. In other words the proper answers are believed in more than the certainty factors; hence it is the latter which get adjusted. This was apparently true with testing MYCIN and has been with many other systems.

The moral of this is do not get carried away with quasi-mathematical formulations which look impressive but do not actually correspond with much real evidence. If you are clear about what the real evidence and expertise is, you should be able to identify which of these kinds of uncertainty you are dealing with and set your testing and amendment priorities accordingly.

10.4 DECLARATIVE AND PROCEDURAL VALIDATION

There is an important distinction in thinking about validation, which is to distinguish **declarative** and **procedural** knowledge. Both categories need to be correct for the expert system to run right. Declarative knowledge unpacks as the question: are the facts, relations, rules correct and consistent? Procedural knowledge unpacks to the question: are these being used in the right way? In other words: are the strategies right? Are rules being accessed in the right order? In the sections below conflict resolution is about procedural knowledge and problems in ordering, whereas network errors are normally going to be relevant to checking declarative knowledge.

10.4.1 Conflict resolution

With rule bases there has to be a method of conflict resolution to cope with the situation where more than one rule might be relevant. The commonest scheme is first-found. This is so common that new entrants do not always notice it exists at first. Implicit in first-found processing is the importance of order of the rules. In ordered rule bases funny effects in processing may be due to rules being disordered. For instance, it is common to have some 'special' rules for particular cases, plus a general rule. In an ordered rule base the specific rules must come before the general rule, or they will never be accessed; this is one of the causes of a system which never seems to access rules which you know should be present. Try to keep closely related rule sets together.

The ordering is simple enough to see in a small rule base, but more difficult in a largish one. Commercial systems where the knowledge editor renumbers the rules for you automatically do not help in this respect, as it makes the rules more difficult to keep track of.

Some systems have more complex conflict-resolution schemes. The expert systems language OPS5 has a choice of resolution methods which can be controlled to some degree by the programmer. This can lead to more complex interactions than first-found ordering, but the basic principle of ensuring that rules fire in the right circumstances remains. Note that conflict-resolution methods affect fundamentally the use of the knowledge base in a way that is not always explicitly stated. Context-dependency may be explicitly stated, but order of course is not. It is not true that all knowledge in a knowledge base is explicitly or declaratively stated, and conflict resolution is an important case in point. In general expert systems encourage facts-as-knowledge to be explicitly stated; these are static. They do not enable procedures-as-knowledge to be explicitly stated in the same way. Dynamic reasoning methods are built-in of course; only one in simple expert systems, and perhaps a choice in the bigger toolkits. Problem-solving procedures, which include knowledge of the best order to apply knowledge are more difficult to state explicitly. The ways of achieving procedural control include conflict resolution and whatever other methods commercial packages may offer; typically a type of rule called a **demon** (which jumps the queue and fires at once if its conditions are true). Just because they are less obvious these rather 'hidden' sources of knowledge can cause implementation errors which have to be fixed during debugging.

10.4.2 Network errors

If using a network-based system, the most common fault is failing to connect all the arcs and nodes up, thus leaving a gap in the network. Formally this is equivalent to leaving out an inference rule. This is quite easy to do in a complicated network. For instance, our engine monitoring system uses connected networks to represent: the physical components and pipes; the mechanical processes, such as shaft rotation; the fluid processes such as combustion and compression, with their inputs and outputs; and the sensor processes measuring all this. Failure to add any one of the many links may result in the system coming to dead stop in running one of its simulation strategies. The model has varying levels of detail including sub-component and sub-process definitions, so that it is not easy to check manually with any certainty of completeness. Because it is a set of connected nets it is difficult to draw graphically, though specific parts can be mapped. One obvious procedure was to input the knowledge base in sections of a small 'natural' size and then check the network links. Boring though it is, an organized approach to doing the work is as everywhere a major factor in easy debugging.

In a network this size we write network-checking utilities to follow the links through, to check each end of an arc is properly defined, and hierarchies complete. For this system the utilities are a set of modules which check various levels or parts of the network, rather than attempt one massive validation. Running these utilities over parts of the knowledge base allows us to confirm that specified parts are good. With large systems there is a very useful general strategy (*à la* Sherlock Holmes) of eliminating as many candidates as possible.

One useful tool for network checking is simply a large whiteboard or sheet of paper. In the early stages of constructing a network it is possible to create a visual map of the knowledge base by drawing it out. As discussed above, rule bases map on to a kind of network, and it can be useful to actually draw this too. In one project we got hold of a set of white formica boards about 10 ft by 4 ft left over from an exhibition, and standing them on end and side by side covered the length of one wall, thus giving ourselves the largest ever whiteboard! We covered it with branches of the network in our knowledge base, which helped considerably in following the cases where there ought to be links to other parts, and so on.

One of things which this makes most glaringly obvious is where the clusters are – related rules using the same items, or nodes in the networks – it gets difficult to add one more line pointing to some crucial item! This is of great help in forcing these clusters to your attention, as you may not have noticed that so many choices were involved here. It is a very useful technique at the point when the knowledge base is emerging from small to medium size, and implicitly helps to review its emerging shape.

If you don't have the whiteboards you can use wallpaper strips pinned side by side inside out. Or you can use print-outs of the knowledge base cut into sections and pasted up, and with connecting lines drawn between them. Look at your knowledge base while you work! Say hello to it when you come in! Scan it idly at coffee! It really helps to get to know it well.

10.5 DEBUGGING WITH SHELLS

One of the difficulties in debugging knowledge bases in shells is that you may be aware of inadequate conceptualization but not able to do much about it because of the limitations of the expressiveness of the shell KRL. For instance, many shells severely limit powers of generalization. The simpler shells do not have class structures, so that if you wish to say

    IF object is a type of superobject
    THEN do this action

for example,

> IF engine is a type of diesel engine
> THEN examine injector heaters

you will have difficulties.

If you can have class structures with inheritance of properties, then you just tag each type of engine as diesel class or petrol class or whatever. Otherwise, assuming that you need to know the engine make anyway you will also have to ask in each case whether it is diesel or petrol. This, as is well appreciated, is a bore for the user, who knows that in most cases the make implies the fuel type: a Leyland truck implies diesel, a Porsche 911 is petrol. And the user will not see why they should have to answer both questions. But as well it is a problem for debugging because the knowledge-base builder has to ensure that the questions are consistently asked in all appropriate cases. This is not quite as simple as it looks, especially as the knowledge base gets bigger and becomes difficult to review in a short hit. You can put all the variants of questions together – but only once. If the versions relate to each of a class of engine then you will more likely want to put all the rules about each class together and you will have to separate all the variants.

10.5.1 Documenting and indexing as control methods

If you have sections of knowledge base for different classes check that all the proper questions are asked in each. Not ensuring this leads to uneven performance in the various sections. Adequate documentation of rules helps here, either by a commented and sectionalized print-out or by a hand-constructed (heaven help us) index. This may seem glaringly obvious but is the kind of thing easy not to bother with at first, and which hardly seems worth the effort of catching up with later (the fate of most good intentions about documentation and commenting). The bigger the knowledge base gets the more it is worth the investment of some external documentation. Anyone creating a knowledge base of more than about fifty rules is likely to run across this problem. It is more than ever true if you are required to work with an inadequately powerful KRL because the knowledge base will be big, verbose and thinly spread, rather than small, powerful and elegant.

10.5.2 Version control and team working

'Go on, you know all about this sort of thing .... Damn, I was sure I had a set of rules in here for coping with the case when there are more than five out-of-bounds figures in this set ... I remember putting them in, it's a real pig to make it report to the user in that silly window ... Oh hell, now I remember I was over in block J working on Ruth's PC ... bet I did it on my backup version ... and now I've done the last two day's stuff on this version. How do I merge knowledge bases

Ben? What do you mean this shell doesn't have a merge knowledge bases facility?!! You're kidding me... aren't you?'

Ho hum. Sorry, no kidding. Difficult though it may be to believe, some shells do not have a merge-knowledge-bases facility; hackers polish up their Pascal or favourite language. Or get typing. Or better still make sure that you keep an eye on which version of the knowledge base you are using.

Team working imposes the same constraints in expert systems as it does in any other programming task. You have to ensure consistency between members of the team. All the points about documentation, specified test sets, version control just apply in spades.

10.5.3 Shell facilities and xreffing utilities

If you have not already discovered it, note that the so-called 'explanation facilities' offered in many shells are more useful to the developer than to the end-user. Many end-users never ask 'why?' or 'how?', but the answer displaying the trail of rules fired is a record of the system's current search path, and is extremely useful for debugging. If you are using a commercial shell with such facilities you can follow a run through checking that each choice has been made as predicted. These facilities are the equivalent of tracing facilities in language implementations.

Some commercial shells keep a dictionary of object names used and will allow the implementer to choose them from a dictionary. This does force you to notice if you have to define something as new when you think it should already exist (misspelling nearly always, or corrupted knowledge base). In general however, shells have better building than validation techniques. With large knowledge bases it is worth writing a cross-referencing utility which constructs a dictionary of what rules contain each object. It should also highlight any object or variable used once only: such an object is redundant because it cannot be used for any kind of inference, and therefore is probably an incorrect reference. With commercial shells it will only be easy to do this if the knowledge base is available in some kind of understandable format – ASCII, text, or some underlying language (e.g. Prolog assertions). Proprietary systems may encode knowledge bases to facilitate access and save space; they usually have a facility for producing a straight text output.

Commercial shells often come with clever knowledge base editors these days. They can be nicer to use than just hacking in a text editor, but some of them indulge in the habit of renumbering their rules when you add a new one. It would be better to create a rule 3.1 if a new one is added between 3 and 4 – but they do not all do it. So do not panic if you think you have lost a rule, check out the renumbering.

10.6 LARGE RULE BASES

There are some specific problems related to testing large sets of rules, of which one is just keeping track of the knowledge base. Modularization is the most obvious important point; put the rules together in chunks. This always gives chunk allocation problems as some rules are relevant in more than one place, but it does allow for internal chunk consistency checking.

Note that the number of rules in a system is not necessarily a good indication of 'rightness' or progress. Like a maturing program, a developing knowledge base should get smaller at times, as well as larger, as you find clusters of individual occurrences which can be generalized into one. These times when the knowledge base becomes more compact are a good sign of progress.

The concept of 'knowledge density' is probably a more useful measure than that of quantity anyway. A hundred relevant and elegant rules are more useful than 1000 verbose ones. Truly elegant expert systems have a good knowledge density, because experts have a good knowledge density. People are fundamentally not good at thinking of a lot of things at once and are very good at 'chunking them up'. Hence experts are experts often because they know which information is really relevant and which can be left out. Although there are genuinely large applications, some of the largest and most cumbersome expert systems have been built by knowledge engineers playing at armchair experts – and it shows.

10.7 MISCELLANEOUS

A couple of miscellaneous tips. Use the 'more_here' principle. Make a rule or an object called more_here, and when you know you're going to need something but are not sure yet what it will be then refer to it as 'more_here'. This is the equivalent of the adventure gamer's dictum 'this cave is still under construction...' and is a handy way of keeping unfinished business tagged.

Another useful trick is to use extra experts in the debugging. Publishers have a practice of using two proof readers for manuscripts because the first proof reader picks up about 70% of the errors and will overlook most of the other 30% on all subsequent readings. Someone else's 30% blind spot is not likely to be in the same places, so a wider net is cast by using two proofers. The same is true with experts, so make use of your experts at this stage as well as at interviewing.

11

Inductive learning for expert systems

RICHARD FORSYTH

With the dramatic rise of expert systems has come a renewed interest in the 'fuel' that drives them: knowledge. For it is specialist knowledge that gives expert systems their power. However, extracting knowledge from human experts in symbolic form has proved arduous and labour-intensive (see Wellbank, 1983). So the idea of machine learning is enjoying a renaissance.

For a computer to refine and re-structure its own knowledge it is necessary to provide a feedback loop, and turn a read-only knowledge base into a programmable-erasable knowledge base. Ultimately this promises an order of magnitude gain in the speed with which expert systems can be constructed (and can adapt to changing circumstances), since they will no longer be held back to the pace at which knowledge engineers can write and debug hand-crafted rule sets. Furthermore, machine induction opens up the exciting possibility of synthesizing totally new knowledge – of discovering concepts and scientific laws that no one has ever thought of.

In this chapter we concentrate on what inductive techniques can offer the knowledge engineer, but it should be apparent from the foregoing that machine learning is not merely a short-cut method of building expert systems; learning is the key to intelligent behaviour, and that is a lesson the AI community will have to learn if artificial intelligence is ever to deserve its title.

Statistical procedures such as classical discriminant analysis and nearest-neighbour classification have proved useful in a number of self-improving systems, as have various cybernetic approaches to pattern recognition (e.g. the Perceptron); but the knowledge they acquire tends to be rather opaque. So this chapter skips over the more mathematically-oriented 'black-box' learning techniques, where only the effectiveness of the system matters, to methods where the resultant knowledge is intended to be accessible to people as well as machines. This makes them more suitable for generating rules that can later be used as part of an expert system's knowledge base, because the knowledge in an expert system should be intelligible to humans.

This involves considering some relatively sophisticated **description languages** (formalisms for representing machine-made knowledge) – in particular, representation schemes capable of expressing structural descriptions, where the relations between parts of an object are important as well as the elementary attributes (or features) of the object.

11.1 THE RULE DESCRIPTION LANGUAGE

The choice of representation for encoding a system's knowledge is at least as important as the details of the learning algorithm it uses. One of the most successful of recent discovery programs, EURISKO (Lenat, 1982 and 1983), owes its success largely to its highly flexible description language. All EURISKO's concepts and heuristics are expressed in a common formalism, as 'units'. Units are frame-like structures that are modified by the discovery rules (other units). Simple syntactic changes in a unit usually lead to meaningful, and possibly valuable, new units. By contrast, small alterations in a conventional program or its data structures are likely to produce nonsense. Thus the space of possible descriptions is characterized by 'gradualness' (Forsyth and Rada, 1986).

It is also very convenient if the representation for the input data is the same as that for the descriptions (or rules) but this is not always the case. When it is, the system is said to employ the 'single representation trick'.

A wide variety of data structures have been used in practical learning systems, from which the obvious conclusion is that there is no ideal representation language for all machine learning problems. However it is important that the representation used is expressive enough for the task in hand.

11.2 LEARNING AS A SEARCH

Tom Mitchell was the first person to link, in print, the two important but previously disconnected AI topics of **learning** and **search**. It can be fruitful to view learning as a search through the space of all possible descriptions for those which are valuable for the task in hand (Mitchell, 1982). The number of syntactically valid descriptions is astronomical; and the more expressive the description language, the more explosive is this combinatorial problem.

Clearly some heuristic method has to be found of guiding the search and thereby ignoring the vast majority of potential descriptions, or concepts, which are useless for the current purpose.

We can try to illustrate the connection between the two fundamental AI notions of search and learning with a simplified weather-forecasting example. Let us suppose that we have a database of weather records and the job of the learning algorithm is to learn how to classify records on the basis of whether the next day will be fine or not. The machine must find a rule for making this discrimination.

Assume further for simplicity's sake that each record contains only four fields. These four variables are: rainfall in millimetres, sunshine in hours, maximum wind gust in knots, and pressure at noon in millibars. Thus two typical records from the training set (the instances used in forming the rule) might be as below.

(1-Apr-87)		(8-Apr-87)	
Rainfall	1.2	Rainfall	0.1
Sunshine	3.5	Sunshine	6.4
Windmax	23	Windmax	13
Pressure	1001	Pressure	1017
[Nextday	Not-Fine]	[Nextday	Fine]

The extra item, Nextday, indicates whether the next day turned out fine or not. For the present purpose, a fine day is defined as having (Rainfall < 0.5) AND (Sunshine > 3.6) i.e. less than half a millimetre of rain and more than 3.6 hours of sunshine. This is the value, derived from the following day's readings, that the system must learn to predict.

Rules can be composed by linking variable names and constants with the following operators.

AND OR NOT ⇔

Thus the rule description language allows Boolean expressions such as

Sunshine < 4 AND Pressure < 1000

with brackets if necessary to avoid ambiguity. This is a relatively simple description language, but it suffices for our purposes.

Given this sort of training data and description language, the learning system can start with an initial description (which may be randomly created) and apply transformation operators to generate its successors. These successors are new descriptions for testing. The most important transformation operators are generalization and specialization. The process is illustrated in Fig. 11.1. For training data we use the 30 days of April 1985 (London readings). Of course in a real meteorological application, we might have tens of thousands of example cases measured on scores of variables.

Each node in the search tree is a decision rule that can be evaluated according to how well it distinguishes days followed by fine weather from days not followed by fine weather. We use here an extremely simple evaluation score, the percentage of correct cases; but rules that apply to less than five cases (out of 30 in the training set) are discarded. They are too rarely applicable. Our search strategy is to generate successors only from rules that have a high evaluation score – i.e. to employ a best-first search method.

The diagram shows that this process can be viewed as a search through a network where the nodes are descriptions (rules) and the arcs are transformations that modify descriptions and thus generate new ones. At each step we show only four successors being generated – two by generalization and two by

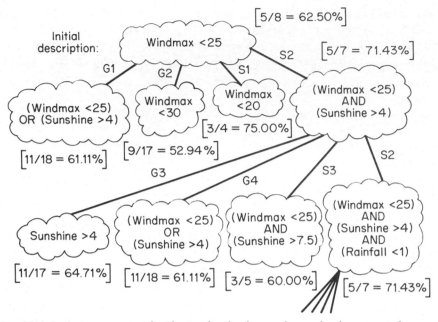

Fig. 11.1 Learning as a search. The top-level rule may be randomly generated or user-supplied. From then on, new rules are produced by applying generalization and specialization operators; such as: G1, add OR condition; G2, increase LT-constant; G3, drop AND-condition; G4, change AND to OR; S1, decrease LT-constant; S2 add AND-condition; S3, increase GT-constant; S4, change OR to AND.

specialization – from the best rule, as defined by our simple evaluation function. In reality, more than four successors would be created at each step.

In this context generalization of a rule means that it applies to more cases and specialization means that it applies to fewer. Thus the operator G1, which adds an OR-condition, makes the resulting expression cover a wider class of examples. On the other hand, the operator S3, which takes an expression of the form

Variable > Constant

and transforms it to

Variable > (Constant + k)

where k is some small increment, makes the rule more specific. It covers fewer cases. There are several methods of automatic generalization and specialization, as we shall see.

Note that the search defines a tree structure, but the underlying search space is a network, because repeated applications of the transformations can regenerate ancestral rules. This corresponds to revisiting a node in the network, and there is an example in the diagram, where

(Windmax < 25) OR (Sunshine > 4)

is generated at two different levels in the tree.

The foregoing is a sketch of an imaginary, and highly simplified, rule-search procedure. We will now look at some real rule-induction procedures, having outlined the basic concepts with the aid of a simple example.

11.3 VERSION SPACE

Mitchell (who first identified induction as a search process) devised an algorithm of his own for searching the space of possible concepts (which he termed the 'version space'). It is known as the 'candidate-elimination' method, and it can be described (to computer programmers) as a cross between the 'Sieve of Eratosthenes' and the 'Binary Chop'.

It constitutes an extremely elegant method (at least with noise-free training instances) of converging on the description of a concept, or a set of descriptions (Mitchell, 1982).

The basic idea behind the candidate-elimination algorithm appears absurd at first glance: list all possible descriptions, then cross off those that do not apply to the training data. (This is its resemblance to the Sieve of Eratosthenes, where prime numbers are found by setting up an array of integers and eliminating the ones that fail a primality test.)

Despite the enormity of the search space, the method becomes practical by utilizing the fact that a partial ordering exists among the descriptions, from general to specific – i.e. any two descriptions can be compared and ranked according to which is the more general. For example, the concept 'brown dog' is more general than the concept 'large brown dog'.

This realization allows the system to maintain two boundary sets – S, the set of the most specific possible descriptions compatible with the training data so far, and G, the set of the most general possible descriptions. Between them, these two finite sets define the edges of a far larger set – the set of all possible descriptions (which is likely to be astronomic in size) – in a compact form.

The S and G sets are gradually made to converge as more and more training instances are examined. (This is where the method resembles the well-known Binary Chop.) The convergence is achieved as follows:

1. When a positive instance is encountered, any description in G that does not cover it is eliminated, and all elements of S are generalized as little as possible so that they cover it.
2. When a negative instance is encountered, any description in S that covers it is deleted, and all elements of G are specialized as little as possible so that they no longer cover it.

Mitchell's masterly exposition convinced many members of the AI community that the rule-induction problem had, in all essentials, been solved. However, li

many theoretically optimal procedures, the candidate-elimination algorithm does not actually work very well in practice. Its chief defect is that it starts to get into trouble with quite modest amounts of noise in the training data.

11.4 QUINLAN'S ID3

Quinlan's ID3 (Interactive Dichotomizer 3) is a general-purpose rule-induction algorithm that has been incorporated into a number of commercial packages (Quinlan, 1982). Given a sample data set to classify, it creates a discrimination tree.

It too is not particularly robust in the face of noisy data, though it could be improved in this respect if it did not always seek a 'perfect' rule. The program works as follows:

1. Select at random a subset of size W from the training set (the 'window');
2. Apply the CLS algorithm (explained below) to form a rule-tree for the current window;
3. Scan the entire database (not just the window) to find exceptions to the latest rule;
4. If there are any exceptions, insert some of them into the window (replacing existing examples if memory space is in short supply) and repeat from step 2; otherwise stop and display the latest rule as the solution.

This procedure actually throws away the latest rule and starts again from scratch on each cycle.

The method of window selection is termed 'exception-driven filtering'. The need for a window arises because the main database may contain hundreds of thousands of cases, and hence be too large to be processed (from backing store) in an acceptable time. Hence it is purely a matter of efficiency.

The CLS algorithm (Hunt *et al.*, 1966) acts as a subroutine of the main program. CLS stands for Concept Learning System and derives originally from work done by experimental psychologists in the 1950s and 1960s. It first appeared as a proposed model of what people do when given simple concept formation tasks, and only later became a computer algorithm, due to Hunt and others. Thus it is an example of AI borrowing from psychology, rather than the other way round.

CLS works by first finding the variable (or test) which is most discriminatory, and partitioning the data with respect to that variable. Quinlan used an information-theoretic measure of entropy (i.e. surprise) for assessing the discriminatory power of each variable, but others have suggested different measures, e.g. the Chi-Squared statistic (Hart, 1985). Having divided the data into two subsets on the basis of the most discriminatory variable, each subset is partitioned in a similar way (unless it contains examples of only one class). The process repeats until all subsets contain data of only one kind. The end-product is

a discrimination tree, which can be used later to classify samples never previously encountered.

ID3 trees performed well on King–Rook versus King–Knight chess end-game problems, where the data is free from uncertainty. Really noisy data, however, such as weather records, leads it to grow very bushy decision trees which fit the training set but do not carry over well to new examples. In the worst case it can end up with one decision node for every example in the training set!

ID3's main shortcomings are:

1. The rules are not probabilistic;
2. Several identical examples have no more effect than one;
3. It cannot deal with contradictory examples (which are commonplace outside the rarefied setting of chess end-games);
4. The results are therefore over-sensitive to small alterations to the training database.

In short, ID3 makes no concessions at all to considerations of statistical sampling. These objections would lose much of their force if ID3 stopped before it reached a subset with no counterexamples at all. Recently a revised version of the algorithm, C4, has been reported by its author (Quinlan, 1986). C4 goes some way towards overcoming the objections listed above.

To give an illustration of ID3 in action, let us imagine that we are giving it data about the flags of various states in the USA. The objective is for it to learn how to distinguish states that joined the Confederacy in the US Civil War (1860–65) from those that stayed loyal to the Union. It is an artificial example, but it serves to illustrate the way the system works. In fact, there are reasons for thinking that confederate states might choose different emblems from those that remained in the Union.

First of all, here is the training data. We have picked 23 states that existed at the time of the Civil War, and augmented our set with the Union and Confederate flags themselves, as well as that of the District of Columbia (which is as federal as you can get, though not really a state at all). This gives 26 examples in all.

The data is presented in conventional feature–vector form, which is the way ID3 expects it. There are nine variables, plus the Type column (U or C) which is the one we want to predict. (See Table 11.1.)

The variables used are as follows. Stars is a count of the number of stars on the flag. Bars are vertical lines. Stripes are horizontal lines. Hues is the number of colours in the flag. Saltire indicates the presence of a diagonal X-shaped cross on the flag. Icon is Y if there is a pictorial design and N if the flag is purely abstract. Humans is a counter of the number of human figures depicted on the flag. (If Icon = N then obviously Humans = 0.) Word is another counter, of the number of words appearing in the flag (as a motto or slogan). Finally Num gives the number of numbers represented: some states put dates, like 1848, on their flag.

Note that this input description language does not allow us to express structural

Table 11.1 Flags of US States.

Flag	Stars	Bars	Stripes	Hues	Saltire	Icon	Humans	Word	Num	Type
Union	50	0	13	3	0	N	0	0	0	U
Confed.	13	0	0	3	1	N	0	0	0	C
Alabama	0	0	0	2	1	N	0	0	0	C
Arkansas	29	0	0	3	0	N	0	1	0	C
Conn.	0	0	0	5	0	Y	0	4	0	U
Delaware	0	0	0	6	0	Y	2	4	2	U
Florida	0	0	0	6	1	Y	1	15	0	C
Georgia	13	1	0	3	1	Y	0	3	1	C
Illinois	0	0	0	6	0	Y	0	6	2	U
Iowa	0	2	0	5	0	Y	0	10	0	U
Louisiana	0	0	0	4	0	Y	0	4	0	C
Maryland	0	12	0	4	0	N	0	0	0	U
Massachussets	1	0	0	4	0	Y	1	6	0	U
Mississippi	13	0	3	3	1	N	0	0	0	C
New Hampshire	9	0	0	5	0	Y	0	7	1	U
New Jersey	0	0	0	5	0	Y	2	3	1	U
New York	0	0	0	6	0	Y	2	1	0	U
N. Carolina	1	1	2	4	0	N	0	3	4	C
Ohio	17	0	5	3	0	N	0	0	0	U
Rhode I.	13	0	0	3	0	Y	0	1	0	U
S. Carolina	0	0	0	2	0	Y	0	0	0	C
Tennessee	3	2	0	3	0	N	0	0	0	C
Texas	1	1	2	3	0	N	0	4	0	C
Virginia	0	0	0	5	0	Y	2	2	0	C
Wisconsin	0	0	0	5	0	Y	2	2	1	C
D.C.	3	0	5	2	0	N	0	0	0	U

Table 11.2 Discrimination Tests.

Test	Union	Confed.
Stripes > 0	3	3
Stripes $\Leftarrow 0$	11	9
Saltire > 0	0	5
Saltire $\Leftarrow 0$	14	7

relationships, such as 'a white star over a blue stripe'. This is one of the problems with feature–vector notation.

CLS begins by looking for the most discriminatory variable, in order to create the root of the decision tree. To do this it constructs a number of frequency tables, at least one for each variable, such as those shown in Table 11.2.

To make these contingency tables the program must pick one or more thresholds when dealing with numeric variables. In other words, the program turns a numeric into a binary (logical) variable by trying various comparison points.

The best discriminator turns out to be

(Saltire > 0)

which is only true for confederate flags, though it is false for both kinds of flag. (The original ID3 could not cope with unrestricted numeric attributes, but it can easily be extended to do so, as we have done here.)

The test (Saltire > 0) is thus established as the root of the tree, as shown in Fig. 11.2.

For the next stage, the left branch can be left alone: it only contains one type of data (confederate). But the right branch needs to be further subdivided, using essentially the same method on the subset of 21 cases for which the top-level test is false.

One of the weaknesses of ID3 appears as the subdivision progresses. It always subdivides the subsets until no single exception remains. So even groups where one kind of data outnumbers the other by, for example, 20 to 1 have to be subdivided. This striving for 100% correct rules is appropriate for chess, where perfection is potentially attainable, but on realistically noisy data it can cause ID3 to generate very bushy trees whose nodes contain very few examples. These are unlikely to be statistically reliable when the tree is later used for classification. Furthermore, large branchy tree structures are difficult for people to comprehend.

Once the tree has been grown, it can be used to make decisions about new examples, by applying the tests and following down the appropriate branches to a terminal node. Thus if we asked, in effect, 'Is Britain a confederate state?' it would reply Yes, because the British flag does have an X-shaped cross. (Well, Britain did lend support to the South during the US Civil War.)

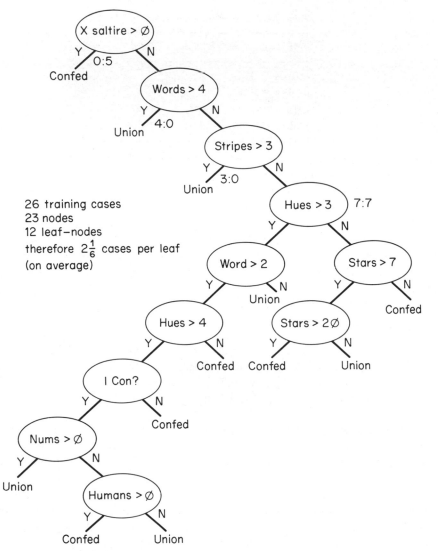

26 training cases
23 nodes
12 leaf-nodes
therefore $2\frac{1}{6}$ cases per leaf
(on average)

Fig. 11.2 Example flag discrimination tree

The decision tree format is quite natural for human readers but it has its problems.

The problem of excessive subdivision could be cured simply by stopping early. For instance, any subgroup that contained fewer than, say, 4% of the training examples could be deemed too small for further division. When the tree was used to categorize new cases and such a node was reached, the system could give a probabilistic answer. Thus, in the diagram, on reaching a node with 3 union and 1 confederate instances, the system could respond with '75% Union' instead of saying 'don't know'. Realistically, such a group is too small to split up any further.

There are many domains where certainty is not attainable, and a probabilistic answer based on a reasonable sample is preferable to an exact answer based on a tiny sample. Systems which halt the subdivision early, based on tests of statistical significance, and systems which prune unnecessary branches off an overly subdivided tree have been reported to out-perform the basic ID3 method. (See Breiman *et al.*, 1984; Bratko and Lavrac, 1987.)

A more serious problem concerns the nature of the description language itself. The decision tree is actually a rather restrictive language. All the tests have to be in the form of a comparison between one variable and one constant, such as (Hues > 3). Tests like

(Stars > = Stripes)

and

(Hues > 4) OR (Humans > 0)

might well prove useful, but the system could never find them. They are literally inexpressible.

This is the price paid for ID3's efficiency. It is relatively quick, but this speed is purchased at a cost. Clearly a more expressive description language would make the tree-growing far more complex; but the poverty of its description language places the burden of devising an effective set of descriptors squarely on the user. Any preliminary calculations or logical operations have to be incorporated in the attributes of the input data before running the program.

ID3 forms the basis of several commercial induction packages marketed, such as ExTran and 1st-class. The ExTran system is not especially good at rule induction on large databases, but it is good at getting experts to formalize their knowledge by presenting tutorial examples. In general it is better with made-up (idealized) training data than with a training set of real examples. Good results have been reported using ExTran as an expert-system building tool by Asgari and Modesitt (1986) and by Michie (1986), among others.

11.5 AQ11 AND INDUCE

The series of programs developed by Michalski and his colleagues at the University of Illinois use more powerful description languages than ID3.

The program AQ11 (Michalski and Larson, 1978; Michalski and Chilausky, 1980) is the one which found better rules for soybean disease diagnosis than a human expert. (See also Chapter 1 of this volume.) For that particular experiment, they collected 630 questionnaires describing diseased plants. Each plant was measured on 35 features (called 'descriptors'). The 36th descriptor was the diagnosis of an expert in plant biology. There were 15 disease categories altogether.

AQ11 generated rules in a language called VL1, where a description is a set of terms called 'selectors'. The rule below (D3), which the system produced for classifying Rhizoctonia Root Rot, illustrates the language.

D3:   [leaves = normal] [stem = abnormal]
          [stem cankers = below soil line]
          [canker lesion color = brown]
OR
          [leaf malformation = absent] [stem = abnormal]
          [stem cankers = below soil line]
          [canker lesion color = brown]

This rule consists of two descriptions linked by an OR: it is a disjunction. Each description happens to consist of four selectors, such as [stem = abnormal], which are linked by logical ANDs. That is to say, AND is implied between selectors, so that a description in VL1 is a conjunction of terms. Each selector compares one variable with a constant (or range of constants).

As a matter of fact, this particular disjunction is trivial. The only difference between the two descriptions, [leaves = normal] versus [leaf malformation = absent], would be unnecessary if the system realized that one was a special case of the other.

This diagnostic rule (D3) and 14 others were generated from 290 training instances. The training set was selected from the 630 cases by a program called ESEL, which picks examples that are 'far apart', or different from each other, to give a broad coverage. Michalski did not report what AQ11 would do with a randomly chosen training set, so the effect of this selection strategy is unclear.

The 15 computer-generated rules were used to classify the remaining 340 cases, with great success. Whereas the human expert's rules gave the correct first choice disease on 71.8% of the test cases, AQ11's rules gave correct first choice on 97.6% of the unseen cases. This performance is in fact a landmark in machine learning: it shows that high-quality expert knowledge can be synthesized from raw data.

AQ11 works in an incremental fashion, each step appending another conjunctive term (i.e. a new selector) starting off from a null description. The idea is to introduce new items of evidence one at a time, or a few at a time, and extend the growing rule to deal with them. The AQ11 method can be outlined in the following pseudo-code.

```
P = {set of Positive instances of the concept}
N = {set of Negative instances of the concept}
A = {answer set, initially empty}
G = {set of most general rules, initially null}
repeat until P is empty:
   [choose an element p from P;
   apply 1-sided Candidate Elimination with p versus
      N using a conjunctive rule language;
   select a description g from G;
   append g to A;
```

remove from P all elements covered by g;
    ]
save and/or display A.

The main step in this top-level algorithm is best understood as a one-sided variant of the candidate elimination algorithm: there is a G set of maximally general descriptions (see Section 11.3) but no S set. The place of the S set is taken by a single example, p. The method specializes G as little as possible to exclude all N (negative examples).

If a single conjunctive description cannot be found to cover all positive examples, AQ11 will generate several, linked by ORs, as we saw with rule D3.

In the soybean work, the system made a complete pass through the data for each disease type, treating cases of that disease as positive examples and all other cases as negative examples. (AQ11 is not a very fast program.) It is also possible for AQ11 to treat previously generated rules as negative examples: this enables it to come up with non-overlapping rules where the categories are mutually exclusive.

AQ11 rules start off very general and become more and more specific. It adds new terms to exclude negative examples, while still covering as many positive cases as possible. The successor of AQ11, Induce 1.2 (Dietterich and Michalski, 1981), works the other way round. It starts with very specific descriptions and keeps on generalizing. It also uses a richer description language called VL2, a form of 'annotated predicate calculus'. This allows quantifiers, functions and relational predicates with more than one argument. A VL2 description of the an arch, for example, could be

(EXISTS A, B, C)
[Touching (A, B)] [Touching (A, C)]
[Ontop (A, B)] [Ontop (A, C)]
[Shape (A) = Pyramid]
[Shape (B) = Block] [Shape (C) = Block]

Induce explores the description space by the method of Beam Search. This is a modified best-first strategy that preserves a small number of descriptions at each stage.

The progress of a Beam Search is illustrated in Fig. 11.3. Here we show the search fanning out upwards. At each level only the seven best nodes are retained. All the other nodes are pruned away, and do not generate any successors. Each node in the diagram represents a description. Upper levels are more general (i.e. cover more cases) than lower ones. In this case the tree grows upwards only. As in Fig. 11.1, the same node/description can sometimes be reached by two or more routes.

Induce employs the Beam Search, as outlined below.

1. Set H to contain a randomly chosen subset of size W of the training instances. (These are also rules which happen to be very specific.)

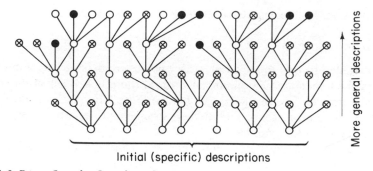

More general descriptions

Initial (specific) descriptions

Fig. 11.3 Beam Search. ●, rule node; ○, parent node; ⊗, pruned node

2. Generalize each description in H as little a possible.
3. Prune implausible descriptions, retaining the best W only. The best are those that are simple and cover many examples; the worst are those that are complex and cover few examples.
4. If any description in H covers enough examples, print it out. If H is empty or enough rules have been printed, stop; otherwise continue from step 2.

We are deliberately vague about the criteria for evaluating descriptions, and hence deciding which ones to prune. Obviously rules should be brief and they should cover many positive and few negative examples, but various trade-offs are possible. Induce provides several preference measures which can be combined to give an evaluation function tailored for a particular application.

Induce works from specific descriptions to more general ones. It is easy to start it off with an initial set because it uses the 'single representation trick'. In other words, the VL2 language expresses both the rules and the training instances. A training instance can be regarded as a highly specific rule – a class with only one member (or possibly a few members if there are repeated examples).

To turn an event description into a rule, or a rule into a more general one, Michalski's program uses a variety of generalization operators. We can illustrate some of them by encoding another flag (this time the national flag of Canada) in a version of VL2.

(EXISTS X, Y, Z) [Background = White]
[Hue (X) = Red] [Hue (Y) = Red] [Hue (Z) = Red]
[Type (X) = Bar] [Type (Y) = Maple Leaf] [Type (Z) = Bar]
[Left-of (X, Y)] [Left-of (Y, Z)] [Left-of (X, Y)]
[Width = 50] [Height = 25]
[Hues = 2]

As well as encoding simple features, such as [Width = 50], VL2 can express structural relationships, such as [Left-of (Y, Z)], which is a step forward from the flag descriptions we used in the previous section. To put it another way, it can handle binary predicates as well as unary ones. It can in fact handle predicates with more than two arguments, if required.

Let us now consider some ways of generalizing this description.

1. Dropping conditions: e.g. delete the last four lines of the above description to create a new description that applies to any flag with a white background and three red objects or regions;
2. Internal disjunction: e.g. [Hue(X) = Red] ⇒ [Hue(X) = Red, Blue]. This now also covers a variant of the Canadian flag with a blue bar on the left-hand side;
3. Relax a constraint: e.g. [Height = 25] ⇒ [Height > 24] or ⇒ [Height < 26]. These effectively introduce disjunctions.
4. Make a constant into a (don't-care) variable: e.g. [Type (X) = Bar] ⇒ [Type (?) = Bar], where the question mark stands for any object, meaning that any object can be a bar. Again, this is a way of introducing an implicit disjunction.

Other methods of generalization have been described earlier. A point which needs stressing is that computers can very easily perform the previously mysterious process called 'generalization' by simple syntactic manipulations. To put it another way: induction by machine is easy; useful induction is hard. The problem is not that machines cannot generalize. On the contrary, there are too many ways of generalizing. This is why Induce only makes minimal generalizations on each cycle (step 2). The successors of a node are produced by applying one generalization operator in only one way.

For example, the dropping-conditions method (no. 1) would cause the generation of 13 successors to the Canadian flag description, since it contains 13 terms. Each successor would differ from the original in having one condition dropped. The program would not drop two or more conditions at once. Nor would it drop a condition and apply another generalizing rule (such as relaxing a constraint) in the same step. For that to happen would require at least two cycles. This is mainly a question of efficiency: if all generalization operators were applied in all possible ways, there would be an astronomical number of new nodes.

The trouble is that even single-change generalizations can lead to an enormous proliferation of descriptions at each stage, especially with an expressive language like VL2. It is highly likely that some which are unpromising in themselves, but which would lead to good descriptions a few more steps down the line, will be pruned away. This ensures that the Induce algorithm is non-optimal (though in practice it performs very well).

One final point about Induce, not so far mentioned, is that it can run the search in two distinct phases. In the first phase it searches the 'structure-only space'. That is to say, it ignores the unary attributes and does a Beam Search using only multi-argument predicates, such as Ontop-of or Left-of. Then, having found a set of descriptions using relational predicates only, it enters a second phase, which is a search of the 'attribute-only space'. At this point the unary features are considered. It is not yet clear, however, whether this two-stage approach is generally useful.

11.6 META-DENDRAL

The Meta-Dendral system (Buchanan, 1976; Buchanan and Mitchell, 1978) has discovered several rules of chemistry that were previously unknown. Specifically it found new cleavage rules that describe how organic molecules, of the Ketoandrostane group and others, break up in a mass-spectrometer. These rules were later incorporated into the knowledge base of Dendral (Buchanan and Feigenbaum, 1978), one of the classic expert systems, which interprets mass-spectra.

The training patterns are produced by an instrument that bombards chemical samples with accelerated electrons, causing them to break up. The fragments are then passed through an electromagnetic field that separates out the fragments with low charge and high mass, which are not deflected much by the field, from those of low mass and high charge, which are deflected considerably. This gives rise to a plot of intensity against mass-to-charge ratio.

A trained chemist can look at such a plot and identify the molecular structure of the compound that produced it by noting where the peaks are. So can Dendral. In doing so it tests its own hypotheses against a simulation of a mass-spectrometer. Meta-Dendral was designed to enhance this internal model of the device by discovering additional fragmentation rules.

Meta-Dendral contains two main programs, Rulegen and Rulemod. Rulegen performs a relatively crude search of the space of potential cleavage rules, using only positive training instances. It moves in the direction from general to specific. It starts with the most general rule possible (that some atomic bond will break) and gradually specializes it. At each stage it creates offspring of existing rules by making them more specific in various ways – i.e. stating more precisely which bonds will break under what circumstances. A descendant rule is retained if:

1. it predicts fewer fragmentations per molecule than its parent (i.e. is more specific)
2. it still predicts fragmentations for at least half of the training molecules
3. it predicts fragmentations for as many molecules as its parent (unless the parent was 'too general').

Rulemod takes the rules produced by Rulegen and performs minor alterations designed to improve their performance – both by generalizing and specializing. In particular, it takes account of negative evidence.

Meta-Dendral can handle noise, which can arise from impurities in the samples, from imperfections in the instrument and from errors introduced by the program that transforms the training instances into a suitable form for processing. In addition, it has achieved respectable performance: some of its discoveries were written up and published in a chemical journal (see Michie and Johnston, 1985).

The real weakness of Meta-Dendral is the fact that its description language is specifically designed to be good for expressing rules about molecular structures and how they spilt up – and for virtually nothing else. However, Meta-Dendral's high performance in its restricted field suggests that building special-purpose learning systems, rather than attempting to use one general induction package on a variety of data, may be a viable strategy.

11.7 BRINGING HOME THE BACON

Another discovery system worthy of note is the Bacon series of programs (Langley, 1977 and 1981).

One of these programs, Bacon. 4, 'rediscovered' – among other things – Ohm's Law, Archimedes's Principle of Displacement, Newton's Law of Gravitational Attraction and almost all of nineteeth century chemistry.

Bacon. 4 is presented with training instances such as Table 11.3.

Here the length of day, length of year, mean distance from the sun, diameter, mass and number of satellites for all the members of the solar system have been tabulated. (We have taken the liberty of including data for Omega Solaris, the totally inconspicuous brown dwarf companion of our sun, which has not yet been discovered – even by Bacon. 4!)

To emulate Kepler, and discover that the square of the orbital period (Year) of a planet is proportional to the cube of its distance from the sun, the program has to note concomitant variations. For example the length of day appears to vary inversely with the diameter, while the year and the distance vary together. This sort of observation leads Bacon. 4 to create new columns in the table, formed by

Table 11.3 Planetary Data.

Planet	Day	Year	Dist.	Diam.	Mass	Moons
Mercury	58.00	0.24	0.39	0.38	0.05	0
Venus	244.00	0.62	0.72	0.95	0.85	0
Earth	1.0	1.0	1.0	1.0	1.0	1
Mars	1.03	1.88	1.52	0.53	0.11	2
Ceres	999.99	4.60	2.77	0.08	0.00	0
Jupiter	0.41	11.86	5.20	11.19	318.35	16
Saturn	0.43	29.46	9.54	9.41	95.30	15
Uranus	0.67	84.01	19.19	4.06	14.60	5
Neptune	0.75	164.80	30.07	3.88	17.30	2
Pluto	6.38	248.40	39.52	0.24	0.08	1
Omega Solaris	3.25	680.00	77.22	19.48	800	7

Table 11.4 Baconian Induction.

	Y	D	Y/D	(Y/D)/D	((Y/D)/D) × Y	(((Y/D)/D) × Y)/D
Mercury	0.24	0.39	0.62	1.61	0.39	1.00
Venus	0.61	0.72	0.85	1.18	0.72	1.00
Earth	1.00	1.00	1.00	1.00	1.00	1.00
Mars	1.88	1.52	1.23	0.81	1.52	1.00
Ceres	4.60	2.77	1.66	0.60	2.76	1.00
Jupiter	11.86	5.20	2.28	0.44	5.20	1.00
Saturn	29.46	9.54	3.09	0.32	9.54	1.00
Uranus	84.01	19.19	4.38	0.23	19.17	1.00
Neptune	164.80	30.07	5.48	0.18	30.04	1.00
Pluto	248.40	39.52	6.29	0.16	39.51	1.00
O. Solaris	680.00	77.22	8.81	0.11	77.55	1.00

The figures are correct to two decimal digits.

fairly straightforward arithmetical combinations of existing ones – using division, multiplication etc.

Bacon.4 proceeds step by step in its search for constancies. This is shown in Table 11.4, where all the variables apart from Y (year) and D (distance) have been ignored.

Bacon.4's first step, having noted that Y and D vary together, would be to divide one by the other, forming the Y/D column. This still varies with D so the next column, (Y/D)/D, is created. Now it has overdone it, but it notices that the new column varies inversely with Y, so it multiplies by Y, giving the fifth column ((Y/D)/D) × Y. This now agrees almost perfectly with D. Eventually it finds a column like the last one, with a constant value to within a pre-defined tolerance. That is what it was looking for. It can be expressed more clearly as $(Y \times Y)/(D \times D \times D)$. In a sense, the program has re-capitulated Kepler's discovery that Y squared equals D cubed.

For exposition, our table cuts out the many blind alleys and red herrings which Bacon.4 would probably explore. (Kepler, too, spent plenty of time on such things.) For example the program, given this data, might well go looking at the relationship of distance with rank position – perhaps even to the extent of re-formulating Bode's notorious 'law', or something like it. Or it might try to relate the number of satellites to the mass of a planet and its distance from the sun. (Readers may care to investigate this for themselves.)

Essentially, Bacon.4's method can be summed up in three rules:

1. If column X has a near-constant value, then formulate a rule involving X;
2. Otherwise, if column X increases as column Y increases, then make a new column of the ratio X/Y and repeat from 1;
3. Otherwise, if column X increases as column Y decreases, then make a new column of the product X × Y and repeat from 1.

Bacon.4, like most scientists, has rather strong preconceptions about the form scientific laws should take – i.e. that the relations between significant quantities should be mathematically simple. Human scientists often express this as an aesthetic principle: that Nature (or God) is clever but not devious; or that the beauty of Truth is its simplicity. Philosophers, however, sometimes take a different view, namely that the human mind is only capable of discovering certain rather simple regularities in nature.

The main drawback of Bacon.4 is that it cannot cope with much noise. It needs a training set without significant exceptions, and thus cannot find approximate statistical laws.

11.8 A DATABASE THAT LEARNS

A learning system rather different from those so far described is the UNIMEM system of Lebowitz (1986). UNIMEM employs a memory organization called GBM, Generalization-Based Memory. Essentially it is a database which reorganizes itself dynamically as new items of information are added. It is much more like human memory than any previous database system: it forms generalized concept descriptions as a by-product of attempting to keep the information it holds organized for efficient retrieval.

UNIMEM is intended to take a series of examples in a domain and store them in permanent long-term memory. As it does so, it notices examples that are similar and generalizes them, forming specialized versions of concepts that can later be used in question-answering tasks. The key idea behind UNIMEM is Generalization-Based Memory (GBM). A system that uses a GBM creates a hierarchy of concepts to describe a situation or domain. It builds up this hierarchy by generalizing from a small number of examples, and then records in memory specific items in terms of the generalized concepts. More specific generalizations are also recorded along with specific examples under the more general cases. GBM involves identifying and defining multiple concepts, as opposed to maintaining a single model of a concept.

UNIMEM has been tested on several domains, including US Universities and Congressional voting records. Two typical concepts derived by UNIMEM from information about the United States are given below.

Features: high urban percentage, low minority percentage, moderate income, low taxes;
Examples: RI, NJ, TX, MI, FLA, OH.
Features: high value of farmland, fairly high population, manufacturing, agriculture, tourism important;
Examples: NC, ARK, TENN, MINN, WI, VA, MO.

Thus UNIMEM forms conceptual clusters. Unlike most of the systems so far described, it does not need to be told whether each case is a positive or negative example of the concept being taught: it decides on its own conceptual structuring.

This is usually called 'unsupervised learning', though Lebowitz prefers the term 'learning by observation'. In addition, UNIMEM is relatively resistant to noise. No concept can be created (or refuted) on the basis of a single example; and although it forms concepts on the basis of small numbers of cases, it maintains the required statistical information to alter its conceptual hierarchy if new and contradictory examples are observed.

UNIMEM is best regarded as a signpost towards a new direction in database design. One day it will be commonplace for databases to restructure themselves as new information arrives. The function of passively recording information will still be there, but in addition to recording data the system will automatically attempt to classify and interpret it – i.e. to notice regularities.

11.9 GENETIC ALGORITHMS

John Holland's theoretical treatment of adaptation (1975) was ignored by the AI community for several years, but recently a number of research groups have used his ideas as the basis for effective learning systems. The basic algorithm has a biological flavour. It deliberately imitates what Darwin and Mendel, among others, have taught us about the process of evolution by natural selection – an exceptionally well-tried method, after three billion years of field testing!

The essence of a genetic algorithm is that the expected number of 'offspring' of a rule is proportional to the success of that rule in the task being learned. This corresponds to the idea of 'survival of the fittest' (a phrase due to Herbert Spencer, not Darwin).

Many people misunderstand the basis on which genetic algorithms work (as indeed many people still misunderstand the theory of biological evolution). The genetic algorithm as a computational procedure is best understood as an advanced form of the 'Monte Carlo' method often used in operational research. Using the basic Monte Carlo approach, a computer simply generates potential solutions, evaluates them and retains the one with the highest score. The longer the system runs, the greater the probability that it will find a solution within a pre-set distance from the optimum. When no analytic or algorithmic solution method is known, the Monte Carlo technique offers a pragmatic fall-back.

Genetic algorithms, however, though based on the use of random choices, take the Monte Carlo idea one stage further by maintaining a population of potential solutions and biasing the search for new candidate solutions towards regions of the search space that have proved successful in past trials. Thus evolutionary methods do not use blind trial and error, but employ a guided heuristic search.

Genetic algorithms have been used in many practical applications. One learning system based on evolutionary principles is the present author's BEAGLE package (Forsyth, 1981; Forsyth and Rada, 1986). The BEAGLE learning algorithm consists of repeating the following procedure for a number of generations, where each generation is a complete run through the training data.

1. Evaluate each rule on every sample with a penalty deducted based on the length of the rule (cf. Occam's Razor);
2. Rank the rules in descending order of merit and remove the worst-performing 50% (approximately);
3. Replace 'dead' rules by applying the MATE procedure to a pair of randomly chosen survivors, thus slicing and re-splicing segments of good rules;
4. Mutate a few randomly chosen rules (but not the best one) and apply procedure TIDY to all new rules, ready for the next generation.

The MATE procedure picks sub-expressions at random from the surviving rules and links them together with a randomly chosen connective.

(The TIDY procedure merely cuts out certain syntactic redundancies such as double negatives, constant sub-expressions and so forth – leaving the pruned rule-tree with the same value but expressed more succinctly.)

A BEAGLE rule looks like a Boolean expression in a conventional procedural programming language, such as C or Pascal. Below are three machine-generated BEAGLE rules.

((BARS < = (POPULATION*RED))&
(RELIGION < (CRESCENT + 0.9998)))

((LANDMASS − ZONE) < = 0.0000)

((PRESSURE − 997) < = MAXTEMP)

The first two were produced when the system was assigned the task of distinguishing Spanish-speaking from non-Spanish-speaking countries on the basis of data about national flags, population, size, geographic location etc. The third rule comes from a weather-forecasting trial where the object was to predict rain on the following day based on temperature, pressure, sunshine and other readings from the London weather centre.

To interpret the first two rules you need to know the meaning of the field names. BARS are the number of vertical bars in the flag. POPULATION is the population of the country in millions. RED equals 0 if red absent, 1 if present in the flag. RELIGION is 0 for Catholic, 1 for other Christian, 2 and above for other faiths/ideologies. CRESCENT is 0 if no crescent moon symbol in flag, 1 otherwise. LANDMASS is 1 for N. America, 2 for S. America, 3 for Europe, 4 for Africa, 5 for Asia, 6 for Oceania. ZONE is 1 for Northeast, 2 for Southeast, 3 for Southwest, 4 for Northwest (with reference to the Greenwich meridian and the Equator).

(There were many other fields in the training data: most of them turned out not to be useful for the task in hand.)

BEAGLE is only one system based on the evolutionary principle. In recent years genetic algorithms have been used for a wide variety of applications (not just rule-learning). To give just two examples: Rechenberg (1984) has employed an evolutionary strategy to design propeller and windmill blades; Goldberg (1985)

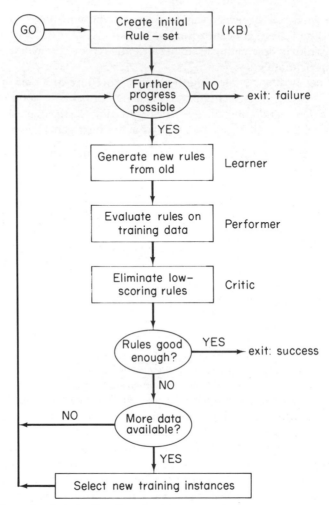

Fig. 11.4 General rule induction flowchart

has employed a genetic algorithm as an adaptive controller optimizing gas flow in a natural gas pipeline.

The great advantage of evolutionary methods is their robustness: they are very general and robust in the face of noise. Their main disadvantage is representational: problem variables are typically coded in terms of fixed-length bit strings (0101**...) to make the operations of mutation, inversion and crossover more easily implemented. This can lead to an inscrutable knowledge representation.

One additional point in favour of genetic algorithms that has not been widely recognized should be mentioned here: they are inherently parallel. In the natural model, many organisms compete for food and mates simultaneously. Evolutionary algorithms are very simplified versions of what goes on in nature, but they share the inherent parallelism of the natural process. At present this parallelism has to be simulated inefficiently on sequential processors. When the new generation of highly concurrent computers arrives, genetic algorithms will look even better than they do today.

11.10 SUMMARY

Conjecture + Refutation is said to be at the heart of all scientific discovery (Popper, 1959). In one way or another, all the systems described here generate potential solutions and then test them, typically discarding the majority.

There are various methods of generation, various measures of quality for the generated rules, various ways of handling training data, and so on. For example, there are model-driven (top-down) generators, guided by prior assumptions about the form of hypotheses (e.g. Meta-Dendral); and there are data-driven (bottom-up) generators, guided by patterns in the training data (e.g. Induce). However, the idea of learning as search provides a framework within which these divergent approaches can be unified.

Figure 11.4 shows a generalized outline of rule-generation as a search process. Numerous variations on the common theme can be obtained by making particular choices about how exactly to fill the boxes. For instance, the production of new descriptions from current descriptions may be predominantly from specific to general, or *vice versa*, or either way. Independently, the evaluation may take account mainly of positive evidence, mainly negative evidence, or both equally.

Likewise the number of plausible rule structures retained on each cycle may vary. In Quinlan's and Winston's programs (Winston, 1984), only a single rule is kept. Other systems keep as many as will fit in RAM. In addition, different systems make different choices about how many training items to focus on at any one time. This can range from examining a single instance at a time (e.g. UNIMEM), through the concept of a window of selected instances (e.g. ID3), to taking the entire training set (e.g. BEAGLE).

Finally, of course, description languages differ greatly. The description language limits what can be learned. Even more important, it determines how well people can understand the results of the learning process. (See also Forsyth and Rada, 1986.)

It is vital that humans should be able to understand knowledge derived inductively by machines, because we have already crossed an important frontier: AQ11 produced a knowledge base superior to any human expert's; EURISKO (Lenat, 1983) devised a 3D logic gate for which a patent was subsequently granted. These are still early days, but it may be understating the case to say that machine induction techniques could transform the field of expert systems. They could eventually transform science as a whole, for once machines take over the creative act of scientific discovery a revolution more profound than the one initiated by Galileo will have taken place. And that changed the world.

11.11 REFERENCES

Asgari, D. and Modesitt, K. (1986) Space shuttle main engine test analysis: a case study for inductive knowledge-based systems involving very large databases. *Proc. IEEE,* 65–71.

Bratko, I. and Lavrac, N. (eds) (1987) *Progress in Machine Learning.* Sigma Press, Wilmslow.

Breiman, L., Friedman, J., Olshen, R. and Stone, C. (1984) *Classification and Regression Trees.* Wadsworth, California.

Buchanan, B. (1976) Scientific theory formation by computer. In J. C. Simon, (ed.) *Computer Oriented Learning Processes.* Noordhoff, Leyden.

Buchanan, B. G. and Feigenbaum, E. (1978) Dendral and meta-dendral: their applications dimension. *Artificial Intelligence,* **11,** 5–24.

Buchanan, B. G. and Mitchell, T. (1978) Model-directed learning of production rules. In Waterman and Hayes-Roth (eds) *Pattern-Directed Inference Systems.* Academic Press, N.Y.

Dietterich, T. and Michalski, R. (1981) Inductive learning of structural descriptions. *Artificial Intelligence,* **16,** 257–94.

Forsyth, R. (1981) BEAGLE: A Darwinian approach to pattern recognition. *Kybernetes,* **10,** 159–66.

Forsyth, R. and Rada, R. (1986) *Machine Learning: Applications in Expert Systems and Information Retrieval:* Ellis Horwood, Chichester.

Goldberg, D. (1985) Genetic algorithms and rule learning in dynamic system control: *Proc. Internat. Conf. on Genetic Algorithms and their Applications,* Carnegie-Mellon Univ., Pittsburgh PA.

Hart, A. E. (1985) Experience in the use of an inductive system in knowledge engineering. In Bramer, M. (ed.) *Research & Development in Expert Systems,* Cambridge University Press, Cambridge.

Holland, J. (1975) *Adaptation in Natural and Artificial Systems.* University of Michigan Press, Ann Arbor, Michigan.

Hunt, E., Marin, and Stone (1966) *Experiments in Induction.* Academic Press, N.Y.

Langley, P. (1977) Rediscovering physics with Bacon-3: *Proc. 5th IJCAI.*

Langley, P. (1981) Data-driven discovery of physical laws. *Cognitive Science,* **5,** 31–54.

Larson, J. and Michalski, R. (1978) Inductive inference of VL decision rules. In Waterman and Hayes-Roth (eds), *Pattern-Directed Inference Systems.* Academic Press, N.Y.

Lebowitz, M. (1986) UNIMEM, a general learning system: *Proc. 7th European Conf. on AI,* Brighton.

Lenat, D. (1982) The nature of heuristics: *Artificial Intelligence,* **16,** 61–98.

Lenat, D. (1983) The nature of heuristics III. *Artificial Intelligence,* **19,** 189–249.

Michalski, Carbonell and Mitchell (eds) (1983) *Machine Learning, Vol. 1,* Tioga Press, Palo Alto, CA.

Michalski, R. and Chilausky, R. L. (1980) Knowledge acquisition by encoding expert rules versus computer induction from examples: a case study involving soybean pathology. *Internat. J. Man-Machine Studies,* **12,** 63–87.

Michalski, R. and Larson, J. B. (1978) *Selection of Most Representative Training Examples & Incremental Generation of VL1 Hypotheses.....* Report 867, Univ. Illinois, Urbana.

Michie, D. (1986) *On Machine Intelligence,* 2nd ed. Ellis Horwood, Chichester.

Michie, D. and Johnston, R. (1985) *The Creative Computer:* Pelican Books, Harmondsworth.

Mitchell, T. (1982) Generalization as search. *Artificial Intelligence,* **18,** 203–26.

Popper, K. (1959) *The Logic of Scientific Discovery*. Basic Books, N.Y.

Quinlan, J. R. (1979) Induction over large databases *Report HPP-79-14*, Stanford University.

Quinlan, J. R. (1982) Semi-autonomous acquisition of pattern-based knowledge. In D. Michie (ed.) *Introductory Readings in Expert Systems*. Gordon & Breach, London.

Quinlan, J. R. (1986) Induction of decision trees. *Machine Learning*, 1, 1.

Rechenberg, I. (1984) *The Evolution Strategy: A Mathematical Model of Darwinian Evolution*. Tech. University of Berlin Report, W. Berlin.

Wellbank, M. (1983) *A Review of Knowledge Acquisition Techniques for Expert Systems*. British Telecom Research, Ipswich.

Winston, P. (1984) *Artificial Intelligence*, 2nd ed. Addison-Wesley, Mass.

12

Expert systems and the knowledge revolution

TOM STONIER

12.1 THE ECONOMICS OF INFORMATION

12.1.1 The importance of knowledge as an input into productive systems

There exists no economic activity without an information input. The palaeolithic hunter tracking the spoor of his prey was using information. The medieval farmer ploughing his field, or his wife spinning fleece were using information. Information may exist in an accumulated form – embedded in the history of a device such as a deep plough or a spinning wheel. Every machine contains within it a history of innovation and invention. This accumulation of information is as important as the accumulation of capital.

Any object or material can be made more valuable by adding information: waste desert land plus information becomes productive crop land. Ignorant labourers plus education become skilled, highly productive operatives. Idle capital plus information becomes revenue-yielding investment. Useless energy like sunshine or ocean waves can be made to perform useful work when you know how. Information can add value not only to other inputs such as land or labour, it can add value to itself. 'Data' may be converted to 'knowledge' by analysing it, cross-referring, selecting, sorting, summarizing, or in some other way organizing the data. Knowledge is more valuable than data, it is data transformed into a meaningful guide for specific purposes. Information added to human beings through education, adds value to those human beings. It is for this reason that education is an ever-growing industry which in the long run will absorb a larger share of the gross national product than any other single economic activity and which will absorb a larger share of the labour force than any other employer.

Information has displaced land, labour and capital as the most important input into modern productive systems. Information reduces the requirement for land, labour and capital; it also reduces the requirements for raw materials and energy. For example, when land becomes very expensive, as it does in the centre of large cities, tower blocks and skyscrapers reduce the *per capita* requirement for land. When tractors displaced horses, large tracts of land dedicated to growing horse fodder became available for other purposes. In both instances information, largely in the form of advanced technology, obviated the inputs of land.

In a similar manner, every time a robot displaces a worker, information in the form of new knowledge and technology is displacing labour. Likewise, the displacement of capital (itself an information concept) may be exemplified by the computer industry: Chris Evans in his book *The Mighty Micro* (Evans, 1979) has pointed out that had the automobile industry made as much progress as had the computer industry over the thirty years since the end of the Second World War, it would have been possible to purchase a Rolls Royce for £1.35, obtain three million miles to the gallon in it, and park six of them on a pinhead – reflecting the reduction in capital, energy and materials inputs.

In addition, as with computers, new information spawns entire new industries, as well as being sold in its own right. Information is the raw material for the fastest growing sector of the economy – the knowledge industry.

It was the economist, Fritz Machlup (1962), who helped define the knowledge industry in the early 1960s and who pointed out that 'education' is the largest of the knowledge industries. Machlup included not only formal educational institutions but also education in the home, the church, and in the armed services. The sociologist, Daniel Bell (1973), extended Machlup's statistics and amplified his concepts. Bell also emphasized the 'centrality' of knowledge in modern economic systems. Marc Porat (1976) updated the pioneering studies of Machlup and Bell in the 1970s. Porat divided the information sector of the economy into two major sub-groups: the 'primary information sector', which includes those firms supplying information, either as goods or services to the market (i.e. other firms and consumers); and the 'secondary information sector', which includes all the information services provided for internal consumption by government and private non-information firms. For example, a manufacturing firm needs to run an office. In fact, as a result of the advances in production technology, the office staff now represents a substantially larger share of the labour force than does the factory.

According to Porat, in 1967 the primary information sector of the United States accounted for 25% of its GNP; the secondary sector accounted for an additional 21%. Therefore, the total economic information activity accounted for 46% of the GNP. Machlup (1980) has pointed out that although Porat's analysis involved different criteria from his own, the overall findings 'are well in tune with the aggregates I had presented. . .'.

Inspired by Porat, the OECD calculated the post-war growth of the information sector for a number of member states (as reviewed by Huppes, 1987). According to the OECD criteria, only 41% of the US economy was included in the information sector in 1970. However, by the 1970s, the information sector had pulled ahead of services, industry, and agriculture in countries like France, West Germany, Sweden, and the UK, comprising roughly a third of each nation's economy. We are now a decade and a half beyond that point, and information technology has become formally recognized in its own right. To give an indication of IT growth: in 1967 there were about fifteen thousand computer terminals in use in the USA, by 1980 there were probably in excess of two million. Computer databases were so scant at that time that on-line searches hardly existed in the 1960s. In the 1970s, the number of on-line searches rose into the hundreds of thousands; while in the 1980s these rose into the millions.

12.1.2 Information as a resource

Information may be sold directly as in electronic databases or in newspapers; information may also be sold as a wealth creator. This is true when an inventor or an author sells a patent or a copyright or provides a licence for others to manufacture an invention. Owning a good patent can be worth a lot more than owning a whole factory. Therefore, information may generate wealth in its own right.

When information is coupled to people, we find that educated and skilled labour tends to be more productive. Hence, there is a continuous selective pressure favouring the educated and skilled, while the uninformed and unskilled are discriminated against. The worker with a shovel is displaced by the bulldozer driver; the filing clerk is displaced by the computer programmer.

Universities provide employment and improve human capital. They also produce new ideas and new industries. Silicon Valley, Oxford and Cambridge are all filled with industries whose manpower and ideas emanated directly from the universities. Of interest to information technologists is the basic research in solid state physics which preceded and led to the transistor. The location of the semi-conductor industry in the early 1950s, prior to the Silicon Valley phenomena, clustered along Route 128 in Boston. Many of the founders of these new companies were graduates of the Massachusetts Institute of Technology, Harvard, and other local universities who frequently either recruited other staff from local universities or consulted with university experts.

12.2 THE RISE OF THE INFORMATION OPERATIVES

Probably the earliest people to make a living as information operatives on a part- or full-time basis were medicine men and priests. In due course they evolved into professional wise men. In ancient Greece, if you were good, you could make a lot of money. Adam Smith calculated how much wealth those most famous of ancient information operatives, the Greek philosophers, made. He came to the conclusion that Socrates, for example, charged ten minae per student and had a hundred such students. Therefore he was making a thousand minae, worth well over three thousand pounds sterling (eighteenth century pounds) for each course of lectures. Another example is Gorgias who made a present to the temple at Delphi of a life-sized statue of himself in solid gold. Plutarch, Plato, Aristotle, all became men of means judging from a variety of accounts.

Today the labour force is dominated by information operatives. That is to say, there are by far more people who make their living working with information than any other single category of worker. Even those working on farms, in factories, or with machinery increasingly need to know more in order to avail themselves of new technology. Information operatives can be categorized into one of the following six categories:

1. A relatively small group involved with creating new information. This includes scientists, artists, statisticians, architects, designers, that is anybody who either creates new information or is weaving new patterns of knowledge from existing information;
2. A large group is involved with the transmission of information. This includes first, telephone operators, postal workers, typists, etc. and second, technical salesmen, journalists and others working in the mass media, and finally a huge industry involving educators of all sorts, including teachers, priests, company training officers, etc;
3. A third group is involved in information storage and retrieval, including filing clerks, librarians, and of course, computer programmers;
4. A fourth category includes the professionals: lawyers, doctors, accountants – people who apply information which they have accumulated inside their heads and it is this expertise which they sell;
5. Then there is a large group of information operatives who are no longer considered part of the labour force, but used to be – students. One must keep in mind that in a country like Britain, right up until World War I the average lad of 12, and most of 10, spent at least half their time in the mines and factories, while the girls worked in the factories, shops, and as domestics. They were part of the labour force which now has been diverted to receiving information;
6. Lastly we have to look at the organization operatives. Modern productive systems involve a complex interaction of land, labour, capital, energy and materials, and a wide range of technology coupled to equally complex transport, communication and distribution systems. In a modern productive system, from the time a kernel of wheat is planted to the time a slice of bread is put in the family toaster, the product undergoes a complex series of processes and interactions. To get these various aspects organized requires not only producers and consumers but also a wide range of middle men and organization operatives – managers.

Managers possess organizational expertise. They create wealth by making the system work. They create new wealth by coupling information to existing organizations or productive systems, thereby reducing the costs of production or by creating new products or services. They must weld the producers into a viable organization, whether they work in factories, farms, or mines or, for that matter, in the art studio or classroom, with a whole host of other information operatives to get the product out to the ultimate consumer. The tools of their trade are the telephone and the pencil, or an extension of these – the typewriter, word processor, telex and so forth (often run by other information operatives).

Organization operatives are among the most highly salaried members of the post-industrial economy because of the important function they have, not merely transmitting information from one individual or group to other individuals or groups, but making complex decisions as to what information goes to whom, where and when. In a large organization managers direct a host of other information operatives who are themselves experts in finance, accounting, legal matters, personnel, industrial relations, advertising, public relations, planners and forecasters, research and development scientists and engineers, new product designers, education and training officers, purchasing agents, marketing experts, office managers, data processing personnel and so forth. Clearly, welding such a mix of expertise into a coherent whole requires great expertise. It is no wonder that managerial skills are amongst the most important and highly valued information skills in our society.

It must be obvious that every one of the above labour categories is engaged in work which will be aided by electronic databases. It also stands to reason that all such databases will acquire some level of advanced organization, most of them evolving into some form of intelligent knowledge-based data system. We will discuss some of these implications later.

12.3 THE RISE OF THE ROBOTS

12.3.1 From energy machines to information machines

The industrial revolution produced machines which extended the human musculature – devices which lifted things or transported things, spun things and wove things. All these involved machines and machinery carrying out manual operations. In contrast, the electronic revolution involved an extension of the human nervous system: telephone and radio, an extension of the ear; film initially based on sight then coupled to sound; television, of course, an extension of both the eye and the ear; and finally, the computer, an extension of the brain. Computers represent a form of machine brain, that is, a device which allows one to do outside of one's head, operations which formerly could only be done internally.

12.3.2 The coupling of energy and information devices

The robots are evolving! They began in a purely electro-mechanical form – primitive devices which were dedicated to carrying out specific routine tasks. These early electro-mechanical devices could change their performance only by altering the hardware, e.g. the wiring or some other part of their structure.

These earliest electro-mechanical devices became displaced by computer-controlled electro-mechanical devices. It now became possible to alter the behaviour or performance simply by means of software changes. The ability to re-program these second-generation robots easily gave them a much greater versatility. However, they were still primitive. A second-generation robot might be programmed to pick up a part, and if the part is not there it would still go through all the motions of picking up such a part even though it would be merely empty air.

The third-generation robots contain built-in sensors and feed-back devices to assess the environment in which they work. This means that they now could respond 'intelligently' to their surroundings. Intelligence refers to the ability to analyse information about the environment and then responding to it appropriately. In the 1980s, this third stage of robot evolution involved an increasing sophistication of both the sensors and the feed-back mechanisms.

This led to the fourth generation of robots: networks of robotized devices connected by, as it were, an artificial neurosystem of sensors and feed-back mechanisms all communicating with each other. Individual robots now could cooperate along an assembly line to carry out tasks, including correcting any mistakes which may arise during the production process. This allowed an entire factory itself to operate like a single gigantic complex machine. One no longer needed human operators to run a factory – only operators to maintain a factory and, where needed, modify it.

The next step will be to give the fully robotized factory-machine a brain. This will be in the factory office and will include expert systems to guide maintenance and self-repair operations, and to guide relationships with the rest of the world. The latter will involve three areas: 1. stock control of raw materials and components (including those needed for repairs) electronically linked to suppliers around the world; 2. direct links with the human decision makers at headquarter office; and 3. links to customers.

In the future, customers will be able to obtain products or services without the intervention of human operators. The matter is analogous to direct dialling an international telephone call. In that instance, customers avail themselves of a fully automated service and need no human operator to intervene in getting their party, perhaps half-way across the world, to answer. Similarly, in the future, via their personal home or office terminal, customers could order a car direct from a factory, specifying their precise individual requirements. The factory office computer would acknowledge and confirm. After checking on their bank account it would set into motion the production of their individual car according to specifications, then make arrangements for delivery. Throughout the process it would check the status of the customer's car and inform him or her. Upon completion and delivery to their home, it would negotiate with their bank computer for the transfer of funds. There would be no need for human intervention except perhaps for the transport of the car to the point of delivery.

Companies making such cars will need human operators for certain kinds of complex maintenance and for modification of the factory, for managerial personnel, and for customer relations in case things go wrong. Not much else. The principal need for low-skilled labour will be for security staff and lorry drivers. The manager will have to fit such a factory complex into the overall international environment. Managers will be involved in negotiating purchases of components (often via their computer to the component factory computers), engage in marketing, fix prices, define the product and company image, worry about cash flows, shareholder pressures, and annual (weekly?) reports, etc. At each point, they will be aided by expert systems. The manager's main function will involve people-to-people interactions. As in the past, managers will need to interact with customers, the public, the government, employees, financial backers, etc.

The above example demonstrates the crucial importance of knowledge as an input into advanced productive (in this case, manufacturing) systems. The fountainhead of future production systems will be a vastly expanded knowledge industry, with knowledge engineering and the creation of expert systems a central component of that industry.

12.4 THE NEED FOR A GENERAL THEORY OF INFORMATION

Information drives modern, post-industrial economies. What is needed today is a new field in economics – information economics. It must address itself to questions such as, how do you measure information in economic terms? How do you measure the productivity of people working with information? One can determine, if with some difficulty, the percentage of the GNP spent on information, but how does one measure the long term impact on the economy? How does one define quantitatively the fruits of invention and information? What percentage of the annual growth of the GNP or of the increase in the quality of life (not always the same thing), is attributable to advances in information or education?

Part of the problem in answering the above questions stems from the fact that we still do not understand the nature of information. Just what is information? Fritz Machlup, who was fully conscious of this problem, organized an interdisciplinary conference on 'information' (Machlup and Mansfield, 1983). A perusal of the resultant volume, which contains many interesting ideas by numerous eminent contributors makes clear that, as yet, there does not exist a satisfactory general theory of information.

In the present article the term information is used in a very broad sense. At one extreme is an individual datum. The simplest datum is an on–off switch, a zero–one, yes–no, binary piece of information. At the higher level, patterns of information comprise knowledge and patterns of knowledge, wisdom.

It may be helpful to make an analogy between information and the textile industry. The raw fleece is equivalent to data, it may be spun into yarn which represents information. The yarn, in turn, may be woven into cloth just as patterns of information may be woven into knowledge. A loom can weave strands of yarn into patterns of cloth. Similarly, a computer can weave strands of data into patterns of information. Cloth, in turn, may be tailored into a suit; and knowledge, properly analysed and digested, may yield wisdom. In this article the term information covers everything from the simplest datum to wisdom. 'Information' should also not be confused with 'intelligence', which processes information in order to make further use of it – nor confuse the creation or existence of information with the transmission of it via a wide variety of communications devices.

The above discussion relates to 'human' information – i.e. information that is perceived, communicated and processed by human brains. However, information may exist outside of the human brain as, for example, inside a computer or inside the brain of another animal. Actually, information may exist in a molecule of DNA. Information may be said to be contained by any system which exhibits patterns of organization. Information is not a human construct, but a property of the universe.

This concept is crucial to the development of a general theory of information (Stonier, 1986b and c). Information has as much physical reality as does matter and energy. It expresses itself in terms of patterns of organization. That is, what mass is to matter, and momentum to mechanical energy, organization is to information.

The reason why 'information' has been overlooked by physicists is two-fold. First, until fairly recently we lacked the historical experience of working with information as an independent entity. Second, just as matter and energy are interconvertible, so are information and energy. Thus it was almost always possible to 'hide' the information component in analysing physical systems. Only sometimes, did energy seem to disappear and required conceptual crutches such as 'potential energy' and 'entropy'.

The concept of energy as something distinct, with a physical reality of its own, is a relatively recent phenomenon in human history. The systematic exploration of 'forces' began only after such forces were apparently 'created' by human invention. Galileo was a military engineer studying the trajectories of cannon balls. Similarly, Carnot and his nineteenth-century colleagues founded thermo-dynamics only after a century of experience with steam engines. Today we are in a comparable situation. The concept of information as something distinct, with an independent reality of its own, reflects our more recent historical experiences. Three are of particular relevance.

First, there were the experiences of the telegraph, telephone, and radio engineers charged with the job of maximizing transmission efficiency. It is no coincidence that among the first to treat information as an independent, abstract quantity were engineers such as R. V. L. Hartley, who in 1928 defined inform-ation as a quantity and provided an equation for its measurement (see review by Cherry, 1978).

Second, and most important, we have now had over four decades of experience with electronic computers. These devices, initially designed as aids for solving lengthy and tedious mathematical computations, rapidly evolved into inform-ation processing systems of increasing complexity and sophistication. They made plain that human information could not only be stored, but manipulated outside of the human brain. This was a dramatic difference.

As long as human information was something static, as in books in a library, it did not seem to arouse much wonder and excitement. Psychologically, information appeared as something dead. The computer has changed our perception of information as something purely static. Inside a computer, information appears to have a dynamic of its own – it appears to have life. Very quickly the excitement of this new experience entered our common culture. Words and phrases such as 'input' and 'output', 'information processing', 'down time', etc., became applied to non-computer situations. Psychologists began to consider the human brain as a highly complex, biological information processor.

The third significant strand in our recent historical experience derives from the findings of the molecular biologists. The unequivocal demonstration that complex molecules such as DNA comprise the carrier of genetic information crowns our collective experience. This experience actually spans millennia of practical animal and plant breeding, as well as the common observation that children tend to resemble their parents.

This genetic information, transmitted from generation to generation, turns out to reside in an inanimate, aperiodic crystal. Both the crystal storing this information, and the code, preceded the appearance of the human brain by at least a billion years. Obviously information may exist in forms wholly separate and distinct from human beings.

It is not possible here to go into detail. The conclusions presented (Stonier, 1986c) may be summed up as follows: a physical system contains information if it exhibits organization. The information content of physical systems is a function which varies directly with organization, and inversely with probability and entropy. Equations in physics which contain reference to time and distance, or to some physical constant, refer to some organizational property of the universe, hence to its information content. Energy and information are readily interconvertible. A quantum of light possesses both energy and information. The equation for the 'relativistic momentum' of particles is consistent with the hypothesis that there may exist particles (infons) which possess neither mass nor momentum, but do retain a velocity, therefore may consist of pure information. Such a conceptualization implies that information is not only an intrinsic property of the universe, but like matter and energy may appear in particulate form.

For knowledge engineering, the development of a general theory of information would be most helpful. Such a theory cannot be developed until the physical reality of information becomes understood. What becomes apparent from an examination of the physics of information is that information involves a system's patterns of organization which may build up to ever greater complexity. Information processing can bring about further organization in a system, leading to more complex, more highly organized patterns of organization. This explains the paradox pointed out by Machlup (Machlup and Mansfield, 1983): '. . . new knowledge can be acquired without new information being received'. That is, just thinking about a subject, without any further information inputs, may still increase a person's knowledge about the subject. By the above criteria, the person has engaged in information 'work' to process the information into the more organized patterns of knowledge – weaving, as it were, the loose strands of information into an integrated cloth.

It is an axiom of information physics that all physical 'work' results in a change in the organization of the universe, hence a change in its information content. Physical work relates to changes in the patterns of matter and energy. Information work relates to changes in patterns of information. It takes energy to engage in information work; information work is merely a special case of physical work.

The above conceptualization of information would be strenuously opposed by Machlup were he still able to enlighten, and enliven us. In his view, the above discussion uses the term information in a 'metaphoric sense'. Information in the 'basic sense' would involve a mind and cognitive processes.

In the present author's view, this conceptualization of information is counter-productive to establishing a scientific basis for knowledge engineering. Information must be understood as an abstract entity like energy. The analysis and processing of information involve 'intelligence'. 'Meaning', for example, is achieved when intelligence is able to process information in such a way as to establish a relationship between a piece of information, and a 'context' in which such information becomes meaningful.

At present, the lack of a general theory of information (not to be confused with Shannon's theory of communication) constitutes a limiting factor, both for developing advanced forms of knowledge engineering, and for developing a science of information economics.

12.5 EXPANDING INTELLECTUAL TECHNOLOGIES

Developing a general theory of information is only one of many intellectual tasks which will need to be accomplished. Another will be the application of expert systems and information technology to achieve reliable forecasts. Weather forecasting already uses IT extensively. Weather systems are complex but perhaps not as complex as other systems, e.g. metabolic systems, ecological systems, economic systems or the political systems which comprise human society.

The reason forecasting is still so inaccurate is that it lacks both a coherent theoretical framework for analysing the future, and a proper method for fleshing out such a theory. The core to the development of the knowledge industry will be the ability to predict business cycles, engage in technological forecasts and, in time, accomplish intellectual feats as unlikely to us today as was predicting eclipses in the Middle Ages. Let us consider some aspects of this area of the knowledge industry.

12.5.1 Expert advice

Some social scientists favour the use of Delphi studies to achieve a consensus on forecasting future developments. However, the best people are often unwilling or unable to cooperate. Also the procedure fails to properly weight the opinions and differentiate between insightful expertise, educated guesses, ignorant folk wisdom, or fanciful speculations. In contrast, in-depth analyses by individuals selected for their expertise and for their creative imagination can be extremely helpful in defining the outlines of future developments. Then, as the concepts mature, it is always helpful to hold a host of meetings ranging from small groups of highly selected experts meeting around a table, to open international conferences and symposia. Such a procedure ought to be one of the prerequisites for creating advanced expert systems.

12.5.2 Trend projection

Certain types of technological developments show characteristic S-shaped growth curves. These are typical curves encountered in biological systems such as those exhibited by bacteria growing in a limited medium. The growth of the world's telephone network (like a mould growing over a petri dish) appears to be amenable to that sort of analysis. Plotting the curve from 1935 to 1985 would probably provide a reasonable guide to anticipating growth to 2010. As a rough rule of thumb, if one wishes to look 25 years into the future, one should look 50 years to the past.

However, trend projections do not anticipate the discontinuities. If, in 1935 one were to look into the future, trend projections of radios would not have predicted that within 25 years most households would have television sets as well. Trend projection of air travel would not have anticipated the emergence of jet planes, much less space travel. And of course, in 1935, the entire world of electronic computers and related information technology was non-existent.

12.5.3 History of technology analysis

Computers are an ideal illustration of a discontinuity in technological development. In 1935, calculating machines were all the commercial world knew about. By 1960 no large, self-respecting organization would any longer consider doing its payroll by anything other than a computer. In 1960, however, home computers were unknown, digital watches and pocket calculators virtually undreamed of. By 1985, such devices were commonplace and the talk was of cryogenic computers, biochips, optical fibres, satellite networks, household robots, and a host of other technological wonders.

Could one have anticipated computers and transistors 50 years ago? The answer is yes, if one knew where to look. By the mid-1930s, Konrad Zuse had clearly defined the concept of general-purpose calculators and had started to build working models at home, while R. W. Pohl had already predicted, in 1933, that electronic valves in radios would be replaced by small solid-state devices (see review by Evans, 1981). If one wants to anticipate technological discontinuities, one needs to look at basic research, then envision two things: 1. the technological possibilities derived from the sciences or other basic technological developments, and 2. the economic or other market forces (such as defence requirements) which transform a discovery or invention into a viable innovation or product.

12.5.4 Economic impact analysis

Firms and countries which avail themselves of IT properly thrive. But how does one measure the value of this IT input? One approach is that exemplified by Albert Fishlow's study on the growth in productivity of American railroads between 1870 and 1910 (as reviewed by Rosenberg, 1983). Fishlow concluded that it would have cost the consumer an additional $1.3 billion to meet the demands of 1910 traffic loads using the much less efficient technology of 1870. Thus the value of improvements in technology (air brakes, automatic couplers, substituting steel for iron rails, more powerful locomotives and more efficient rolling stock) allowed for trains carrying bigger pay loads, faster. The value of these improvements reduced costs by $1.3 billion.

Using this technique one ought to make in-depth studies of insurance, banking and other commercial activities who are large consumers of IT. Specifically, how much would it have cost to run the volume of insurance business in 1985 using 1960 technology? How about 1935 technology when the telephone system was still relatively small and computers non-existent? By means of such case studies, one should be able to obtain insights into what the impact was in the past, and is likely to occur in the future.

12.5.5 Input/output analysis

Among the most useful forms of analyses in economics is Leontief's input/output analysis (Leontief, 1986). If reliable information is available for constructing an input/output matrix, it becomes possible to forecast how changes in one part of the economy affect other parts. Leontief was in fact one of the earliest users of computers and may be said to be the creator of the first expert system in the social sciences.

The main disadvantage with an input/output matrix is that it is relatively static. One could make it more dynamic by making the assumptions that technology changes post-industrial economies. It does so because of three unique properties of information/technology:

1. The growth of information and technology is virtually irreversible. It is possible to forget some things and ignore others, but once something becomes known it is almost impossible to unknow it. Similarly, once something has been invented, one can't uninvent it;
2. The growth of information and technology is exponential. The more is known

and the more has been invented, the easier it is to know still more, and invent still more;

3. There is no foreseeable upper limit to the growth of knowledge or inventions.

No other component of the evolving human societal system has these properties – not the ecological, not the economic, not the political – that is why the growth of information and technology is the main driving force in human social evolution.

12.5.6 Systems analysis of human societies

Human societies evolved from hominid societies. The dominant determinant of animal societal evolution is the environment. Among primate societies today, such ecological pressures are still paramount. With the emergence of technology among the early hominids, the relationship between hominid societies and their environment changed. Weapons, fire, speech, and the domestication of plants and animals meant that neither predation nor the variation in food supplies were as important as formerly. By the end of the Neolithic Revolution cultural evolution began to supersede biological evolution because the two great problems confronting almost all animals – getting enough to eat, and not being eaten – had been largely solved. Instead, relationships with con-specifics – neighbours and enemies – became more important.

Human cultural systems represent the most advanced extension of evolving biological systems. The idea that human social systems evolve may be traced back at least to the philosophers of the eighteenth century Enlightenment. Adam Smith, for example, described the considerable progress made by British society between pre-Roman times and the eighteenth century (Adam Smith, *The Wealth of Nations*, Book Two, Chapter III). At that time the concept of evolution, as we know it, did not exist. It was more a sense of the gradual but continuous betterment of the human social condition.

We associate the idea of cultural evolution with Herbert Spencer. Spencer, however, misperceived human cultural evolution in that he considered the evolution of cultural systems to involve the same processes as the evolution of biological systems. He failed to appreciate that cultural evolution had transcended biological evolution – the increasing reliance on learned, rather than instinctive behaviour had altered the process of evolution. Culture in the present context is defined as a society's communal database upon which it draws to define belief systems and accepted modes of behaviour patterns. Cultural evolution differs from biological evolution in at least three fundamental respects: 1. it is goal oriented; 2. it can be Lamarckian; and 3. its rate of change is vastly accelerated.

1. The emergence of human consciousness as a result of the evolution of the primate nervous system introduced a discontinuity into the process of evolution. No longer was evolution dependent on random variation, followed by the selection of successful variants. Human cultural evolution became goal-oriented.

Instead of waiting for the environment to have an impact on the system (in this case human society), the system analysed, then altered the environment so as to enhance the system's survivability. After ten thousand years of human cultural evolution, a planet which originally could sustain, at best, several million hominids, now sustains several billion people.

2. Lamarck postulated that the neck of the evolving giraffe became extended because its ancestors had stretched their necks to reach the leaves higher up on the trees. It was the stretched neck, according to Lamarck, which was inherited by all subsequent descendants. In contrast, Darwin and Wallace derived the great insight that the variations in biological systems were random. It was the selection of successful variants which gave evolving systems their apparent direction. Giraffes with longer necks had a higher chance of survival, therefore were more likely to reproduce.

In human, cultural evolution, the Lamarckian mechanism can operate. If an individual wishing to get to the top of a tree, invents a ladder – then all descendants of that individual can use that ladder. Hence 'the inheritance of acquired characters' – a heresy in biological evolution – is a basic feature of cultural evolution.

3. This also accounts for the speed of cultural evolution. Instead of bumbling around for generations, relying on random variations, which only incrementally solve the mismatch between a biological system and its environment (in this case short-necked ungulates and tall trees), goal-oriented cultural evolution allows a non-incremental solution (e.g. a ladder) to appear in one generation.

Since the dawn of humanity, social evolution has been driven by technological evolution. What makes information technology so interesting theoretically is that, from here on in, IT will drive technological evolution just as technology has been driving social evolution.

12.5.7 The international dimension

Post-industrial economies are transnational (see Stonier, 1983). No amount of refined analysis of the economy within any one country can provide an accurate assessment of the future. One of the great tasks of economists must be to create a global input/output table which then, using computers, can provide a world model of the present economy. A number of economists, including Leontief (1986), have been engaged in global modelling for some time. When this work is completed, it will provide a powerful new tool for the knowledge industry.

Technology transcends political boundaries. Technology drives social evolution. Human societies are evolving into a single global society, the modes of production in advanced information economies are becoming increasingly transnational. Just as the requirements of an industrial economy made obsolete the European feudal states, replacing them with nation-states, so today do we witness the gradual decay of the traditional European nation-states in favour of a European Community.

In due course, other parts of the world will evolve into similar regional states which, in turn, will coalesce until we will have achieved a single global political institutional framework.

IT greatly accelerates the process of globalizing human society. The development of expert systems will become increasingly significant in this process. It behoves knowledge engineers, therefore, to eschew parochialism and develop a global frame of reference when working on databases and expert systems.

12.6 THE IMPACT OF EXPERT SYSTEMS ON SOCIETY

The development of expert systems will have an impact on society in at least three distinct, though interrelated ways. First, there will be the direct impact at the micro level – on the specific enterprise each individual expert system is designed to aid. Earlier, we discussed how a fifth-generation robotized automobile factory might operate. In fact, General Motor's 'Saturn' project is moving precisely in that direction (as reviewed by Huppes, 1987). There will be a direct link from dealer showroom to factory floor – a factory no longer organized as an assembly line but a series of working units. Both the workers at these units, and the managerial structure will engage in quite different work practices. As Huppes points out, under the impact of automation the project is busy de-Taylorizing, de-hierarchizing, and de-bureaucratizing one of the world's largest companies.

Expert systems will play a role in all advanced automated systems. They will have an even more direct and profound effect on various professions such as medicine, the law, the military, oil exploration, etc. The emergence of these systems portends changes in daily work habits, in client relationships, in organizational structures, and in employment patterns. Just as scribes disappeared when everybody learned to read and write, so will many professionals whose current function is merely that of walking databases, become obsolete as databanks evolve into globally accessible expert systems.

Finally, computers and intelligent, knowledge-based systems will have a profound impact on education. The possibility of a computer-based education (CBE) system with a concomitant shift over the next few decades from school-based, back to home-based education has been discussed elsewhere (Stonier, 1979; Stonier and Conlin, 1985).

This brings us to the second category of impacts. Expert systems, as part of the overall thrust of IT, will alter the intellectual infrastructure of society. Whereas expert systems applied directly to solve specific problems merely represent another form of advanced technology, *in toto*, expert systems constitute a meta-technology. A meta-technology is a technology which affects vast areas of existing technology. One classic example of a meta-technology is the steam engine. Initially invented to pump water out of mines, it subsequently became a meta-technology as it gave rise to a class of power machines which could be coupled to a wide range of other existing mechanical devices – wagons on rails (to create locomotives), ships (to create steamships), looms (to create power looms), presses (to create power presses), etc. What we think of as the industrial revolution, represented to a large extent, the impact of that meta-technology (Stonier, 1983).

A more relevant example of a meta-technology involves the adoption of the printing press in Europe in the fifteenth century. Although Chinese and Korean printing presses antedated the European printing press by centuries, the ideographic nature of the Chinese written word, prevented its effective use. Only a very small number of scholars were literate. In contrast, in Europe, with a phonetic written language which was universally understood (Latin), the level of literacy, particularly among clerics, was very much higher. Therefore, there was a large market for the output of printing presses in Europe and it was no accident that the early output of printed books was largely confined to religious tracts. The 1569 edition of the Huguenot Psalter involved printing 35 000 copies. Consider how many monks slaving away in their cells, copying out one book at a time would have been required for a comparable effort. In the long run, however, of greater significance to European progress were schoolbooks like Erasmus' *Colloquia* for Latin students, De Villedieu's *Doctrinal* for teaching grammar, textbooks such as Besson's *Theatre of Instruments*, and others written by Ramelli, Veranzio, Branca and Zonca connecting the arts and crafts of the classical period. Even more important were the new works on metallurgy, mining and chemical technology by Biringuccio, Agricola, Ercker and Lohneiss. No area of technology remained unaffected by the printed word. Unlike their medieval predecessors, the craftsmen of the late sixteenth century were in a position to consult the descriptions and instructions of their trans-European colleagues (Stonier, 1983).

It has always been a mystery why sometime around the seventeenth century Europe began to dramatically outpace the other great civilizations such as China. At least one of the factors, and perhaps the most important, was the increasingly widespread use of the printed word. In a sense, this development constituted the first major breakthrough in creating an effective trans-European collective memory. In due course, books became supplemented with newspapers and periodicals, and by the twentieth century, the electronic revolution created radio, telephone, film and television, as the Communicative Era emerged to provide the planet with a highly efficient, global societal nervous system. The matter has been examined in greater detail elsewhere (Stonier, 1986a).

Electronic data storage will have as profound an impact on the intellectual infrastructure of society as did the printing press. Expert systems will be central. The new global intelligence system will solve most of the economic, social and political problems which currently plague us. Half a millennium ago, the printed word was instrumental in spreading new ideas and experiences so as to usher into Europe, a new era – the Mechanical Era (Stonier, 1976). This era saw the conquest of diseases, while the frequent famines of the seventeenth century gave way to food surpluses. Similarly, the excesses of slavery, absolute monarchy, and other undesirable cultural traits vanished. So, in the Communicative Era will we see the institution of war disappear, dictatorships replaced by democratic regimes, an equitable distribution of vastly expanded resources, and a general improvement in the quality of life for all (see Stonier, 1983). That is the good news.

The bad news is, that it will also initiate an evolutionary process which will inevitably lead to the displacement of humanity as we know it. This is the third, and long-term impact of expert systems. Expert systems represent advanced memory systems for machine intelligence; and the creation of machine intelligence represents a radically new phenomenon in this part of the universe. The combination of machine intelligence and human society represents a stable new system capable of evolving. The situation is analogous to one which occurred several thousand million years ago when the organization of matter and energy underwent a radical transformation during the geological evolution of our planet. At some point during this evolution, molecular systems acted in new synergistic combinations to transcend earlier inorganic systems and generate Life. The combination of machine intelligence and human society will also act in new synergetic combinations to transcend present biological systems and generate Intelligence (Stonier, 1976).

12.6.1 Why computers will end up smarter than people

When we use the term 'evolution', we tend to apply it to the evolution of biological systems. Yet, all persistent systems exhibiting organization, evolve. In a changing environment, all organized systems undergo change. Such change either leads to an increase in entropy, as the organized system succumbs to environmental pressures and loses its organization, or alternatively, the system contains sufficient information to extract energy and information from its environment thereby setting the stage for its own survival and further evolution.

Evolving systems are characterized by an increase in information content as reflected by the increase in the complexity of their organization. Such complexity of organization involves an increase in self-regulatory, self-sustaining homoeostatic activities.

In the evolution of machine intelligence, new characteristics may emerge, and be inherited in a matter of milliseconds. This is the first reason why machine intelligence will outpace human intelligence. In the history of technology, there has never been a pace comparable to the advances in computers. It took 66 years from the time of the Wright Brothers' first flight at Kitty Hawk to the time when men walked the moon. Even if computers evolved no faster than aircraft, we should be on the machine intelligence equivalent of the moon by the year 2010.

The second reason centres on the concept that although at this point in time, computers are nothing more than idiot-*savants*, that does not mean that things will always be so. As both our knowledge of the human brain and our ingenuity in manipulating electronic systems grow, the computer will become more of a *savant* and less of an idiot.

The whole field of contextual analysis, for example, must sooner or later bear fruit in allowing machine intelligence to be able not only to perform logical operations and act as an inference machine, but to begin to comprehend the context in which such operations are carried out.

The third reason relates to self-reproducibility. Computers have started to help human engineers design the next generation of computers and in theory could some day reproduce themselves like DNA molecules. To consider the computer similar to other tools is to overlook the inherent self-replicating capacity of machine intelligence.

The last reason, and theoretically the most important, is the fact that whereas we can extend human knowledge, we cannot physically expand the human brain. There are no such limitations on machine intelligence. This means ultimately that we can create devices into which we can stuff all human knowledge and all human neurological capabilities. It is the height of delusion to think that computers can never become more intelligent than people. Instead of deluding ourselves we must begin to think out the implications.

12.7 CONCLUSIONS AND WARNING

The mechanics of information technology are advancing rapidly. Our ability to organize data logically, to devise ever more ingenious algorithms, and to simulate systems with increasing sophistication, reflects our skills at mathematics, programming, and logic. In due course, we will overcome the epistemological problems which comprise the limiting factor in creating advanced expert systems.

Helpful and useful as such systems will be, they could also create serious distortions in our culture. The industrial revolution produced enormous suffering during its inception. Towards the end of the industrial era, although many of the early problems had been solved, it had created a sort of social monster which was largely brawn and very little brain – a global society with a military technology which could destroy our civilization without having developed the political technology to make certain that we wouldn't – a global society in which the affluent sector worried about food surpluses while the poorer sector suffered famines and death from malnutrition. Are we about to embark on creating a new social monster – one which will be all brain and no heart?

It must be clear that our education system is poorly geared to providing the kinds of people needed to meet the challenges of the next century. The failure is two-fold. Firstly, at the narrow economic level there is inadequate training which fails to keep up with the rapid increase in information inputs into all forms of employment. The tendency is to produce skilled operatives too slow and too late and at the same time keep producing them after they are no longer needed. The second flaw is more serious. It is the inability to produce people of sufficiently broad background to be able to understand issues and be able to communicate effectively with experts in other areas. It is probably true to say that the majority of decisions made in Britain and to a lesser extent in many other Western countries, are made by technological illiterates. At the same time most engineers, data processors, scientists, that is, technical experts of all sorts, are humanistic and social illiterates.

Expert systems may help. Probably they will. However, we might now be creating a new kind of social monster whose conceit is that all problems may be solved by using the logic and algorithms of a clever chess player. Chess is a zero-sum game. Human existence is not. Devising an expert system to advise a chess player will not lead to fatal errors. Devising an inappropriate expert system to advise a government could lead to disaster. Obviously, we need to create an intellectual technology to help solve human problems including those in economics, politics, belief systems, education, and our culture in general. However we must become increasingly cautious and conservative about compounding complexities.

By applying to highly complex systems which are still poorly understood (e.g. economic systems), new sets of complexities which themselves may also be poorly understood (e.g. information systems), we are producing new levels of un-certainties, while at the same time creating the delusion of greater accuracy. There is always the danger that people, forever seeking simple solutions, will accept the outputs of machine intelligence with much greater faith than is warranted. These concerns are even more worrying, when we look at the rapid pace of military technology.

Finally, the knowledge industry utilizing expert systems, and IT in general creates the conditions which will lead to the evolution of humanity beyond itself. As Forsyth and Naylor (1985) have pointed out earlier: 'Humanity has opened two Pandora's boxes at the same time, one labelled genetic engineering, the other labelled knowledge engineering. What we have let out is not entirely clear, but it is reasonable to hazard a guess that it contains the seeds of our successors.'

Chris Evans (1979), in considering these steps into the unknown quotes H. G. Wells' *Things to Come*: '. . . once Man has taken the first step down the path of knowledge and understanding, he must take all those that follow. The alternative is to do nothing, to live with the insects in the dust.' Libraries and electronic databases represent humanity's collective memory. Expert systems will come to represent humanity's collective wisdom. As such they could give us the wings to soar out of our earthly dust. Will we be able to do so wisely?

Acknowledgement: the author wishes to thank Ms M. Ellison for her patient assistance in producing this manuscript.

12.8 REFERENCES

Bell, D. (1973) *The Coming of Post-Industrial Society*. Basic Books, New York.
Cherry, C. (1978) *On Human Communication*, 3rd ed. MIT Press, Cambridge, Mass.
Evans, C. (1979) *The Mighty Micro*. Victor Gollancz, London.

Evans, C. (1981) *The Making of the Micro*. Victor Gollancz, London.

Forsyth, R. and Naylor, C. (1985) *The Hitch-Hiker's Guide to Artificial Intelligence*. Chapman and Hall, London.

Huppes, T. (1987) *The Western Edge*. Kluwer, Dordrecht, Holland.

Leontief, W. (1986) *Input-Output Economics*. 2nd ed., Oxford University Press, Oxford.

Machlup, F. (1962) *The Production and Distribution of Knowledge in the United States*. Princeton University Press, Princeton, New Jersey.

Machlup, F. (1980) *Knowledge and Knowledge Production*. Princeton University Press, Princeton, New Jersey.

Machlup, F. and Mansfield, U. (1983) *The Study of Information*. John Wiley & Sons, New York.

Porat, M. (1976) *The Information Economy* Center for Interdisciplinary Research, Stanford University, California.

Rosenberg, N. (1983) *Inside the Black Box*. Cambridge University Press, Cambridge, UK.

Stonier, T. (1976) The natural history of humanity: past, present and future. Inaugural Lecture, Bradford University (17 Feb 1976). 48 pp [Reprinted in *Int. Jour. Man-Machine Studies* **14**, 91–122 (1981)].

Stonier, T. (1979) Changes in Western society: educational implications. In T. Schuller and J. Megarry (eds), *World Yearbook of Education 1979: Recurrent Education and Lifelong Learning*. Kogan Page, London, pp. 31–44.

Stonier, T. (1983) *The Wealth of Information: A Profile of the Post-Industrial Economy*, Thames/Methuen, London.

Stonier, T. (1986a) Intelligent networks, overview, purpose and policies in the context of global social change, *ASLIB Proceed.* **38**, 269–74.

Stonier, T. (1986b) Towards a new theory of information. In *Telecommunications Policy*, **10**, 278–81.

Stonier, T. (1986c) What *is* information? In *Research and Development in Expert Systems III*, Cambridge University Press, Cambridge, pp. 217–230.

Stonier, T. and Conlin, C. (1985) *The Three Cs: Children, Computers and Communications*, John Wiley & Sons, Chichester, UK.

Bibliography

Specific references can be found at the end of each chapter in this book. The aim of this bibliography is to provide a general reading list for those who want to broaden and deepen their knowledge about the field of expert systems.

Aleksander, I. and Burnett, P. (1984) *Re-Inventing Man*. Penguin Books, Middx.

Alty, J. L. and Coombs, M. J. (1984) *Expert Systems: Concepts and Examples*. NCC Publications, Manchester.

Alvey Directorate (1982) *The Alvey Report*. HMSO, London.

Anderson, J. and Bower, G. (1973) *Human Associative Memory*. Holt, N.Y.

Asgari, D. and Modesitt, K. (1986) Space shuttle main engine test analysis: a case study for inductive knowledge-based systems involving very large databases. *Proc. IEEE*, 65–71.

Bachant, J. and McDermott, J. (1984) R1 revisited after four years in the trenches. *AI Magazine*, **5**, 21–32.

Brachman, R. J. and Levesque, H. J. (eds) (1985) *Readings in Knowledge Representation*. Morgan Kaufmann, Los Altos, CA.

Bramer, M. (ed.) (1985) *Research and Development in Expert Systems*. Cambridge Univ. Press, Cambridge.

Bratko, I. (1986) *Prolog Programming for Artificial Intelligence*. Addison-Wesley, Wokingham, Berks.

Bratko, I. and Lavrac, N. (1987) (eds) *Progress in Machine Learning*. Sigma Press, Wilmslow, UK.

Breiman, L., Friedman, J., Olshen, R. and Stone, C. (1984) *Classification and Regression Trees*. Wadsworth & Brooks, Monterey, CA.

Burton, M. and Shadbolt, N. (1987) *POP-11 Programming for Artificial Intelligence*. Addison-Wesley, Wokingham, Berks.

Charniak, E. and McDermott, D. (1985) *Introduction to Artificial Intelligence*. Addison-Wesley, Reading, Mass.

Cognitive Science, Special Issue (1985) Connectionist models and their applications: *Cognitive Science*, **9**, (1).

Cohen, P. and Feigenbaum, E. (1982) *The Handbook of Artificial Intelligence*, Volume 3. Pitman Books, London.

Dietterich, T. and Michalski, R. (1981) Inductive learning of structural descriptions. *Artificial Intelligence*. **16**, 257–94.

Dreyfus, H. and Dreyfus, S. (1985) *Mind over Machine*. Macmillan/The Free Press, New York.

Ernst, G. and Newell, A. (1969) *GPS: A Case Study in Generality and Problem Solving*. Academic Press, New York.

Feigenbaum, E., Buchanan, B. and Lederberg, J. (1971) On generality and problem solving. *Machine Intelligence*, **6**.

Feigenbaum, E. and McCorduck, P. (1984) *The Fifth Generation*: Michael Joseph, London.

Fodor, J. and Pylyshyn, Z. W. (1988) Connectionism and cognitive architecture: A critical analysis. *Cognition*, in press.

Forsyth, R. (ed.) (1984) *Expert Systems: Principles and Case Studies*, 1st edition. Chapman and Hall, London.

Forsyth, R. and Rada, R. (1986) *Machine Learning: Applications in Expert Systems and Information Retrieval*: Ellis Horwood, Chichester.

Gashnig, J. (1982) Prospector: An expert system for mineral exploration. In D. Michie (ed.) *Introductory Readings in Expert Systems*, Gordon & Breach, New York.

Goodall, A. (1985) *The Guide to Expert Systems* Learned Information. Oxford, England.

Graham, I. and Jones, P. L. (1988) *Expert Systems: Knowledge, Uncertainty and Decision:* Chapman and Hall, London.

Greenwell, M. (1988) *Knowledge Elicitation: Principles and Practice:* Ellis Horwood, Chichester.

Hart, A. (1985) The role of induction in knowledge elicitation. *Expert Systems*, **2**, 24–8.

Hart, A. (1986) *Knowledge Acquisition for Expert Systems*. Kogan Page, London.

Hayes-Roth, F., Waterman, D. A. and Lenat, D. B. (1983) *Building Expert Systems*: Addison-Wesley, Reading, Mass.

Hinton, G. and Anderson, J. (eds) (1981) *Parallel Models of Associative Memory*. Erlbaum, New Jersey.

Hofstadter, D. (1985) *Metamagical Themas*. Viking, New York.

Holland, J. (1975) *Adaptation in Natural and Artificial Systems*. University of Michigan Press, Ann Arbor.

Holland, J. H., Holyoak, K. J., Nisbett, R. E. and Thagard, P. R. (1986) *Induction: Processes of Inference, Learning and Discovery*. MIT Press, Mass.

Jackson, P. (1986) *Introduction to Expert Systems*. Addison-Wesley, Reading, Mass.

JIPDEC (1981) *Preliminary Report on Study and Research on Fifth Generation Computers*. Japan Information Processing Development Centre, Tokyo.

Kidd, A. (1985) What do users ask? In M. Merry (ed.) *Expert Systems 85*, Cambridge Univ. Press, Cambridge, pp. 9–19.

Lakatos, I. (1976) *Proofs and Refutations: the Logic of Mathematical Discovery*. Cambridge University Press, Cambridge.

Langley, P., Simon, H., Bradshaw, G. and Zytkow, J. (1986) *Scientific Discovery: Computational Explorations of the Creative Process*. MIT Press, Mass.

Lawler, R., Du Boulay, B., Hughes, M. and MacLeod, H. (1986) *Cognition and Computers*. Ellis Horwood, Chichester.

Lenat, D. (1982) The nature of heuristics. *Artificial Intelligence*, **19**, 189–249.

Lenat, D. (1983) Eurisko: A program that learns new heuristics and domain concepts. *Artificial Intelligence*, **21**, Nos. 1 & 2.

McCorduck, P. (1979) *Machines Who Think*. Freeman, San Francisco.

McCulloch, W. (1965) *Embodiments of Mind*: MIT Press, Mass.

Medawar, P. (1969) *Induction and Intuition in Scientific Thought*. Methuen, London.

Michalski, R., Carbonell, J. and Mitchell, T. (1983) *Machine Learning: An Artificial Intelligence Approach*, Tioga Publishing Corp., Palo Alto, CA.

Michalski, R., Carbonell, J. and Mitchell, T. (1986) *Machine Learning: An Artificial Intelligence Approach, Volume 2*, Morgan Kaufmann Publishers, Los Altos, CA.

Michalski, R. and Chilausky, R. (1980) Learning by being told and learning from examples . . . *Internat. J. of Man-Machine Studies*, **12**, 63–87.

Michie, D. (ed.) (1982) *Introductory Readings in Expert Systems*, Gordon & Breach, London.

Michie, D. (1986a) *On Machine Intelligence*, Ellis Horwood, Chichester.

Michie, D. (1986b) The superarticulacy phenomenon in the context of software manufacture, *Proc. Royal Soc., A*, **405**, 185–212.

Michie, D. and Johnston, R. (1985) *The Creative Computer*, Pelican, London.

Minsky, M. and Papert, S. (1969) *Perceptrons: An Introduction to Computational Geometry*, MIT Press, Boston, Mass.

Mitchell, T. (1982) Generalization as search, *Artificial Intelligence*, **18**, 203–26.

Naylor, C. (1983) *Build Your Own Expert System*, Sigma Press, Cheshire.

Newell, A. and Simon, H. (1972) *Human Problem Solving*, Prentice-Hall, New Jersey.

Partridge, D. (1986) *AI: Applications in the Future of Software Engineering*, Ellis Horwood, Chichester.

Pollitt, S. (1986) Reducing complexity by rejecting the consultation model as a basis for the design of expert systems, *Expert Systems*, **3**, 234–8.

Popper, K. (1972) *Conjectures and Refutations* (4th edition), Routledge and Kegan Paul, London.

Pylyshyn, Z. and Demopoulos, W. (eds) (1986) *Meaning and Cognitive Structure*, Ablex Publishing, New Jersey.

Rosenblatt, F. (1962) *Principles of Neurodynamics*, Spartan Books, London.

Schank, R. (1982) *Dynamic Memory: A Theory of Reminding and Learning in Computers and People*, Cambridge University Press, Cambridge.

Shortliffe, E. (1976) *Computer Based Medical Consultations: MYCIN*, American Elsevier, New York.

Simon, H., Langley, P. and Bradshaw, G. (1981) Scientific discovery as problem solving, *Synthese*, **47**, 1–27.

Spiegelhalter, D. and Knill-Jones, R. (1984) Statistical and knowledge-based approaches to clinical decision-support systems, *J. Royal Statis. Soc.*, **147**, 35–77.

Stonier, T. (1986) Towards a new theory of information. *Telecommunications Policy*, **10**, 278–81.

Uhr, L. (1966) *Pattern Recognition*, Wiley, New York.

Wiener, N. (1948) *Cybernetics*, MIT Press, Mass.

Winograd, T. and Flores, F. (1986) *Understanding Computers and Cognition*, Ablex, New Jersey.

Winston, P. (1984) *Artificial Intelligence* (2nd edition), Addison-Wesley, Mass.

Wong, S. K. M., Ziarko, W. and Ye, R. L. (1986) Comparison of rough-set and statistical methods in inductive learning, *Internat. J. Man-Machine Studies*, **24**, 53–72.

Yazdani, M. (ed.) (1986) *Artificial Intelligence: Principles and Applications*, Chapman and Hall, London.

Zimmermann, H.-J. (1987) *Fuzzy Sets, Decision Making and Expert Systems*, Kluwer Academic Publishers, The Hague, Holland.

Index